PRAISE FOR PREVIOUS EDITIONS OF

Louisiana
Off the Beaten Path ®

"To learn more about our own state, buy a copy of Gay Martin's guidebook. . . . [I]t qualifies as a bible for those who want to roam the roads of Louisiana."
—*Times-Picayune,* New Orleans

"A conversational, in-depth, parish-by-parish guide to towns and attractions."
—*Louisiana Life* magazine

"Nowhere in the United States are there more unique places than in Louisiana. . . . I've been back there twice, and this guide makes me want more."
—*Endless Vacation* magazine

"Designed to bring the traveler into contact with Louisiana culture and traditions . . . this is an important adjunct to any standard guide to the state."
—*Midwest Book Review*

Help Us Keep This Guide Up to Date

Every effort has been made by the author and editors to make this guide as accurate and useful as possible. However, many changes can occur after a guide is published—establishments close, phone numbers change, hiking trails are rerouted, facilities come under new management, etc.

We would love to hear from you concerning your experiences with this guide and how you feel it could be improved and be kept up to date. While we may not be able to respond to all comments and suggestions, we'll take them to heart, and we'll make certain to share them with the author. Please send your comments and suggestions to the following address:

The Globe Pequot Press
Reader Response/Editorial Department
P.O. Box 480
Guilford, CT 06437

Or you may e-mail us at: editorial@GlobePequot.com

Thanks for your input, and happy travels!

INSIDERS' GUIDE®

OFF THE BEATEN PATH® SERIES

Off the Beaten Path®

EIGHTH EDITION

louisiana

A GUIDE TO UNIQUE PLACES

GAY N. MARTIN

INSIDERS' GUIDE®

GUILFORD, CONNECTICUT
AN IMPRINT OF THE GLOBE PEQUOT PRESS

The prices, rates, and hours listed in this guidebook were confirmed at press time. We recommend, however, that you call establishments to obtain current information before traveling.

To buy books in quantity for corporate use or incentives, call **(800) 962–0973** or e-mail **premiums@GlobePequot.com**.

3 9082 10251 3077

INSIDERS' GUIDE®

Text design by Linda Loiewski
Illustrations by Carole Drong
Maps created by Equator Graphics © Morris Book Publishing, LLC
Spot photography throughout © age fotostock/SuperStock

ISSN: 1539-3763
ISBN-13: 978-0-7627-4202-8
ISBN-10: 0-7627-4202-X

Manufactured in the United States of America
Eighth Edition/First Printing

To my husband, Carlton,
who remains wonderful—"Here is for Papou."

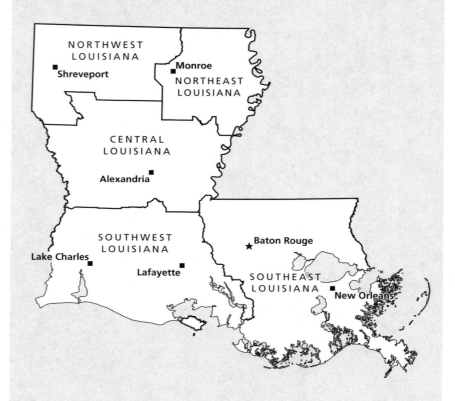

NORTHWEST
LOUISIANA
■ Shreveport

Monroe
■
NORTHEAST
LOUISIANA

CENTRAL
LOUISIANA
Alexandria ■

SOUTHWEST
LOUISIANA

Lake Charles
■
Lafayette ■

★ Baton Rouge

SOUTHEAST
LOUISIANA ■ New Orleans

Contents

Acknowledgments

Merci beaucoup to all the terrific people who helped me with past editions of this guidebook. Because that list grew so long over the last seventeen years, I cleared the decks and started over. So, in random order, here goes: Elizabeth Taylor, Darienne Wilson, Carolyn G. Kolb, Beverly Gianna, Larry Lovell, Donna O'Daniels, Tanya Leader, Gerald Breaux, Kelly Strenge and the Lafayette crew, Shelley Johnson, Megan Monsour, Tico Soto and the Lake Charles bunch, Anne and Dr. Lee J. Monlezun, A. C. Boudier, Danny Young, Jeff Richard, Karen Primeaux, Vergie Banks, Bruce Odell, Sandra Day, David Savoy, Cindy R. Breaux, Fran Thibodeaux, Dona Degatur Richard, Warren A. Perrin, Melanie Melancon, Judge Tim Ellender, Stacy Brown, Brandy Evans, Kevin Kelly, Jeremy Langlois, Ann Johnson, Toby Traylor, JoAnn and Dan Gray, Christine DeCuir, Lucette Brehm, Tom Fitzmorris, Bonnie Warren, Marda Burton, Jessica D. Guillot, Mary Miller, Marjorie Collamer, Virgie Ott, and Carolyn and Bill Mason.

For the chefs, restaurateurs, and cooks who contributed recipes for this edition, *merci mes amis*. I also want to acknowledge the Louisiana Office of Tourism, the New Orleans Convention and Visitors Bureau, the New Orleans Tourism and Marketing Corporation, and the many chambers, bureaus, and parish tourism offices throughout the state for their help with this project.

A special thank you goes to Lori Boatfield for her invaluable research assistance and to my husband, Carlton, for his help in myriad ways. And as always, hugs to family and friends, who continue to offer encouraging words and assure me I'll meet my next deadline.

Introduction

First, let's get that horrible H-word out of the way. As the world knows, the 2005 hurricane season proved to be the most destructive in recorded history. On August 29, Hurricane Katrina devastated coastal areas of Mississippi and Louisiana, leaving a legacy of death and destruction in her wake. Along with heavy damage to four parishes and New Orleans, the breakdown of city levees compounded the catastrophe. Less than a month later, on September 24, Hurricane Rita struck Southwest Louisiana, severely impacting six parishes and the city of Lake Charles.

How does all this affect the traveling public? Tourism officials remind visitors that 85 percent of the state sustained little or no storm damage. New Orleans proper is once again a great destination offering its usual superb cuisine, wonderful music, and a storied 300-year history. True, the historic heart of New Orleans escaped with minor damage, but the devastation of low-lying neighborhoods and surrounding areas remains a study in horrors.

New Orleans continues to rank as one of the world's top culinary destinations. At press time, the Louisiana Restaurant Association reported that 1,168 restaurants and retail food establishments were open in Orleans Parish and 1,657 in Jefferson Parish. (For updated information, visit www.lra.org.)

Currently, more than 180 hotels are open with 27,155 hotel rooms operational in the Greater New Orleans area. Before Katrina, the room inventory numbered 38,000. As more hotels finish their remodeling phases, rooms are becoming available on a daily basis. At this time, the Louis Armstrong International Airport offers 103 flights daily, a good percentage of pre-Katrina's 166 flights per day.

With this year's fabulous Mardi Gras and Jazz Fest, said a spokesman, the city proved it can host major events successfully. The best way to show your support is by visiting. So what are you waiting for?

My own love affair with Louisiana began about four decades ago—and shows no signs of cooling down. During the late '80s, I started in-depth research for this guidebook, now in its eighth edition. At that time, the state's welcome centers dispensed tourism literature bags touting LOUISIANA—AS AMERICAN AS CRAWFISH PIE. Since then, other slogans have come and

meetthe louisianafamily

Louisiana's residents represent a rich ethnic mix. This includes not only the famous French heritage but also the Scotch-Irish-English background common to many white southerners. Other groups—African American, Hispanic, and Native American, along with Vietnamese, German, Lebanese, and even Hungarian—add to the cultural gumbo of the state.

gone, but this remains my favorite because it suggests something of the state's uniqueness.

Cultural distinctions jump out at you each time you encounter a word that appears unpronounceable at first (example: Zwolle, a small town near Toledo Bend on the state's western border, rhymes with *tamale*).

A list of how Louisiana differs from other states could start with the legal system. As Stanley reminds Stella in a *Streetcar Named Desire,* ". . . we have something in Louisiana called the Napoleonic Code." And consider the Long dynasty and that cast of colorful characters associated with past political regimes. Consider too that much of our unique political activity is carried out in what we call parishes, not counties—carryovers from the original divisions drawn by the Roman Catholic Church.

weather-wise

Given the humid, subtropical (meaning not-quite-tropical) climate of the state, summers can be hot in Louisiana. Winters, blissfully, are mild. Hurricanes can be a coastal-area hazard. Whatever the season, prepare for rain.

Louisiana dishes up diversity in the arts as well. What other state could possibly serve as a setting for *Divine Secrets of the Ya-Ya Sisterhood?* And where else would you ever see an official portrait of the governor with Blue Dog? It's true. Blue Dog shares the canvas with Louisiana's governor, Kathleen Babineaux Blanco.

And who's Blue Dog you say? Internationally acclaimed Cajun artist George Rodrigue conjured up Blue Dog in 1984, and the image soon grew to pop-icon status. Both Rodrigue and Governor Blanco hail from New Iberia, and so does novelist James Lee Burke.

Of course, Louisiana's cuisine is as unusual as our other cultural offerings and, as you'll learn, holds a unique importance here.

Research is the heart of writing, especially travel writing, and lucky is the writer whose research leads her through Louisiana. Something about describing this extraordinary state always seems to send me to my kitchen. (Fortunately, a flight of stairs separates my keyboard from my cutting board.)

Many New Orleanians agree with this famous quote by Ella Brennan: "In some places, they eat to live—in our town, we live to eat."

And it's true. You'll understand why when you travel through our gastronomic wonderland.

Or perhaps you're already familiar with Louisiana's cuisine. Cajun restaurants have proliferated beyond state borders (a friend previously visited one in a remote area of Australia), and packaged Cajun foods, spices, and cookbooks are now readily available to fuel further interest in this celebrated cuisine. Basically French country cooking, Cajun cuisine utilizes fresh indigenous ingredients—rice, peppers, herbs, game, and fish—notably the ubiquitous crustacean called crawfish. Aqua-culture, the growing of crawfish and catfish in shallow ponds, plays a significant role in Acadiana's economy.

The natives will gladly demonstrate the proper way to peel a crawfish and patiently explain it again. If, on the third try, you still don't get the hang of it, they'll probably do it for you. Then, all you have to do is dip it in some delectable sauce. (You might prefer to leave the head-sucking to the locals.)

Louisiana's innovative chefs may tempt you to eat yourself into a coma with pan-seared foie gras, crab and sweet corn bisque, etouffee, jambalaya, soft-shelled crab in sherry sauce, shrimp and artichoke salad, oysters (nude or in sublime sauces), pompano *en papillote,* smoked salmon with tasso, and classic crème brûlée or variations thereof. Menus feature everything from broiled, baked, boiled, blackened, steamed, and fried fish to delectable concoctions of gumbo, shrimp Creole, crabmeat crepes, crawfish bisque, eggplant pirogue, and more. With cuisines ranging from Acadian, Creole, and haute French to Southern—well, what more can be said?

Perhaps only a question—is there a way to take all this home?

For food enthusiasts who want to extend their enjoyment of Louisiana's cooking, this edition contains recipes reflecting the state's varied cuisine, from the fruit-filled creations of peachy Ruston to the renowned meat pies of Natchitoches, to mouth-watering chicken and dumplings, generously shared by the rstaff at Lea's Lunchroom in Lecompte. Specialities from Cajun country, Baton Rouge, and New Orleans may inspire you when you're having trouble coming up with ideas for dinner.

If I haven't included that special recipe you're looking for, chances are you'll find it in your travels, at least if you keep your eye out for cookbooks, which abound here. In each region you'll come across excellent cookbooks featuring local specialities, which is not surprising in a state that takes food seriously and regards cooking as an art.

atleisure

Renowned for its richness of outdoor activities, Louisiana refers to itself as a "Sportsman's Paradise"—as in the longtime state license plate motto. Fishing and hunting are much-favored leisure activities. Among spectator sports, loyalties are divided between professional football's New Orleans Saints and the popular college teams, such as the LSU Tigers and Tulane University's Green Wave.

Tasting your way through the state you will probably understand the results of a personal poll I took in my Louisiana travels. Asking residents "What's the best thing about Louisiana," I heard the answer, "the food," as much as I heard, "the people." The other answers described Louisiana amenities you may want to get acquainted with: fishing, hunting, the history, the climate, and the "flowers that bloom all year long."

As you plan your itineray, you'll no doubt first be struck by the state's shape—another example of its uniqueness. Its shape is like a boot or perhaps a Santa Claus stocking, raveling at the toe. We think of it as the natives do, dividing it simply into two parts—North Louisiana and South Louisiana, with New Orleans as a third entity. North and south merge at Alexandria, in the middle of the state.

For the purpose of clustering regional attractions, this book breaks the "boot" into five sections. Starting with the northwestern region, the text moves from west to east in zigzag fashion, culminating in the southeastern area on the doorstep of New Orleans. "The city that care forgot" would serve as a fitting finale for a Louisiana holiday, and several enticements, such as the Garden District and Vieux Carré (French Quarter), are suggested as part of a New Orleans itinerary. As the state's principal tourist magnet, New Orleans hardly qualifies as being off the beaten path; however, it would be a shame to miss some of this grand city's unique attractions.

From blues, jazz, and Cajun to country, swamp rock and pop, and progressive zydeco, music starts with a capital M in Louisiana. Fans flock from afar to Plaisance for the annual Zydeco Festival, where the music's hot and so's the temperature (but the heat doesn't daunt the dancing, clapping throngs).

Because Louisianians love festivals, practically any topic is good enough for a celebration—possums, peaches, pecans, poke salad, pirates, sweet potatoes, frogs, catfish, rice, oil, omelettes, crawfish, and the list goes on. (Incidentally, despite what your biology teacher may have told you, the proper term here is crawfish—not crayfish.)

The merrymaking, which always includes good music and great food, can also feature such festivities as frog derbies, crawfish-eating contests, and pirogue races. At Morgan City's long-running Shrimp & Petroleum Festival, two big boats meet in a bow-to-bow "kiss" as the king and queen lean forward from their respective decks for a traditional champagne toast. Of course all the world knows about the state's biggest festival, Mardi Gras (French for "fat Tuesday"), with its magic, music, and mystique. To enhance your visit to a particular area, find out about any nearby festivals—they fill the calendar.

The state boasts a number of the South's grand plantation manors, and many are mentioned in this guide. If you're a history buff, be sure to check the area through which you're traveling for other showplaces that may be in the same vicinity. Some historic homes, not open on a regular basis, can be visited by appointment. A great number, especially along River Road, offer year-round tours. Best of all, many of these mansions now open their doors to travelers, inviting them to sleep in canopied beds, wake up to coffee delivered on a silver platter, and enjoy a full plantation breakfast of grits, ham, eggs, and biscuits or perhaps sugared stacks of French toast with sausages. For a different slant on life along River Road, visit Laura, a Creole plantation and the American home of the legendary Br'er Rabbit tales.

You can also take a look at the lifestyles of early citizens who endured hardship and privation. Their customs and contributions are commemorated in museums across the state—from the Acadian Village and Homer's Ford Museum to Shreveport's Pioneer Heritage Center and Baton Rouge's Rural Life Museum.

Some general observations: North Louisiana's culture and topography resemble those of surrounding states—Mississippi, Arkansas, and Texas. This area is primarily Protestant. In contrast, most of South Louisiana's landscape features marshes, swamps, bayous, and bottomlands. Predominantly Catholic, many of its inhabitants descended from the French Acadians, who were forced by England to leave Canada in 1755. *Evangeline,* Longfellow's epic poem, tells their story. In time the pronunciation of "Acadian" was reduced to "Cajun." Known for their *joie de vivre,* or joy of life, Cajuns treasure their ancestry, and many still speak the Cajun-French language.

The state's economy took a big dip during the '80s when gas and oil prices plummeted. Although the financial landscape continues to reflect the ups and downs of the oil industry, the economic sector has broadened considerably during the past two decades. Tourism, for example, generates funds for the state, and its related industries are major sources of employment. Before Hurricane Katrina, the state's tourism and cultural economy amounted to a $10.4 billion business.

Other areas of diversification include a broader retail base, an expanded health care industry, and an innovative approach to agriculture, reflected in new harvesting techniques, hybridization programs, and state-of-the-art equipment. With sugarcane, rice, and aquaculture (raising crawfish and catfish in shallow ponds) as major industries, agriculture plays a vital role. Alligator ranching certainly qualifies as innovative, and Louisiana leads the world in alligator production—and preservation.

One native recommends "calling any place before you visit, as this is the country, and folks are liable to just leave and go fishin'." When traveling off the beaten path or before driving long distances, take this advice because dates, rates, times, attractions, and facilities *do* change.

For a free Louisiana tour guide or road map of the state, call (800) 33–GUMBO. For more information, check out www.louisianatravel.com.

For help in planning a visit to the Big Easy, click on www.NewOrleans Online.com, the official tourism Web site of the city of New Orleans. Here, you can book a room in your preferred location and price range, check out restaurants, and order a free guidebook called *New Orleans: The Official Guide to the City* with money-saving coupons.

Unless otherwise noted, all museums and attractions with admission prices less than $5.00 per adult will be designated as modest. A restaurant meal (the price of a single entree without beverages) listed as economical costs less than $8.00, moderate prices range between $8.00 and $20.00, and entrees more than $20 are classified as expensive. As for accommodations, those that cost less than $80 per night will be listed as standard, an overnight stay falling in the $80 to $150 range is labeled moderate, and lodging more than $150 is designated deluxe.

Louisiana possesses many wonderful, tucked-away towns and special spots—more than can be included in this volume. If this sampler whets your appetite for a statewide exploration of your own, you'll discover a smorgasbord of tempting offerings. Take along your curiosity and your appetite when you head for Louisiana and let the good times roll! Or, as they put it in Cajun country, *"Laissez les bons temps rouler!"*

FYI

There's plenty to love and learn about the state of Louisiana. Here are some fun-filled facts and practical health notes that will better prepare you for your off-the-beaten-path adventure.

SYMBOLICALLY SPEAKING

Louisiana has a wealth of state symbols. The two state songs are the not-too-well-known "Give Me Louisiana" and the perennial favorite "You Are My Sunshine," composed by former Louisiana governor Jimmie Davis. The state amphibian is the green tree frog; the state insect, the honeybee; the state fossil, petrified palmwood; the state wildflower, the iris; and the state dog, the Catahoula hog dog (a usually blue-eyed hound with distinctive whorls in its coarse black-and-white or grayish coat, said to be descended from early Spanish dogs).

The official Louisiana state seal shows a pelican feeding three young birds, with the motto "Union, Justice, Confidence" below. Perhaps significantly, the early Louisiana explorer Iberville captained a ship named *Pelikan* in a seventeenth-century victory over the English in Canada.

HEALTH NOTES

Exercise common sense: That's the best health information you need before any vacation. There are, however, a few things to keep in mind.

Because of the weather in Louisiana, pay special attention to temperature changes. Drink lots of water when it's hot. Stay dry and wear warm clothing in the winter—Louisiana duck hunters can be in danger of hypothermia when sudden cold fronts arrive in the marshes. Follow water safety rules and wear your life jacket in any watercraft. Obey all weather warnings from the media—if they say get out, go immediately.

Tuck in your shirt and pull your socks over your pant cuffs when you walk in the woods—Lyme disease ticks are found in the state, mainly in the Florida Parishes. Out in the wild, look where you walk: Snakes and poison ivy are both avoidable hazards. Nature is bountiful in Louisiana, but don't nibble on fruits, berries, or mushrooms in the wilderness unless you are absolutely sure of their identity.

In larger cities practice good sense. Don't walk alone on dark streets. Stay with the lights and the crowds. Obey the laws. And use alcohol in moderation. Even on vacation you still need a designated driver.

After all, you're going to want to come back here and fall in love with Louisiana all over again.

Northwest Louisiana

Northwest Louisiana (on a map, the top of the back of the boot) boasts the greatest range of temperatures in the state. The all-time high was 114 degrees in Plain Dealing and the low was minus 16 degrees recorded in 1886 in Minden.

Geologically speaking, this is the oldest part of the state. Louisiana's "hill region" includes the Sabine Uplift, around which curve outcrops of rock strata called "wolds." The Nacogdoches Wold (named for a town in nearby Texas) includes Driskill Mountain, which rises to 535 feet above sea level in Bienville Parish. The Red River and various tributaries and old channels drain the area.

The close proximity of Texas is readily seen not just in the hot weather but also in the local culture, a nice blend of South-western and Louisiana Southern that finds chicken-fried steak on the menu as well as shrimp and crawfish, and Wrangler jeans as proper attire for most local events.

Shreveport, the second-largest city in Louisiana, and Bossier, its across-the-Red-River sister city, constitute the commercial center of this section of the state.

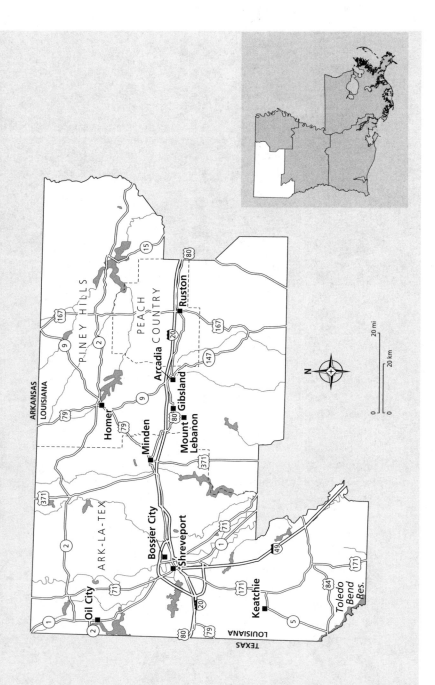

Ark-La-Tex

Entering Louisiana at its northwest corner, a person can stand in three states at the same time. North of Rodessa, the Three States Marker shows where the borders of Louisiana, Texas, and Arkansas all converge. Shreveport and Bossier City, farther south, serve as the hub for a 200-mile radius known as the *Ark-La-Tex.* The Shreveport-Bossier area makes a convenient starting point for exploring other portions of Louisiana. From here you can either proceed eastward or you can angle south into the central section. Both regions provide plenty of off-the- beaten-path attractions.

Named for the Native Americans who once lived here, Caddo Parish was created in 1838. The Caddo (or Kadohadacho) Native Americans who occupied the surrounding forests sold one million acres to the United States government on July 1, 1835.

Afterward, with the discovery of oil, the area turned from happy hunting grounds to hootin' and hollerin' hysteria almost overnight. In one year land values jumped from 50 cents an acre to $500 an acre. Oil City sprang up to become the first wildcat town in the Ark-La-Tex. The resulting large red-light district and influx of rough characters gave the town an unsavory reputation.

When you enter today's Oil City via Route 1 from the state's northwestern corner, you'll find a small, quiet hamlet with few reminders of its brawling boomtown days. To learn more, head for the *Louisiana State Oil and Gas Museum* (318–995–6845) at 200 South Land Avenue (Oil City's main street).

GAY'S FAVORITES IN NORTHWEST LOUISIANA

American Rose Center
Shreveport

Ark-La-Tex Antique and Classic Vehicle Museum
Shreveport

Ford Museum
Homer

Germantown Colony Museum
Minden

Kisatchie National Forest
Homer

Louisiana Downs racetrack
Bossier City

Louisiana State Oil and Gas Museum
Oil City

Meadows Museum of Art
Shreveport

R. W. Norton Art Gallery
Shreveport

Sci-Port Discovery Center
Shreveport

Town of Keatchie

Currently the complex consists of three buildings dating from the early 1900s plus a new museum with galleries highlighting the culture and the role of oil and gas in the area's history.

Start your tour in the new 12,000-square-foot facility. You'll see an adjacent caboose and displays of early oil field equipment, railroad artifacts, old photographs, Native American relics, a collection of pearls found in mussels from Caddo Lake, and other items relating to the area's history.

A ten-minute video presentation acquaints you with North Caddo Parish's history. Take a self-guided tour to learn some of the region's colorful legends, such as the story of an Indian chief who divided his extensive land holdings between his twin sons. Each brave was told to walk for two and a half days—one toward the rising sun and the other toward the setting sun. The eastward-bound son received Louisiana's Natchitoches area as his legacy, and the other's inheritance was the region around Nacogdoches, Texas.

The museum is open Monday through Friday from 9:00 A.M. until 4:00 P.M.

After touring the museum, step outside to see the century-old bank and post office, which was moved from nearby Trees City. A security system now protects the small bank, although none was there when the bank did a booming cash business.

Perhaps the closest Oil City comes to its lively past occurs each spring when citizens celebrate the oil industry with their *Gusher Days Festival.* On tap are such events as arts-and-crafts exhibits, street dancing, parades, and a beard contest. Previous festivals featured a spirited competition in which local businesspeople vied for the dubious distinction of being named Miss Slush Pit.

Not only was the first oil well in Northwest Louisiana drilled in this area, but the world's first marine well was drilled in nearby Caddo Lake. Until May 1911, when this original offshore well was completed, underwater drilling remained in the realm of theory.

Water sports enthusiasts will appreciate Caddo Lake for other reasons. The large cypress-studded lake, which can be reached via Route 1, offers opportunities for boating, skiing, fishing, hunting, and camping. Consulting your map you'll see that the lake also spills over into Texas.

Continue to 8012 Blanchard-Furrh Road, where you'll find the *Walter B. Jacobs Memorial Nature Park* (318–929–2806)—2.9 miles east of Longwood (Route 169) and 2.8 miles west of Blanchard (Route 173). Dedicated to nature's preservation, the park invites those who want to use it for walking, hiking, photography, painting, writing, bird-watching, or simply the pure enjoyment of being outdoors.

At the interpretive building you'll see an exhibit on predators and prey, coiled live snakes in glass cages, and a colony of bees in action. Other displays feature mounted specimens of native wildlife such as a Louisiana black bear, coyotes, and river otters. One of the building's classrooms contains "feel" boxes, helpful for using a hands-on approach with students. Youngsters can reach inside a box, guess what object they're touching, and then describe it for their classmates. This leads to follow-up discussions on different aspects of nature. (I was relieved that my box contained an antler instead of something squirmy.)

Trail and terrain maps are given to visitors who want to hike through the 160-acre park of pine, oak, and hickory forest. Markers identify natural features and animal habitats along the trails. Local woods are populated by deer, snakes, lizards, turtles, rabbits, squirrels, opossums, raccoons, armadillos, and other animals. Plant lovers will want to check out the medicinal and herb garden and the wildflower trail.

The park provides a picnic area with pavilion for people who want to pack a lunch and spend the day. Also two full-time and two part-time naturalists are available to arrange guided tours, present programs, teach sessions, and, in general, share expertise.

You can visit from 8:00 A.M. to 5:00 P.M. Wednesday through Saturday and from 1:00 to 5:00 P.M. on Sunday. The park is closed New Year's Day, Easter, Thanksgiving, and Christmas Day. Admission is free. Check out www.caddo parks.com for more information.

Don't miss the ***American Rose Center*** (318–938–5402) at 8877 Jefferson-Paige Road, Shreveport. Located just off Interstate 20, the American Rose Center is 5 miles east of the Texas state line and about 10 miles west of downtown Shreveport. Take exit 5 and follow the signs.

Now America's national flower (Congress made it official in 1986), the rose reigns supreme here at America's largest rose garden. The American Rose Society, established in 1892, also makes its headquarters at the center. Recent additions to the center include Klima Rose Hall, an education and visitor's facility, as well as a gift shop with great items for your favorite gardener. You can stroll along pathways edged by split-rail fences to see more than sixty-five individual gardens spreading over the site's currently developed fifty-seven acres. You don't have to be a rose expert to appreciate the beauty of this place. A label next to each planting provides such pertinent information as the rose's name, type, and heritage. Like the flowers themselves, the names are intriguing: White Masterpiece, New Year, Show Biz, French Lace, Angel Face, Touch of Class, Double Delight, and Sweet Surrender are among the rose varieties you can see here. While sampling this buffet of blossoms, be careful when you sniff—bees like the roses, too.

The Windsounds Carillon Tower rises impressively from plantings of award-winning roses in reds, pinks, yellows, mauves, and a medley of other

rosamonstrosa

A personal favorite: By far the oddest flower at the American Rose Center is the *Rosa monstrosa,* an all-green flower with petals the same color as its leaves. It has a certain creepy charm and must look rather like roses do to the color-blind.

colors. You'll also find a picturesque log cabin chapel, a gift shop, sundials, gazebos, inviting benches, and picnicking facilities. The gardens and chapel serve as a beautiful backdrop for more than one hundred weddings a year.

Christmas in Roseland makes the place more magical than ever with such entertainment as choral groups, soloists, dancers, and storytellers. Displays include illuminated wire sculptures depicting the Nativity scene, Eiffel Tower, Statue of Liberty, a spotlighted group of large wooden Christmas card panels designed and painted by area students, and other festive displays.

You can visit the Rose Center from April through October between 9:00 A.M. and 5:00 P.M. weekdays, 9:00 A.M. to 6:00 P.M. on Saturday, and 1:00 to 6:00 P.M. on Sunday. Holiday hours, from Thanksgiving through New Year's Eve (except for Christmas Day), change to 5:30 to 10:00 P.M. daily, and the gates close at 9:30 P.M. Admission. Take a look at www.ars.org for answers to your rose-growing questions.

Continue into **Shreveport,** now big and bustling. The city truly qualified as an off-the-beaten-path kind of place before Captain Henry Miller Shreve appeared on the scene in 1833 to unclog the Red River. Using snag boats, Shreve and his crews divested the river of a logjam known as the "Great Raft," which extended some 180 miles—a project that took five years and cost $300,000. Later the town that sprang up on the banks of the Red River was named in honor of Captain Shreve. It's a safe bet to say that today the captain would not recognize his riverfront, which has taken on a Las Vegas look with dockside riverboat gaming, specialty shops, lounges, live music, and crowds courting Lady Luck via video poker, blackjack, craps, roulette, slots, and similar pursuits.

The Louisiana legislature officially recognized Shreveport as a town in 1839. During the Civil War Shreveport served as the state's capital for a short time. The last place in Louisiana to concede defeat, its official Confederate flag was not lowered until Federal troops arrived to occupy the city.

Start your visit to Shreveport with a drive through the historical Highland-Fairfield area, a setting for many of the city's elegant mansions. Fairfield Avenue, one of Shreveport's most attractive streets, features grand houses in a diversity of architectural styles. One of these lovely homes, **Fairfield Place** (318–222–0048), in the city's Highland Historic District, can be your base while here. When Janie Lipscomb first saw this classic Victorian house located at 2221 Fairfield Avenue, she fell in love with it and immediately signed a sales contract on the hood of her car.

With two crews of carpenters and artisans, she worked day and night seven days a week for the next five months to restore the home and convert it into an elegant guest house. The bed-and-breakfast facility was opened in 1983. Dating from the 1870s, the home still contains many of its original brass light fixtures and much of its copper hardware.

A former dental hygienist, Janie has effervescence and energy that serve her well in her current career as innkeeper. "I've tried to give each room and suite everything I ever wanted in a hotel room," she says, "and eliminate everything I hate about hotel rooms." Janie's an avid gardener, and you will admire her well-kept grounds and flower gardens. She serves full gourmet breakfasts with rich Cajun coffee and usually offers an afternoon tea cart with light refreshments. Rates range from moderate to deluxe, and credit cards are accepted. Click on www.fairfieldbandb.com for more information.

While tooling around downtown Shreveport, stop by ***Ark-La-Tex Antique and Classic Vehicle Museum*** (318–222–0227) at 601 Spring Street. Here, on

TOP ANNUAL EVENTS IN NORTHWEST LOUISIANA

Holiday in Dixie
Shreveport, April
(318) 865–5555

Mudbug Madness
Shreveport, May, Memorial
Day Weekend
(318) 222–7403

Mayhaw Festival
Marion, weekend of Mother's Day
(318) 292–4716

Louisiana Peach Festival
Ruston, fourth week in June
(318) 255–2031

Red River Revel Arts Festival
Shreveport, first week in October
(318) 424–4000

Louisiana State Fair
Shreveport at Louisiana State
Fairgrounds, last week in October
(318) 635–1361

Christmas in Roseland
Shreveport, Friday after Thanksgiving
through December 30
(318) 938–5402

December on the Red
Shreveport-Bossier, December 30
(800) 551–8682

the premises of a 1920s automobile assembly area and showroom, you'll view a choice selection of vintage vehicles. At one time, you could purchase a Graham truck or Dodge car here. Now you'll see an assortment of antique automobiles, all polished to a high sheen and "peopled" with mannequins in period costumes. There are also motorcycle exhibits and a room focusing on the firefighting profession with antique fire trucks and related equipment. More than forty classic cars from private collections throughout the country and abroad may be admired at any given time, and exhibits rotate every six months. Tools, toys, historic photos, and related items complement the nostalgic settings. The facility, which stages special events, houses a gift shop and an automotive library; some exhibit vehicles are for sale. The museum is open Monday through Saturday from 10:00 A.M. to 5:00 P.M. Admission. Check out these gems at www.carmuseum.org.

backtonature

One pleasant way to dawdle away a Shreveport afternoon is on the paths and by the fountains of the **R. S. Barnwell Memorial Garden and Art Center,** (318–673–7703), 601 Clyde Fant Parkway. This art gallery and plant-and-flower-exhibit facility is free and open daily. Stroll through the sculpture garden and a specially scented garden, or simply enjoy the quiet greenery you'll find along the walkways. Before some recent landscaping you could find bonus vegetation: Pokeweed growing on the slopes of the nearby Red River levee attracted lots of busy gatherers each spring for poke salad.

Afterward, continue your sentimental journey by taking in **Spring Street Historical Museum** (318–424–0964), only a few steps away. Here at 525 Spring Street, you'll get a real feel for the city's history. Built as a bank in 1865 and recently restored, this fine structure with its cast-iron balcony is one of the town's oldest existing buildings. An eight-minute video presentation acquaints you with the city's early history. Rotating exhibits allow the museum to showcase its historical collections of furniture, clothing, jewelry, firearms, books, and newspapers.

Don't miss seeing the upstairs with its permanent collection of Victorian furnishings. Beautiful period pieces include American Chippendale chairs that date from 1760 to 1775, paintings from the 1800s, various pieces of carved rosewood furniture, an 1878 cherry and walnut organ that has been restored to playing condition, a child's harp, a melodeon, and a Persian carpet. You'll also see a chair that belonged to Shreveport's famous madam (who received a three-month bank loan for her business and repaid it within two weeks). Hours are from 10:00 A.M. to 4:00 P.M. Tuesday through Saturday. Modest admission.

While in the area you can stop for a meal at the **Blind Tiger** (318–226–8747) on the corner of Spring and Texas Streets in historic Shreve Square. Hark-

OTHER ATTRACTIONS WORTH SEEING

Lake Bistineau State Park
Doyline
(318) 745–3503 or (888) 677–2478.
This park has facilities for camping
and cabin and boat rentals. State
parks make a welcome break in a
driving vacation, even if you don't stay
overnight. For information on camping
and rentals, write to Lake Bistineau
State Park, 103 State Park Road,
Doyline 71023, or call (877) 226–7652,
the reservations number for all
Louisiana state parks.

Louisiana State Fairgrounds
3015 Greenwood Road, Shreveport
(318) 632–2020
Even when it's not fair week (last
week in October) the Louisiana State
Fairgrounds are worth visiting for the
Louisiana State Exhibit Museum.
Inside the marble rotunda, a long,
circular corridor leads past dioramas
of Louisiana industry and life. You'll
find an oil refinery, a sulfur mine, a salt
dome, an Indian village . . . in short, a
wealth of small tableaux that explain
Louisiana, along with murals, other
exhibits, and an art gallery.

Sci-Port Discovery Center
820 Clyde Fant Parkway
(318) 424–3466 or (877) Sci–Port
This hands-on science museum on
Shreveport's riverfront offers some
200 programs and interactive exhibits.
Here you might lie on a bed of nails and
learn why and how you can do this
without flinching or screaming. Besides
participating in Sci-Port's interactive
discovery areas, you can take in an
engrossing IMAX production on a 60-
foot dome screen. Open daily, Monday
through Friday from 10:00 A.M. to 5:00
P.M., Saturday from 10:00 A.M. to 6:00
P.M., and Sunday from 1:00 to 6:00 P.M.

Shreveport Sports Arena
3207 Pershing Boulevard, Shreveport
(318) 752–BUGS (2847)
Although snow is something of a rarity
in the area, there's ice galore at Hirsch
Coliseum, and it's exciting to watch
the Shreveport Mudbugs battle it
out with other professional hockey
teams from November through March.
Check www.mudbugshockey.com
for schedules.

Spirit of the Red River Cruise
820 Clyde Fant Parkway on the
Shreveport riverfront across from
Sci-Port Discovery Center
(318) 424–3576
See the city from a different perspective
with a tour of Red River and Cross
Bayou. You can also view wildlife in
its natural habitat.

ing back to the time of Prohibition and speakeasies, when saloons operated behind facades or "blinds" such as museums with wild animal displays to mask back rooms where alcoholic beverages were sold, the restaurant's name serves as a reminder of the town's past.

Erected in 1848, the building burned in 1854 and was rebuilt later to house several businesses, including the Buckelew Hardware Company. The interior echoes the nostalgic theme with stained glass, dark wood paneling, brass rails, and Tiffany chandeliers.

courthouse
copycat

President Harry S. Truman liked Shreveport's Caddo Parish Courthouse (500 Texas Street) so much that he used part of its design for his presidential library in Independence, Missouri.

"Our menu offers plenty of variety, although the emphasis is on seafood," says Rick Sloan, who with Glenn Brannan owns the Blind Tiger. Consider an appetizer of tiger wings or pigskins for starters, then try one of the snapper specialties. The restaurant also serves a Cajun sampler of five different entrees as well as great steaks and hamburgers. Prices are moderate. Hours are from 11:00 A.M. to 10:00 P.M. Monday through Thursday, 11:00 A.M. to 11:00 P.M. Friday and Saturday, and noon to 9:00 P.M. Sunday The bar is open all night—until 6:00 A.M. daily, except Sunday when it closes earlier.

Located at 619 Louisiana Avenue in Shreveport, the **Strand Theatre** (318–226–1481) is a must-see, although parking can present a problem. Be sure to notice the dome and the exterior's decorative details as you approach. Now restored to its previous grandeur, the neobaroque theater originally opened in 1925 with the operetta *The Chocolate Soldier*. Listed on the National Register of Historic Places, the 1,636-seat theater boasts an organ of 939 pipes, ornate box seats, and gilt-edged mirrors. The interior features a color scheme of rich burgundy with gold accents. Don't forget to look up at the magnificent ceiling and dazzling chandeliers.

Reopened in 1984, this downtown landmark again attracts crowds for performances that range from ballet and musical extravaganzas on ice to touring Broadway hits. The Strand is open Monday through Friday from 9:00 A.M. to 5:00 P.M. for performances, or by appointment. Modest admission.

Continue to the **Meadows Museum of Art** (318–869–5169), located at 2911 Centenary Boulevard in Shreveport 71104, on the Centenary College campus. The museum's permanent collection includes works by such artists as Mary Cassatt, Diego Rivera, Alfred Maurer, George Grosz, and others. Also, you'll see the work of Louisiana artists such as Clyde Connell, John Scott, Maria Lopez, Clementine Hunter, Lucille Reed, Langston McEachern, and Jack Barham. The museum hosts from three to six temporary exhibitions throughout the year.

"Many works on view from the permanent collection during 2006–2007 have been recently conserved or newly acquired," said director Diane Dufilho. Learn more about the museum's holdings and exhibitions at www.meadows museum.org.

The Meadows Museum showcases the work of French academic artist Jean Despujols. On request, visitors can view the museum's award-winning film,

Indochina Revisited: A Portrait of Jean Despujols. This twenty-eight-minute documentary will provide some glimpses into the life and work of an extraordinary artist. A seven-minute slide presentation also offers an overview of the Despujols collection.

From December 1936 to August 1938, French artist Jean Despujols made his way through French Indochina's interior, capturing its people and landscapes with pencil, ink, oil, charcoal, and watercolor. This rare collection of 360 works is personalized by excerpts from a diary he kept while traveling through the remote areas of Vietnam, Laos, and Cambodia. Despujols moved to Shreveport in 1941 and became an American citizen in 1945. His collection (hidden at his parents' home in France) survived World War II only to disappear in transit later when the artist requested that it be shipped to him in America. Lost for seven months during the trip from France, the valuable collection surfaced in Guadeloupe, where it had mistakenly been unloaded. The treasure finally arrived in Shreveport in December 1948.

The Smithsonian Institution exhibited Despujols's works in 1950, and *National Geographic* borrowed twenty-one of his paintings to illustrate a 1951 article on Indochina. Despujols died in 1965, and his works were kept in a Shreveport bank vault. In 1969 Centenary College alumnus Algur H. Meadows purchased the collection, presented it to the college, and also provided funds for a museum to house the rare body of work.

The Meadows Museum is open to the public from noon to 4:00 P.M. Tuesday, Wednesday, and Friday; from noon to 5:00 P.M. on Thursday; and from 1:00 to 4:00 P.M. Saturday and Sunday. Admission is free.

Multiple treasures await at the **R. W. Norton Art Gallery** (318–865–4201), surrounded by forty landscaped acres that showcase masses of azaleas each spring. Designed in a contemporary style, the gallery at 4747 Creswell Avenue, Shreveport, houses twenty-five exhibition rooms. Here is one of the three largest collections in the country of American Western paintings and sculptures by Frederic Remington and Charles M. Russell, as well as Flemish tapestries (ca. 1540) and works by Corot, Auguste Rodin, Sir Joshua Reynolds, and other masters. In addition to its collections of decorative arts, sculptures, and paintings spanning four centuries, the Norton Gallery offers a reference/research library. Except for national holidays, the museum is open from 10:00 A.M. to 5:00 P.M. Tuesday through Friday and 1:00 to 5:00 P.M. Saturday and Sunday. Admission is free. Check out current and upcoming exhibitions at www.rwnaf.org.

After a visit to the art gallery, take Route 1 to the campus of Louisiana State University in Shreveport. Near the northeast corner of the campus you'll find the **Pioneer Heritage Center.** The complex is composed of several authentic plantation structures that give you a picture—outside the pages of a history book—of how the area's early settlers lived.

The Webb and Webb Commissary serves as a visitor center where you'll get an overview of the operation and an interesting history lesson about the pioneers who settled the northwest corner of Louisiana. The building itself is typical of a company store in an agricultural community, where purchases could be made on credit before a crop was harvested and paid off later when the crop was sold.

You'll come away with a new appreciation for modern dentistry after seeing the dental drill displayed in the doctor's office at the Pioneer Heritage Center. There's also a collection of medical and surgical instruments from the "olden days." One room contains displays of various herbal home remedies.

You'll see the restored 1856 "Big House," a frame antebellum cottage from Caspiana Plantation, and an outside kitchen. A nearby structure, the Thrasher log house, illustrates the dogtrot style. The dogtrot (an open passage supposedly favored by the family dogs) provided a cool covered area for performing household chores during hot weather. The complex also features an equipped blacksmith's shop and a small church.

The Pioneer Heritage Center serves as a "history laboratory" for area schools and visitors. For information on special events or to schedule a tour, call (318) 797–5339. The complex closes for major holidays and from mid-December through February. Admission is modest, and children get in free. Learn more at www.lsus.edu/pioneer.

At *Savoie's,* "The Cajun Restaurant" (318–797–3010), located at 2400 East Seventieth Street, you can sample special Cajun dishes in a North Louisiana locale. Savoie's offers such delights as court bouillon (*koo boo-YON*), crawfish stew, shrimp, oyster or catfish po'boys (submarine sandwiches for "poor

Webb and Webb Commissary at Pioneer Heritage Center

boys"), stuffed crab, and jambalaya. You also can opt for steaks—a rib-eye or a filet mignon that comes with french fries and coleslaw.

If it's lunchtime and you're in a hurry, order from the items with stars—they require less time to prepare. Try the shrimp fettuccine or the Louisiana fried oysters with jambalaya.

Open daily, the restaurant operates from 11:00 A.M. to 10:00 P.M. Monday through Saturday, and 11:00 A.M. to 9:00 P.M. Sunday. Prices are moderate.

Before continuing east, you may want to sweep south a short distance for a look at a charming little town called *Keatchie* (*KEY-chi*—the second syllable sounds like the *chi* in "child").

To reach Keatchie, about 25 miles southwest of Shreveport, take U.S. Highway 171 south (the Mansfield Road), then turn west on Route 5. Incorporated in 1858 as Keachi, the town takes its name from a Native American tribe of Caddo ancestry. You will see a sign that says WELCOME TO HISTORIC KEACHI because Travis Whitfield (318–933–8371) and other members of the local heritage foundation worked hard to get the original spelling restored.

Predominantly Greek Revival, which Travis describes as "kind of a Parthenon temple style," much of the town's architecture dates from the 1840s and 1850s and is on the National Register of Historic Places. A short drive takes visitors by three Greek Revival–style churches, the large Keatchie Plantation Store, the Masonic Hall, and a Confederate cemetery. On Highway 172 west of downtown stands the 1852 Keatchie Baptist Church, originally the chapel for a women's college (no longer in existence). Future plans call for a cultural center on what was once the campus. If your visit coincides with Independence Day, you can enjoy an old-fashioned fun-filled evening from 7:00 to 9:30 P.M. with games, homemade ice cream in a variety of flavors, and a fireworks finale. The Keatchie Fourth of July celebration usually attracts around 1,000 people. Another popular event, which takes place the third Sunday of December, features a program of classical and seasonal music performed by a string quartet at the Presbyterian Church with a home tour scheduled afterward.

Next, you can head southeast to historic Natchitoches (described in the section on Central Louisiana) via Interstate 49 or return to Shreveport for an eastward thrust.

Traveling east, Bossier City begins where Shreveport ends. Bossier boasts a well-beaten path, Louisiana Downs, one of the country's top racetracks for Thoroughbreds.

Also in Bossier City, just across the Red River from downtown Shreveport, you'll find the *Louisiana Boardwalk,* an enticing shopping and entertainment destination. As the state's first lifestyle center, this venue offers outlet shopping, an entertainment district, and riverfront dining. Visitors can hop aboard the

Magnolia Belle Trolley, a breezer-style trolley patterned after those of the 1920s and 1930s.

The state's first Bass Pro Shops Outdoor World here lures more than fishermen and hunters. The facility offers equipment for hiking, backpacking, wildlife viewing, camping, outdoor cooking, and more. Look for the Alligator Pit at the front of the store, popular with both tourists and shoppers.

If shopping's not your favorite sport, the Boardwalk offers lots more—a movie theater, bowling alley, carousel rides, live entertainment, riverfront dining, dancing water fountains, and gaming. Visit www.louisianaboardwalk.com for current and upcoming events.

The *Touchstone Wildlife and Art Museum* (318–949–2323) is located 2.2 miles east of the Louisiana Downs racetrack at 3386 U.S. Highway 80 East, near Bossier City. Founded by professional taxidermists Lura and the late Sam Touchstone, this natural history museum features hand-painted dioramas as backdrops for mounted mammals, birds, and reptiles from all over the world. The collection contains more than 1,000 specimens of wildlife displayed in habitats simulating their natural environments. Sam practiced "taxidermy in action," and all his animals are engaged in lifelike pursuits. Be sure to notice the giraffe and the family of red foxes as well as the 310-pound gorilla that died at age twenty-seven in a zoo.

Take the nature trail behind the museum and see some mesquite growing, a rarity for Louisiana. Also on display are collections of insects, Native American artifacts, war relics, and antique tools. The museum is open Tuesday through Saturday from 9:00 A.M. until 5:00 P.M. Winter hours run Thursday through Saturday 9:00 A.M. to 5:00 P.M. Parking is free, and admission is modest.

treefacts

Forestry is an important factor in Louisiana's economy because paper mills demand vast quantities of wood pulp pine trees. New varieties of the loblolly pine can be brought to market in only nine years.

Continue east from Bossier City, by way of either I–20 or U.S. Highways 79–80, and you'll arrive in Minden. Take time to drive along Minden's brick streets to see the downtown area with antiques shops and several homes on the National Register of Historic Places.

Located 7 miles northeast of Minden (and some 30 miles east of Shreveport), you'll find the *Germantown Colony Museum* (318–377–6061 or 318–377–4240) on Museum Road off Germantown Road. Watch for signs. Several German families established a village here in 1835, and their furniture, documents, letters, tools, and other artifacts are exhibited both in replica buildings and in original cabins made of hand-hewn logs.

On display is a copy of an 1826 document signed by an archduke ordering Count von Leon (who became the group's leader) to leave Germany. In Pennsylvania the count and his wife met other German families who shared similar religious beliefs. They joined forces and began a journey south to the Minden area, the site they selected to establish a community. During the trip the count died of yellow fever at Grand Encore, Louisiana. Undaunted, the countess carried on and saw the group's goal of establishing a self-sufficient religious colony fulfilled. Germantown functioned as a communal system for more than three and a half decades. The countess earned money by giving music lessons. (Her pupils came from Minden.) Other colonists performed work according to their talents and interests. The group grew grape and mulberry trees for making jellies and wine.

You'll see the cabin where the countess lived and the kitchen–dining hall where the colonists gathered for

minden's indianaties

Minden's founder, War of 1812 veteran Charles Veeder, purchased 160 acres of land for his new hometown and moved here from Rushville, Indiana, in 1835.

meals, as well as reproductions of a smokehouse (on the site of the original), a doctor's cottage, and a blacksmith shop with authentic equipment. All the buildings contain items that the Germantown settlers used, and a map shows where other structures, such as barns and workhouses, once stood.

On the walls of the countess's cabin, you can see remnants of the original wallpaper that she ordered from New Orleans. Among the interesting items on display are the countess's piano, Count von Leon's coronet, the colony's book of laws, German Bibles, ledgers, and slave passes.

The museum is open Wednesday through Saturday from 10:00 A.M. until 3:00 P.M. and also by appointment. Admission is modest.

Piney Hills

Travel south on Route 154 for about 3 miles to *Gibsland.* Each year on the weekend closest to May 23, the town stages its *Authentic Bonnie and Clyde Festival* with robbery reenactments and more civilized events such as an antique car parade and a street dance. Gibsland's *Authentic Bonnie and Clyde Museum* contains newspaper accounts and photos relating to the criminal careers of the gunslinging couple. Check with the town hall for more information.

Afterward, continue south on Route 154 to Mount Lebanon. Located on a downtown corner, the *Stagecoach Museum* offers a glimpse of yesteryear; hours vary.

From Mount Lebanon continue south for 5 miles. Here under Ambrose Mountain's shady pines stands a simple marker denoting the ***Bonnie and Clyde Ambush Site.*** The notorious couple had vowed never to be taken alive. At this spot a surprise attack by Texas Rangers brought the fugitives' spree of bank robberies to a screeching halt. The stone marker, erected by the Bienville Parish Police Jury, reads AT THIS SITE MAY 23, 1934, CLYDE BARROW AND BONNIE PARKER WERE KILLED BY LAW ENFORCEMENT OFFICIALS.

One local legend has it that during an attempted robbery of a Ruston bank, the couple took an undertaker as hostage. Clyde's bargain: the man's life for his future services. He was released in Arkansas when Clyde extracted a promise from the mortician to make him "look good" after the inevitable occurred. Later, upon learning the couple had been killed, the undertaker traveled to the Arcadia funeral home (where the bodies had been taken), determined to keep his end of the bargain. Although he found the two corpses beyond salvaging, he was allowed to restore one of Clyde's hands.

After your visit return to Mount Lebanon and continue north to the intersection of US 80. Travel east on this road until you reach ***Arcadia.*** This small town, along with near-by Homer, Athens, and Sparta, all took their names from ancient Greece.

In Arcadia you can stop by the ***Bienville Depot Museum*** to see a permanent exhibit of memorabilia related to Bonnie and Clyde as well as other items of local history. Located downtown, the ca. 1884 depot stands across from City Hall. Arcadia also hosts ***Bonnie & Clyde Trade Days*** on Route 9 about 2.5 miles south of town. This monthly event takes place the weekend prior to the third Monday.

For more information on local attractions in northern Bienville Parish, such as ***Driskill Mountain,*** Louisiana's highest point, call Bill Atteridge at the ***Civil and Korean War Naval Museum*** (318–263–8247), 153 Museum Road in Arcadia. The museum is open Thursday through Saturday from 10:00 A.M. to 4:00 P.M. and from 1:00 to 4:00 P.M. on Sunday. Mr. Atteridge,

Bonnie and Clyde Ambush Site

who has constructed more than 1,100 models of Civil War ships for twelve museums, is currently gathering information for a Bonnie and Clyde Tourism Trail. His collection includes eighty Civil War models and twenty-seven Korean models. Free admission.

Homer, located 23 miles north of Arcadia, can be reached by taking Route 9 north, which runs into US 79 just outside town.

Proceed to Homer's town square. On the square's south side, you'll see the *Ford Museum* (318–927–9190), located at 519 South Main Street. This museum owes its existence to a German infantry officer's helmet, which inspired the museum's collection. When Herbert S. Ford's sons retrieved the helmet from the town dump, he embarked on a personal campaign to preserve for posterity other items of historical significance.

In 1918 Ford started his collection, and as he accumulated additional artifacts, storage became a problem. At various times the collection occupied a room at the local high school, a railroad car, and the town hall. This remarkable assemblage now has a permanent home in the handsome Hotel Claiborne, a building that dates from 1890.

Downstairs you will see interpretive exhibits for each of the area's major development stages, starting with a dugout canoe and other Native American artifacts. Illustrating Claiborne Parish's pioneer period is an authentic log cabin moved from nearby Haynesville. The structure had to be dismantled and then reassembled inside the museum. Other items of interest at the Ford Museum include a moonshiner's still for making corn whiskey, a scale for weighing cotton bales, an 1830 loom, a collection of handwoven overshot coverlets, and an 1868 Grover and Baker sewing machine. You'll also see a ca. 1832 piano brought by barge and oxcart from New Orleans to nearby Minden. The museum also features a collection of thirty plantation bells, which came from schools and farms throughout the parish.

Don't miss the upstairs area, where individual rooms focus on various themes. You'll see a series of historical settings featuring a doctor's office, chapel, school, general store, hotel room, military room, and the like. Also on display are antique firearms (including Confederate weapons) and a doctor's buggy that was used in a John Wayne movie, *The Horse Soldiers,* filmed in nearby Natchitoches.

Even though the Ford Museum could be considered off the beaten path, about 2,000 persons find their way to this fascinating facility each year. Community volunteers play a major role in the museum's operation. Monday, Wednesday, and Friday hours are from 9:00 A.M. to noon and from 1:00 to 4:00 P.M. To see the museum on other days, call for an appointment. There is a modest admission charge. Learn more at www.ford.claiborneone.org.

From the Ford Museum you can walk across the street to the ***Claiborne Parish Courthouse,*** in the middle of Homer's town square. A classic example of Greek Revival architecture, the structure was completed in 1861 and is still in use. The courthouse served as the departure point for area soldiers mustering for the Confederate cause and remains one of only four pre–Civil War courthouses in Louisiana. Some artifacts from the courthouse are displayed at the Ford Museum.

From Homer, take State Route 2 east to Bernice, a distance of about 25 miles.

You will enjoy a stop at the ***Bernice Depot Museum*** (318–285–2433) and adjacent park. Located at Louisiana and Main Streets, the restored 1899 railroad depot features exhibits on railroading, such as its Rock Island memorabilia and a 1938 wooden caboose called *The Captain Henderson*. You'll also see material on local "Big Woods" history. Open Monday through Friday, the museum's hours are 10:00 A.M. to noon and 1:00 to 3:00 P.M., or by appointment.

Afterward, take U.S. Highway 167 to Ruston, about 20 miles south.

Peach Country

You are now in Lincoln Parish, in the heart of peach country. From mid-March through early April, this region becomes a landscape of blooming peach trees. ***Mitcham's Farms*** (318–255–3409), located just outside Ruston north of I–20 off Highway 544 on Mitcham Orchard Road, offers fresh peaches for sale from mid-May through mid-August; a retail store with peach products stays open all year. Visit www.mitchamfarms.com for some background and peachy products.

Ruston hosts the annual ***Louisiana Peach Festival,*** which has been chosen one of the Southeast Tourism Society's top twenty events for June. Besides eating lots of peach ice cream, festival-goers can enjoy a parade, treasure hunt, cooking contests, craft exhibits, and musical entertainment.

Founded in 1884 as Russ Town, the city of ***Ruston*** was named for Robert E. Russ, who gave the Vicksburg, Shreveport, and Pacific Railroad some acreage to build a railroad and town site on his property. An early center of culture, Ruston was the site of the Louisiana Chautauqua, a summer program providing opportunities for citizens to immerse themselves in music, drama, art, and the like. The parish is now home to two universities, Grambling and Louisiana Tech.

The ***Lincoln Parish Museum*** (318–251–0018), 609 North Vienna Street, Ruston, serves as a good starting point to begin your exploration of this inviting city. Housed in the lovely Kidd-Davis home, built in 1886, the regional museum features a collection of period furniture, paintings, and other items of historical interest. In the entry hall be sure to notice the hand-painted wall murals that illustrate the Chautauqua and scenes from local history.

You'll see a dollhouse, exquisitely furnished with tiny period pieces, on display downstairs and another on the second floor. The museum's upstairs exhibits feature various collections such as vintage wedding dresses and original textiles designed during the 1930s as part of the government's Works Progress Administration program. Other displays include household items ranging from cornshuck brooms and kitchen utensils to antique radios and tools.

The museum is open Tuesday through Friday from 10:00 A.M. to 4:00 P.M. and on Saturday and Sunday by appointment.

Jimmie Davis, twice governor of Louisiana (1944–48 and 1960–64) and professional country-music artist and composer, started his singing career in 1928.

Peaches, Peaches Everywhere

Kaylon Thompson French created the following dish featuring Ruston peaches to complement a Cornish hen/wild rice combination. Her recipe took top honors in a past Peach Cookery Contest and proved so delectable the judges could not stop with a sample taste or two. Rumor has it they tossed restraint to the winds and all but licked the platter clean.

Peach-A-Doodle-Do

4 Cornish hens	1 cup peach jelly or preserves
1 tablespoon Cajun seasoning	1 teaspoon ground cinnamon

Preheat oven to 350° F. Clean hens and cavities. If desired, the hens may be cut in half lengthwise. Place hens in a shallow 9" x 13" roasting pan, skin side up. Season with Cajun seasoning to taste and roast 25 minutes. Meanwhile, place peach jelly or preserves in a microwave-safe container and melt in a microwave oven for approximately 1 minute. Consistency should be loose, not runny or boiling. Stir cinnamon into melted jelly. Remove hens from oven and brush with melted jelly until fully coated. Return to oven and roast for another 20 minutes. Baste once more 5 minutes before serving. Discard remaining glaze. Remove from oven and serve with the following:

Wild about Peaches Rice

2 boxes wild rice (fast cooking)	1 small package of walnut pieces
4 tablespoons peach preserves	1 small bunch of green onions, chopped

In a nonstick boiler, prepare rice according to directions on box (including spice packet and butter). Approximately 2 minutes before the cooking time has finished, stir in peach preserves and walnut pieces. Cover boiler and finish cooking. Remove from heat. Garnish with chopped green onions.

One of his original songs, "You Are My Sunshine," became a hit in 1939 and was later recorded in thirty-four languages. Until his death, Davis paid an annual visit to the Homecoming held at the ***Jimmie Davis Tabernacle,*** south of Ruston in Jackson Parish. The revival-style Homecoming, which is held the first Sunday in October, attracts lots of folks. Everyone is invited to bring a dish and enjoy an old-fashioned dinner and a fish fry on the grounds. (At many places in the South, dinner is served at midday, with a lighter supper in the evening.)

Professional gospel groups from across the country join the function held on the site of Davis's parents' home close to the Peckerwood Hill Store. The Tabernacle, built in 1965 by a group of Davis's friends, is located near the junction of Highways 542 and 811 midway between Quitman and Jonesboro.

In Ruston be sure to stop by the ***Piney Hills Gallery*** (318–255–1450), located at 212 North Vienna Street in the Dixie Center for the Arts. Original works, ranging from traditional and contemporary crafts to fine arts by some forty North Central Louisiana artists, are displayed in this consignment sales gallery.

You'll see paintings, pottery, quilts, crocheted items, holiday ornaments, stained glass, jewelry, lamps, sculpture, calligraphy, and photography. Also on display are textile arts, wood carvings, and handmade musical instruments. Articles at the gallery can range in price from $2.00 to $2,000.00. The gallery is open from 9:00 A.M. until 2:00 P.M. Monday through Friday and closes on holidays.

Unique pieces from the ***Kent Follette Pottery Studio*** are among the gallery's distinctive offerings. Kent Follette, a nationally acclaimed potter, maintains a studio at 1991 Pea Ridge Road. You can visit the Follette Pottery Store (318–513–9121) at 2401 South Service Road West. Hours are 10:00 A.M. to 5:00 P.M. Monday through Saturday. Take a look at www.follettepottery.com to see some of the artist's work.

At some point during your Ruston visit, plan to stop by the ***Log Cabin Smokehouse*** (318–255–8023), located a quarter mile north of I–20 at 1906 Farmerville Highway. Housed in an 1886 dogtrot home of hand-hewn logs, the eatery serves barbecue sandwiches or hickory-smoked beef, turkey breast, ham, pork ribs, steaks, burgers, and sausage. Prices are economical to moderate. From Monday through Friday,

hotoffthegridiron

Grambling State University at Grambling, near Ruston, is one of Louisiana's historic African-American colleges. What it is best known for, though, is the large number of its alumni who go on to play pro-football—more than most schools could ever hope for. Drive around the stadium grounds and note the signage directing the media. What the sports reporters know is that if you want to see what the National Football League will look like in the future, go to a Grambling game and read the team roster. And don't miss the halftime show!

serving hours run from 11:00 A.M. to 2:00 P.M. and from 4:30 to 9:00 P.M. Hours are from 11:00 A.M. to 9:00 P.M. on Saturday. Closed Sunday.

Youngsters will enjoy seeing *Idea Place* in Woodard Hall on the campus of *Louisiana Tech University,* located on the town's west side. This children's museum features hands-on exhibits designed to encourage both you and the kids to investigate scientific and mathematical concepts and have fun at the same time. For an appointment between 8:00 A.M. and 5:00 P.M. Monday through Friday, call (318) 257–2866.

Tech is also *the* place in Ruston to get ice cream—both cones and large containers—filled with such flavors as blueberry cheesecake and the old standbys vanilla, strawberry, and chocolate. During summer months you can enjoy peach ice cream, and at Christmastime, peppermint and rum raisin flavors are available. Thanks to the college's cows, you can also purchase other premium dairy products: fresh milk (including chocolate), cheeses, and butter along with rolls and bread—all at extremely reasonable prices. These products are sold daily at the *Louisiana Tech Farm Salesroom,* located behind Reese Hall (about 1.5 miles south of the main campus) just off US 80 West. You can line up with local students and professors Monday through Friday from 8:30 A.M. to 5:30 P.M. (With advance notice visitors can tour the nearby dairy plant, which processes these products.)

Places to Stay in Northwest Louisiana

ARK-LA-TEX

Best Western Chateau Suite Hotel
201 Lake Street
I-20, exit 19A
Shreveport
(318) 222–7620 or
(800) 845–9334

Best Western of Minden
1411 Sibley Road
Minden
(318) 377–1001

Clarion Hotel
1419 East Seventieth Street
Shreveport
(318) 797–9900 or
(800) 424–6423

Days Inn
4935 West Monkhouse Drive
Shreveport
(318) 636–0080 or
(800) DAYS–INN

Fairfield Place
2221 Fairfield Avenue
Shreveport
(318) 222–0048

Hampton Inn
1005 Gould Drive
Bossier
(318) 752–1112 or
(800) HAMPTON

Holiday Inn Express–Airport
5101 Westwood Park Drive
Shreveport
(318) 631–2000

Holiday Inn Financial Plaza
5555 Financial Way
Shreveport
(318) 688–3000

MEDJOY Bed & Breakfast
601 Ockley Drive
Shreveport
(318) 861–4424

Ramada Inn & Conference Center
4000 Industrial Drive
Bossier
(318) 747–0711

2439 Fairfield—A Bed & Breakfast
2439 Fairfield Avenue
Fairfield Avenue at Prospect Street
Shreveport
(318) 424–2424

PEACH COUNTRY

Days Inn
I–20, exit 86
1801 North Service Road
Ruston
(318) 251–2360 or
(800) DAYS–INN

Hampton Inn
3315 North Trenton
Ruston
(318) 251–3090 or
800–HAMPTON

Places to Eat in Northwest Louisiana

ARK-LA-TEX

Blind Tige,
120 Texas Street
Shreveport
(318) 226–8747

Chianti
6535 Line Avenue
Shreveport
(318) 868–8866

Columbia Café
3030 Creswell Avenue
Shreveport
(318) 425–3862

Country Tavern
823 Brookhollow Drive
Shreveport
(318) 797–4477

Ernest's Orleans Restaurant and Lounge
1601 South Spring Street
Shreveport
(318) 226–1325

Gumbo Daddy's
365 Broadway Street (at
Louisiana Boardwalk)
Bossier City
(318) 742–2233
www.gumbodaddy.com

Herby K's
1833 Pierre Avenue
Shreveport
(318) 424–2724

Murrell's
539 East Kings Highway
Shreveport
(318) 868–2620

Ralph and Kacoo's
1700 Old Minden Road
Bossier
(318) 747–6660

Savoie's, "The Cajun Restaurant"
2400 East Seventieth Street
Shreveport
(318) 797–3010

Semolina
4801 Line Avenue
Pierremont Mall
Shreveport
(318) 868–6884

Strawn's Eat Shops
(three locations)
125 Kings Highway
Shreveport
(318) 868–0634

East 70th Street
Shreveport
(318) 798–7117

2335 Airline Drive
Bossier
(318) 742–8484

Wilson's Bistineau Inn
630 Horseshoe Bend Road
Doyline
(318) 987–2228
www.lakebistineau.com/
wilsons

PEACH COUNTRY

Log Cabin Smokehouse
1906 Farmerville Highway
Ruston
(318) 255–8023

Ponchatoulas
109 East Park Avenue
Ruston
(318) 254–5200

Rabb's Steak House
2647 South Service
Road West
Ruston
(318) 255–1008

Sundown West Tavern Patio & Grill
111 Park Avenue
Ruston
(318) 255–8028

FOR MORE INFORMATION

Arcadia Chamber of Commerce
P.O. Box 587
Arcadia 71001
(318) 263–9897

Homer Chamber of Commerce
519 South Main Street
Homer 71040
(318) 927–3271

Kisatchie National Forest
2500 Shreveport Highway
Pineville
(318) 473–7160 or
3288 Highway 79, 71040
(318) 927–2061
(for information on recreation and
accommodations in this national forest)

Ruston-Lincoln Parish Tourist Commission
104 East Mississippi Street
Ruston 71273
(318) 255–2031 or (800) 392–9032
www.rustonlincoln.com

Shreveport-Bossier Convention and Visitors' Bureau
629 Spring Street
Shreveport, 71166-1761
(800) 551-8682
www.shreveport-bossier.org

There are visitor centers at 100 John
Wesley Boulevard in Bossier City and
in the Pierre Bossier, South Park, and
St. Vincent Malls.

Webster Parish Convention and Visitors Bureau
P.O. Box 819
110 Sibley Road
Minden 71058
(318) 377–4240 or (800) 2–MINDEN
www.visitwebster.com

Area newspapers include the *Minden
Press-Herald* in Minden; the *Bienville
Democrat-Ringgold Record* in Arcadia;
the *Bossier Press-Tribune* in Bossier
City; the *Guardian-Journal* in Homer;
the *Daily Leader* in Ruston; and the
Shreveport Times in Shreveport. The
Times will have the most comprehensive
entertainment listings for the area.
When near a university, always pick up
a copy of the school paper; the local
entertainment listings might be useful
(and sometimes there are good coupons
to clip).

Northeast Louisiana

The top northeast corner of Louisiana has some of its richest land along the river bottoms. This is mostly farming country; soybeans predominate, cotton was once king. Settlements grew up along river shipping points.

The area near Monroe has natural gas reserves for mineral wealth. Economically this is a region of sharp contrasts, with a unique cultural blend that affords visitors a pleasant experience among friendly folk.

The upper part of Louisiana is much more akin to nearby Southern states than to the French-Catholic culture near the coast. Notice that older homes look a little different here—the typical saltbox-style Cajun cottage and the New Orleans Victorian shotgun give way to simple farmhouses and the occasional dogtrot (center breezeway) house that derives from log cabin construction.

Cotton Country

After leaving Ruston, travel east on Interstate 20 to **West Monroe,** the first of several stops in Ouachita (*WASH-a-taw*) Parish. You won't find a more inviting place to take a driving break than **Kiroli Park** (318–396–4016). Located at 820 Kiroli

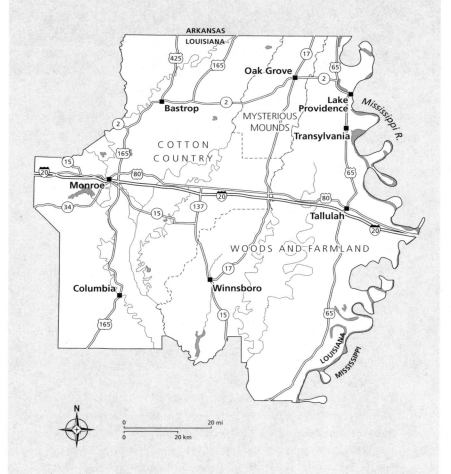

(*ka-ROLL-ee*) Road, the park's entrance is framed by tiers of flower beds. Nature trails for hiking and paved paths for jogging provide a pleasant interlude. With a park permit and state license, you can try your luck in the fishing pond. The 150-acre park also features picnic facilities, tennis courts, a lodge, playgrounds, an amphitheater, a conservatory, and rest rooms.

Formerly used as a Boy Scout camp, the park is now owned and operated by the City of West Monroe. There's a modest admission fee.

For a look at works by area artists, visit the **Ouachita River Art Guild Gallery** (318–322–2380). Located at 308 Trenton Street, West Monroe, the fine art sales gallery features original watercolor, oil, and acrylic paintings, stained glass items, pottery, sculpture, jewelry, calligraphy, and other art forms. The gallery is open from 10:00 A.M. to 5:00 P.M. Tuesday through Saturday.

Antiques buffs will want to save time for exploring **Antique Alley** in

car-window forestry

Driving along I–20 you get a good view of Louisiana forests. Note that the vegetation near the highway is different (and denser) than that back in the woods. More sun, different roadside soils, and mowing by the highway department create a different ecosystem here. Country roadsides are where you find blackberries (late May) and pokeweed (for edible poke salad, late March and early April).

In the woods the predominant upper-story (tallest) trees are pine (shortleaf and loblolly, some grown from planted seedlings and some natural), plus oak and hickory trees. On the highlands you will see more pines. In the lowlands you will see more hardwoods, which shed leaves in winter.

West Monroe. Between Trenton Street's 100 and 300 blocks, you'll find a concentration of antiques and gift shops with more than twenty dealers, along with several art galleries and eateries. These renovated shops are housed in downtown buildings dating from the 1880s. Inventories feature American and European antiques, Oriental vases and rugs, silver, crystal, linens, primitives, baskets, railroad and nautical artifacts, quilts, Coca-Cola memorabilia, jewelry, coins, original paintings, and other decorative objects. Most shops are open Tuesday through Saturday from 10:00 A.M. until 5:00 P.M.

Continue east until West Monroe merges with **Monroe.** For a fine dinner, try **Warehouse No. 1 Restaurant** (318–322–1340) at One Olive Street. The eatery, which retains its original roof and flooring, occupies a restored warehouse on the Ouachita River. Featured menu items include Louisiana catfish, blackened jumbo shrimp, red snapper, and rib-eye. Prices are moderate to expensive. Restaurant hours are 11:00 A.M. to 2:00 P.M., Tuesday through Friday for lunch. Dinner hours run from 5:00 to 9:00 P.M. Monday through Thursday and 5:00 to 9:30 P.M. Friday and Saturday; closed Sunday.

In Monroe head north to 2006 Riverside Drive, the location of the ***Biedenharn Museum and Gardens*** (318–387–5281 or 800–362–0983), which consists of the Biedenharn family mansion and Elsong Garden and Conservatory, with piped music, splashing fountains, and a profusion of blooming plants, and a collection of rare Bibles. Because of a fire, the Bible Museum is now closed, but plans are in the works for an expanded facility. "We anticipate reopening the Bible Museum by spring of 2008," said Ralph Calhoun, executive director. "We're also adding a Coca-Cola Museum. We see this as the silver lining of a very black cloud, and we're coming back better than ever." Until then, visitors can continue to tour the Beiderharn home and gardens.

A world-renowned concert contralto who once performed in Europe, Emy-Lou Biedenharn was forced to return to America when World War II brought her successful operatic career to an abrupt halt. Upon arriving at her Monroe home in 1939, her father, Joseph A. Biedenharn (Coca-Cola's first bottler), presented her with an original John Wycliffe Bible. This gift inspired her to start collecting rare Bibles. She later bought the next-door mansion to contain her vast collection and named it Elsong (for "Emy-Lou's Song").

The theme gardens are gorgeous. You'll see the Garden of Four Seasons with its marble cherubs, an Oriental garden featuring a gazebo and potted bonsai specimens, the Plants of the Bible Garden adjacent to the museum, the Ballet Lawn (where a bride was being photographed when I visited), and other delightful settings.

Except on national holidays, the facility is open Monday through Saturday from 10:00 A.M. to 5:00 P.M. and Sunday from 2:00 to 5:00 P.M. Admission is free. Visit the property at www.bmuseum.org.

GAY'S FAVORITES IN NORTHEAST LOUISIANA

Biedenharn Museum and Gardens
Monroe

Louisiana Purchase Gardens and Zoo
Monroe

Masur Museum of Art
Monroe

Poverty Point State Historic Site
Epps

Tensas River National Wildlife Refuge
Delhi

Biedenharn Museum and Gardens

Take time to drive through Monroe's square-mile ***Historic District,*** which overlooks the Ouachita River. Founded by Don Juan Filhiol, the original settlement was known as Fort Miro. Later the town's name was changed to Monroe in honor of the first steamboat to pass that way. Be sure to notice the Ouachita Parish Courthouse. At 520 South Grand Street, near the site of old Fort Miro, stands the frontier-style ***Isaiah Garrett House,*** a redbrick structure that dates from 1840.

Continue to ***Masur Museum of Art*** (318–329–2237), a modified English Tudor–style building at 1400 South Grand Street. In addition to the museum's permanent collection of paintings, graphics, sculpture, photographs, and other artworks, traveling exhibits are featured throughout the year.

A remodeled carriage house serves as an on-premises workshop for art classes. Staff members conduct tours through the museum, which is open Tuesday through Thursday from 9:00 A.M. until 5:00 P.M. and Friday through Sunday from 2:00 until 5:00 P.M. Admission is free.

early
mon-ro(e)ver

In his far-ranging expedition in the 1540s, explorer Hernando de Soto visited present-day Monroe and wrote about crossing the "Washita," as he spelled it, River.

At the ***Louisiana Purchase Gardens and Zoo*** (318–329–2400), 1405 Bernstein Park Drive, Monroe, you can enjoy a delightful outing. Stroll along tree-lined paths and take a leisurely cruise on a canopied pontoon boat along Bayou Safari. The Louisiana Territory's historic events and points of interest serve as the park's theme and a backdrop for an animal population that ranges between 450 and 550. The zoo is especially noted for its primate collection; its large group of lemurs (whose forebears came from Madagascar) were all bred on the premises.

In the Louisiana Purchase exhibit, you'll see animals typical of those roaming the region more than two centuries ago—black bears, bison, mountain lions, white-tailed deer, and wild turkeys.

Among lush gardens with live oaks and a host of flowering plants, the zoo offers a gift shop and concessions. Except for Christmas Day, the facility is open 10:00 A.M. to 5:00 P.M. daily. Admission is modest; children two and under are admitted free.

Continue south on U.S. Highway 165 to *Columbia* in Caldwell Parish. Don't miss the *Martin Homeplace* (318–649–6722) about a mile north of Columbia on Martin Lane off US 165. Watch for the turnoff sign to this historic property, a two-story ca. 1878 farmhouse at 203 Martin Place Road.

The Martin Homeplace offers a glimpse of rural life during the early 1900s. Canned jellies from wild fruits make splashes of purple, green, red, and gold on scallop-edged pantry shelves. Martin Homeplace is open Thursday and Friday from 10:00 A.M. to 4:00 P.M. Donations welcome. Visit www.martinhome place.org

As a result of Columbia's participation in Louisiana's Main Street program (a project of the National Trust for Historic Preservation), many once-forgotten structures have been rescued and restored, such as the unique *Schepis Museum* (318–649–9931). Head for 106 Main Street at the levee, where you'll see this structure topped by life-size statues of George Washington and Christopher Columbus beneath a bald eagle's spread wings. Built by Italian architect John Schepis, the former mercantile store resembles a Renaissance-style palazzo of the mid-fifteenth century.

The museum, with rotating exhibits every two months, showcases Louisiana artists and offers travel information. One of the museum's past exhibits showcased the 1927 Flood and its devastating impact on eleven states. Other exhibits have featured black-and-white photography depicting rural life in Louisiana from 1939 to 1963 and bayous and wetlands. Hours are Tuesday through Saturday from 9:00 A.M. to 5:00 P.M. Free admission.

After seeing the museum's current exhibit, step next door to the ***Watermark Saloon*** (318–649–0999), the last building before the levee. The oldest saloon on the Ouachita River, the Watermark dates back to the steamboat era during the reign of King Cotton. Hours are 10:00 A.M. to midnight, Monday through Saturday.

Directly across the street, ***The Captain's Quarters*** (318–649–0105) at 103 Main Street, makes a handy place to headquarter while exploring Columbia. Owner Emma Jean Richardson carries out a nautical theme throughout this bed-and-breakfast in a house more than 110 years old. The front door with its etched-glass riverboat design, 14-foot ceilings, original light fixtures, and wood flooring also features a back courtyard. Behind the home, another guest house offers three bedrooms and two baths. Rates are standard to moderate. Check out www.cptquarters.com for more information. Enjoy a continental breakfast here or start your day with a pastry and specialty coffee at ***The Columbia Coffee Shop,*** a few steps away at 111 Main Street. Sip a cappuccino or espresso and use your laptop to catch up on e-mail. Besides a variety of coffees, teas, and soft drinks, owner Greg Richardson offers cinnamon rolls, muffins, and cookies along with Blue Bell ice cream, and much more. Also, you'll find a

First United Methodist Church

selection of books, magazines, and original art. Hours run Monday through Saturday from 7:00 A.M. to 8:00 P.M. and Sunday from 9:00 A.M. to 5:00 P.M.

After strolling along Main Street and browsing for antiques, plan a drive by the nearby ***First United Methodist Church.*** Ask someone to point you in the direction of this picturesque building, painted dark green with white trim. Constructed from plans brought from Europe by a church member and completed in 1911, the church is listed on the National Register of Historic Places. If time permits, plan a walking tour through the town's hillside cemetery. At this point, you can easily continue south on US 165 to Alexandria and launch an exploration of the state's central section or continue your sight-seeing through the state's northeastern corner.

fishyguests

Although catfish farming is more common in the delta area of neighboring Mississippi, there are some commercial catfish ponds in Louisiana. The strangest "tourists" to discover these attractions are the cormorants, fishing birds that come up from their usual haunts on the Gulf to fish in these productive waters. These large black birds with long necks usually perch on utility lines.

Proceed to Bastrop—the seat of Morehouse Parish—north of Monroe. Across from the Morehouse Parish Courthouse on the town square, you'll see the ***Rose Theater,*** restored and used for local productions throughout the year. Call (318) 283–0120 for a recording that provides information on current or upcoming events. Tours are available by reservation.

Before leaving Bastrop, follow US 165 east until it becomes Mer Rouge Road. You'll pass right by the ***Snyder Memorial Museum and Creative Art Center*** (318–281–8760) at 1620 East Madison Avenue, Bastrop. Housed in a brick building with a roof of red tile, the museum contains furniture from the eighteenth and nineteenth centuries, an Oriental rug in an unusual design, clothing, maps, documents, china, and kitchen utensils. In the living and dining rooms, notice the antique oak furniture with legs carved in a barley-twist design. The museum also features a country store with old-fashioned merchandise, Native American artifacts, historic documents, and monthly art exhibits.

A separate carriage house holds old farm implements, sidesaddles, cotton scales, and a horse-drawn hearse from the 1800s. The grounds offer gardens and picnic facilities, and the museum is open Tuesday through Friday from 9:00 A.M. until 4:00 P.M. or by appointment. There is no admission charge.

From Bastrop take Route 133 south until you reach Route 134, which leads east to Epps. Located slightly northeast of Epps (and 15 miles north of Delhi) on Route 577 off Route 134, you'll discover Poverty Point State Historic Site, one of North America's most remarkable archaeological wonders.

Mysterious Mounds

If you happen to fly over Louisiana's northeastern corner during winter months when the earth is not camouflaged by foliage, you can see the outline of a great bird with a wingspan of 640 feet. This bird mound was built some 3,000 years ago by the advanced people of Poverty Point.

The mind boggles to think about the millions of loads of dirt (carried in baskets of animal skin and woven materials and weighing perhaps fifty pounds a load) required to create the site's huge complex of concentric ridges and ceremonial mounds. This tremendous undertaking involved not only tedious labor but also a high degree of engineering expertise. Now known as **Poverty Point State Historic Site** (318–926–5492 or 888–926–5492), the area is as archaeologically significant as England's Stonehenge.

"A whopping total of 1 percent of Poverty Point has been excavated so far," says manager Dennis LaBatt. But that 1 percent tells a remarkable story. When these ridges and mounds were built along Bayou Macon between 1700 and 700 B.C., they were the largest earthworks in the Western Hemisphere. Poverty Point's inhabitants, evidently a bird-revering people, possessed an uncanny degree of astronomical awareness; two of the aisles line up with the summer- and winter-solstice sunsets.

Excavations have uncovered numerous articles of personal adornment, many with bird motifs. Pendants, bangles, and beads of copper, lead, and red jasper appear among the finds. Designs feature various geometric shapes, bird heads, animal claws, locusts, turtles, clam shell replicas, and tiny carved owls. Artifacts also include stone tools, spears, and numerous round earthern balls used for cooking.

When LaBatt stages a cooking demonstration to show visitors how the cooking balls may have been used, he heats fifty balls and puts them in a pit;

lotsa atl-atls

The Atl-Atl *(at-ul at-ul)* is a bit of early technology known at Poverty Point in its heyday. It is a spear-throwing aid— a wooden hand-grip supports the spear and enables the thrower to increase range and accuracy. Covering the distance of a football field would be no problem.

The guides at Poverty Point State Historic Site will demonstrate how one works and let you try your hand. And, you can make your own.

OTHER ATTRACTIONS WORTH SEEING

Downtown Columbia
Stop and walk about in this pleasant old steamboat stop. Main Street has been revived and focuses on the Ouachita River. Columbia was the hometown of former Louisiana governor John McKeithen.

Lake D'Arbonne State Park
P.O. Box 236
Farmerville 71241
(318) 368–2086 or (888) 677–5200
Excellent fishing (buy a license!) and water sports on a man-made lake. Lots of places to picnic.

The Univeristy of Louisiana University at Monroe
On the eastern side of Monroe
There is always something interesting to see on a university campus. The library will have exhibits, there will be art displays, and you can pick up the campus newspaper for events.

he then places venison or fish (wrapped in green leaves) on the heated balls. The food is covered with fifty more balls and allowed to cook slowly.

You can explore the park on foot—it takes between one and two hours to complete the 2.6-mile walking trail—or you can opt for a ride in an open-air tram, which seats forty-four adults. The forty-five-minute tram tour operates from March 1 to October 31 and features stops at Mound A, Mound B, Mound C, and the terrace ridges.

At the visitor center, an audiovisual presentation provides some background on Poverty Point, and you'll see displays of artifacts found on the site. There are also picnic facilities here. If you visit Poverty Point during summer, you may see an archaeological dig in progress. Several state universities schedule digs during this time, and visitors are welcome to watch the excavations.

Poverty Point's hours are from 9:00 A.M. to 5:00 P.M. seven days a week year-round, excluding Thanksgiving, Christmas, and New Year's Day. Admission is modest; senior citizens and children under twelve are admitted free.

The area surrounding Poverty Point is agricultural country, and the terrain is flat. Along the road you'll see pastureland, crops, cotton gins, and sawmills.

Woods and Farmland

After leaving Poverty Point, head south to Delhi and take U.S. Highway 80 east, watching for a sign to turn right onto a gravel road to reach ***Tensas River National Wildlife Refuge*** (318–574–2664). To reach the visitor center, continue south to the end of Quebec Road. (When I entered the refuge via a nearby dirt road, five white-tailed deer leaped across the trail in front of me.)

The Tensas (*TEN-saw*) Refuge's visitor center is a large, rustic building with a rough-cedar exterior. Here you can pick up a refuge map and see dioramas and exhibits of birds, mammals, and reptiles indicative of regional wildlife. The building also houses an auditorium where films and slide shows on the refuge's activities may be viewed. The Hollow Cypress Wildlife Trail, extending about a quarter of a mile, takes you to an observation platform. Along the way you may see birds, squirrels, and, yes, snakes.

As part of the National Refuge System, Tensas serves as a protected habitat for native wildlife such as the Louisiana black bear. According to the Fish and Wildlife Service, some sixty to one hundred of these bears currently roam the Tensas woods (including the refuge and surrounding forests in Madison Parish).

The Louisiana black bear inspired America's beloved teddy bear. Although the story varies as to locale, it seems that President Theodore Roosevelt, while on a hunting trip to the deep South, wanted to shoot a bear. He once wrote, "I was especially anxious to kill a bear . . . after the fashion of the old Southern planters, who for a century past have followed the bear with horse and hound and horn. . . ." Members of Roosevelt's hunting party, knowing of his keen desire to bag a bear, captured a black bear and tied it to a tree—an easy target for the president. Roosevelt's refusal to shoot the helpless animal resulted in much publicity, triggering several editorial cartoons. Soon after the hunting incident, a New York shopkeeper named Morris Michtom came up with the idea of marketing some stuffed toy bears made by his wife, Rose. He called them "Teddy's Bears," and the president gave his approval. The Michtoms' cuddly bears became an instant success, and the rest is history.

Radios have been placed on 200 black bears to monitor their activity in a program aimed at preserving and improving their habitat. The radio collars emit signals, which enable refuge personnel to keep track of the bears' whereabouts.

According to Talbert Williams, a range technician at the refuge, "These small black bears are barely holding their own." Talbert, who was born in a log cabin on the banks of the Tensas River, served for more than three decades as a state game warden before going to work for the federal government to "save these woods." He can tell you plenty of local stories, including anecdotes about Ben Lilly, a legendary hunter from these parts.

This habitat also provides food and shelter for many other animals, including the bobcat, otter, raccoon, mink, squirrel, woodchuck, wild turkey, barred owl, and pileated woodpecker, as well as thousands of waterfowl and other migratory birds.

In this bottomland forest you'll also see a great variety of trees—several kinds of oak, three or four species of elm, cypress, sweet gum, maple, black locust, honey locust, red haw, and others. Spiky palmetto, muscadine vines, shrubs, and other plants grow here as well.

Deep in the heart of the woods stand the ruins of an old plantation house—about ten handmade-brick pillars (from 10 to 12 feet tall) are all that remain of the former three-story structure. Also hidden in the forest are an old cemetery with eight or nine tombstones and the towering chimney of a pre–Civil War cotton gin.

Primitive canoe launches plus two new boat launches allow visitors to explore parts of the refuge by water. Some public hunting is allowed here, but hunters need to familiarize themselves with refuge regulations. Deer hunting permits, which must be requested in advance by writing or phoning, are issued on the basis of drawings. The refuge is open year-round for fishing, but no camping is allowed. As Talbert says, "If you like the natural things, this is the place to come."

The public is welcome to visit the refuge, which offers an active environmental education program, any time of the year. Except for holidays the visitor center is open Monday through Friday from 8:00 A.M. until 4:00 P.M. For further information contact the Refuge Manager, Tensas River National Wildlife Refuge, 2312 Quebec Road, Tallulah 71282, or visit www.fws.gov/tensas river.

After exploring the refuge, head northeast to *Tallulah.* In this area of flat farmland, you'll drive past pecan groves, pastures of grazing cattle, and fields of soybeans, cotton, rice, and wheat.

Tallulah was founded in 1857 and is said to have been named by a traveling railroad engineer in honor of his former sweetheart back home (after he was jilted by a local lady). A bayou winds its way through town and is especially lovely during the holiday season, when lights from a series of Christmas trees placed in the water reflect across its surface.

During the early 1900s Tallulah was the site of a government laboratory where experiments were conducted to find a weapon in the war against the boll weevil. By the 1920s aerial crop-dusting techniques were being developed here. In 1924 Delta Airlines (then called Huff Daland Dusters) entered the picture and established the first commercial crop-dusting company.

Traveling north on U.S. Highway 65 takes you to East Carroll Parish and the town of Transylvania, a tiny community with a spooky name. *Transylvania General Store* (318–559–1338) stands adjacent to a small post office; beyond looms a white water tower emblazoned with a black bat.

The store has attracted sightseers from England, Italy, Iceland, Japan, and even Romania's Transylvania—including a visitor who identified himself as a descendant of Count Dracula.

Besides food, dry goods, and hardware, the owners sell life-size rubber bats, skull replicas, and about 250 dozen T-shirts a year—with a bat logo. (Be sure to take a peek at the "baby vampire bats" in a lighted box.)

You can get cold soft drinks here and order sandwiches of your choice as well as hamburgers, fried chicken, and plate lunches. The store, open Monday through Saturday from 6:30 A.M. until 5:30 P.M., is closed on Sunday.

After leaving Transylvania, continue north on US 65 (a direct route through the state's northeastern corner to Arkansas) for 10 miles to **Lake Providence,** located on a 6-mile-long oxbow lake that appeared on the local landscape when the Mississippi River couldn't decide which way to go.

According to parish lore, the town's name sprang from early years when Captain Bunch and his band of pirates attacked and robbed travelers on the Mississippi. If settlers got past Bunch's Bend, they thanked Providence for their safe passage. Fortunately, today's visitors don't have to worry about pirates and can stop to enjoy the lake's recreation opportunities.

thejamesboys

The town of Oak Grove, near Lake Providence, was said to be frequently visited by outlaws Jesse and Frank James, who were such pleasant house guests that they were known to help local kids with their homework.

Located downtown at 208 Lake Street, the **Ole Dutch Bakery** (318–559–1574) offers French, honey whole wheat, and cinnamon breads and other specialties. A perennial favorite, the poppy seed bread is made with almond, butter, and vanilla flavorings and topped with a glaze. Owners Kathy and Marlin Wedel also operate an adjoining cafe where you can enjoy lunch; the single daily special might range from a traditional Mennonite recipe to upside-down pizza or cheese enchiladas. The cafe's wooden tables and chairs were made by Marlin's brother, Errol. The business actually started in Kathy's kitchen. Her home-baked goods made from traditional Dutch and German recipes proved popular, and the Ole Dutch Bakery opened its doors in 1983. Hours are Tuesday through Friday from 6:30 A.M. until 5:00 P.M. and on Saturday from 6:30 A.M. to 4:00 P.M.

Afterward, continue to **Byerley House** (318–559–5125) at 600 Lake Street (also US 65) in Lake Providence. This restored Victorian structure serves as a visitor and community center. Here you can collect information and maps on local and state attractions, enjoy free coffee (or lemonade during summer months), unpack a picnic lunch in the park across the street, or stroll on the pier over the lake. Byerley House is open from 9:00 A.M. to 5:00 P.M. Monday through Friday.

A 500-foot overwater nature walk adjacent to Byerley Park offers a view of **Grant's Canal** through 300-year-old cypress trees. Part of the Civil War Discovery Trail, the channel proved to be a military failure for General Grant in his attempts to find an alternate way to slip Union gunboats past Vicksburg's heavy fortifications during his Southern attack.

Continue to the **Louisiana State Cotton Museum** (318–559–2041), located a couple of miles or so north of town at 7165 US 65 North, for an overview of the history of cotton and its impact on westward expansion, society, culture, and the economy. Exhibits focusing on the period from 1820 through the 1930s interpret cotton's leading role in the state's heritage and its influence on life in Louisiana and the South as a whole. You'll see a large cotton gin (supposedly the state's first electric version) plus other museum exhibits and pavilions on the grounds. In early fall, you may get a chance to pick cotton on the premises. The site offers picnic facilities with RV parking nearby. Hours are from 9:00 A.M. to 4:30 P.M. Monday through Friday. Admission is free.

To see another agricultural product in its various phases, continue north about 8 miles on US 65 to **Panola Pepper Company** (318–559–1774) until you see the sign directing you east to Panola, about a quarter of a mile off the highway at 1414 Holland Delta Road. Owner Grady Brown will line up a guide to give you a tour (except during the hottest summer months). From planting to pickling peppers, there's something seasonal and interesting to see at this family cotton plantation, which has diversified into food processing.

The company's country store stocks hot sauces, packaged mixes, gourmet mustards, pepper-stuffed olives, and seasonings. Panola Gourmet Pepper Sauce makes a great souvenir, although hard-core pepper lovers may prefer the Bat's Brew or Vampfire Hot Sauce (inspired by nearby Transylvania). For the undecided, Panola offers a variety pack. The store also carries home accessories, aprons, T-shirts, golf balls, and other gift items. Store hours are 8:00 A.M. to 5:00 P.M. Monday through Friday, with tours available from 9:00 A.M. to 4:00 P.M. Or you can visit www.panolapepper.com.

Before leaving the northeast section, consider taking US 65 south toward Newellton in Tensas Parish. **Winter Quarters State Historic Site** (318–467–9750 or 888–677–9468), the only plantation home along the banks of Lake St. Joseph that was not torched by Yankee troops during the Vicksburg Campaign, is located at 4929 Highway 608, 6 miles southeast of Newellton (and north of St. Joseph). The original structure, a three-room hunting lodge, was built in 1805 by Job Routh. The plantation grew to more than 2,000 acres. Later,

Routh's heirs added several rooms and a gallery to the lodge. In 1850, Dr. Haller Nutt and his wife, "Miss Julia" (Routh's granddaughter), bought the property and enlarged the house again.

Grant's Vicksburg Campaign brought many changes to Winter Quarters Plantation. The Union army marched south through Tensas during the spring of 1863, carrying out General William Tecumseh Sherman's orders to destroy everything not needed by Union troops. Fifteen plantation homes lined the banks of Lake St. Joseph before the Union troops passed through. When they left, only Winter Quarters remained standing.

According to a letter written by Dr. Nutt and dated October 1863, he and his family were in Natchez, Mississippi, when Union troops tramped through Tensas Parish. His overseer, Hamilton Smith "obtained letters of protection in my [Dr. Nutt's] name from advance officers of this army," Generals McPherson and Smith. Thus, Winter Quarters Plantation was saved. Regrettably, Union army stragglers destroyed all outbuildings, livestock, and crops.

The mansion, which overlooks Lake St. Joseph, features front, back, and side verandas. Furnished with period pieces, the house also contains documents, personal records, copies of diaries, and memorabilia from the Civil War period. Be sure to notice the rare billiard table, ca. 1845. Except for Thanksgiving, Christmas, and New Year's Day, the site is open daily from 9:00 A.M. until 5:00 P.M. Modest admission.

Places to Stay in Northeast Louisiana

COTTON COUNTRY

The Captain's Quarters
103 Main Street
Columbia
(318) 649–0105

Days Inn
5650 Frontage Road
Monroe
(318) 345–2220

Fairfield Inn
401 Constitution Drive
West Monroe
(318) 388–3810 or
(800) 228–2800

Hampton Inn
1407 Martin Luther
King Drive
Monroe
(318) 361–9944 or
(800) 426–7866

Holiday Inn Holidome
I–20 and US 165 Bypass
Monroe
(318) 387–5100 or
(800) 465–4329

La Quinta Inn
1035 US 165
Bypass South
Monroe
(318) 322–3900 or
(800) 531–5900

Ramada Limited Motel
1601 Martin Luther
King Drive
Monroe
(318) 323–1600 or
(800) 2–RAMADA

MYSTERIOUS MOUNDS

D'Arbonne Lake Motel
101 Dori Drive
Farmerville
(318) 368–2236

Preferred Inn
1053 East Madison Avenue
Bastrop
(318) 281–3621 or
(800) 227–8767

WOODS AND FARMLANDS

Best Western Winnsboro
4198 Front Street
Winnsboro
(318) 435–2000

Super 8 Motel
144 Highway 65
Tallulah
(318) 574–2000

Places to Eat in Northeast Louisiana

COTTON COUNTRY

Canard's
2500 North Seventh Street
West Monroe
(318) 325–5012

Chateau
2007 Louisville Avenue
Monroe
(318) 325–0384

The Columbia Coffee Shop
111 Main Street
Columbia

**Cracker Barrel
Old Country Store**
309 Constitution Drive
West Monroe
(318) 325–5505

Danken Trail
7702 DeSiard Street
Monroe
(318) 343–0773

Genusa's Italian Restaurant
815 Park Avenue
Monroe
(318) 387–3083

La Bella Vita
407 Constitution Drive
West Monroe
(318) 998–6900

Scott's Catfish & Seafood
2812 Cypress Street
West Monroe
(318) 387–6212

**Warehouse No. 1
Restaurant**
One Olive Street
Monroe
(318) 322–1340

WOODS AND FARMLAND

Brown's Landing
120 Brown's Landing Road
Winnsboro
(318) 435–5291

Country Pride
224 Highway 65 South, exit 171
Tallulah
(318) 574–5900

The Dock
1829 Lake Street (US 65)
Lake Providence
(318) 559–DOCK

**Jehovah Java Gourmet
Coffee Bar**
218 North Hood Street
Lake Providence
(318) 559–7430

Jesse's Steak and Seafood
3942 Front Street
(Highway 15)
Winnsboro
(318) 435–9948

Ole Dutch Bakery
208 Lake Street
Lake Providence
(318) 559–1574

San Marcos
4198 Front Street
Winnsboro
(318) 435–0002

FOR MORE INFORMATION

Doorway to Louisiana, Inc.
600 Lake Street
Lake Providence 71254
(318) 559–5125

**Monroe–West Monroe Convention
and Visitors Bureau**
P.O. Box 1436
West Monoe 71294-1436
601 Constitution Drive
West Monroe 71292
(318) 387–5691 or (800) 843–1872

**Winnsboro–Franklin Parish
Tourist Center**
3826 Front Street
Winnsboro 71295
(318) 435–7607

Area newspapers include the *News–Star* in Monroe (largest in the region, should have activities listings weekly), the *Banner–Democrat* in Lake Providence, the *Caldwell Watchman* in Columbia, the *Bastrop Daily Enterprise* in Bastrop, the *Franklin Sun* in Winnesboro, and the *Madison Journal* in Tallulah.

Central Louisiana

Central Louisiana is crossed by rivers and streams, with the old meanders of the Red River and even the Mississippi River still marked in the region's geology. The area around Marksville is on a raised terrace of land, but like most of Louisiana, the general characteristic of the terrain is flat. Rich soil and a long growing season made agriculture, especially of cotton, profitable along the rivers.

Around A.D. 100 the area was home to a Native American culture (named Marksville for its location) of mound building with distinctive pottery. This part of Louisiana was later the gateway to the Spanish colonies of the West, with an early frontier outpost just outside Natchitoches, a city that itself dates to the early eighteenth century.

Woodland and Water

About midway between Shreveport and Lake Charles on U.S. Highway 171, you'll find *Hodges Gardens* (800–354–3523), a site that lures visitors year-round. Created by conservation-minded A. J. Hodges, this forest retreat was once barren land, stripped by timber companies. During the 1940s Hodges replanted thousands of acres with pine trees to bring to pass this

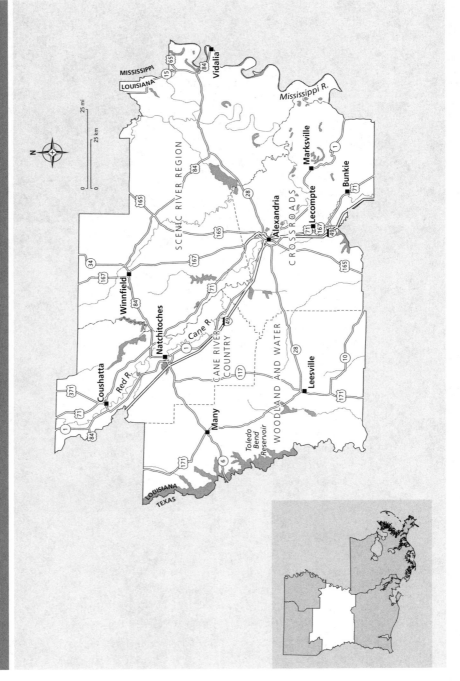

CENTRAL LOUISIANA

outdoor wonderland containing staggered gardens of formal plantings and hill-sides strewn with wildflowers. Near the entrance of the main garden area, you'll see a petrified tree—supposedly thousands of years old.

A stone quarry serves as a striking backdrop for moss-covered rocks, waterfalls, and a profusion of wildflowers and other plants. Although featured flowers vary with the season, there's always a lavish display. Acres of daffodils, tulips, and other multicolored bulbs herald spring; camellias, dogwood, and azaleas blazing in reds, corals, and hot pinks confirm the season's arrival. With summer come assorted annuals and thousands of roses bursting into dazzling bloom. Fall furnishes vibrant displays of chrysanthemums—a fantasy in red, pink, purple, yellow, bronze, and white.

Wending your way along pebbled concrete walks that lead past streams and cascading waterfalls, you'll enjoy rainbows of blossoms with sweet aromas. Although the formal gardens are accessible only on foot, you may drive from point to point within the complex. Along the way various panoramic observation points provide breathtaking views. The 4,700 acres of pine forest also serve as home to various birds and animals. You'll see squirrels, wild turkeys, and deer (some 700 deer inhabit these woods). Barbados and mouflon sheep and buffalo roam pastures bordering a large lake on the property.

Rental boats for fishing are available. Two picnic areas—one nearby equipped with a vending area and rest rooms and the other (without these facilities) in a more remote setting—provide pleasant places for enjoying lunch or a snack. The grounds also offer lakeside cabins, a conservatory, green-houses, and a gift shop.

Except for Thanksgiviing Day, Christmas Eve, Christmas Day, and New Year's Day, the gardens are open daily from 8:00 A.M. to 5:00 P.M., and admission

GAY'S FAVORITES IN CENTRAL LOUISIANA

Bayou Folk Museum
Cloutierville

Briarwood
Natchitoches

Kent House
Alexandria

**Los Adaes State
Commemorative Area**
Robeline

Melrose Plantation
Natchitoches

Toledo Bend Lake

Town of Natchitoches

is charged. For more information contact Hodges Gardens, P.O. Box 340, Florien 71429. Check out the property at www.hodgesgardens.com.

Across the road from the entrance to Hodges Gardens is **Emerald Hills Golf Resort** (800–533–5031), where you may want to hit a few, have dinner, or stay overnight. Visit www.emeraldhillsresort.com for more information.

To reach **Fisher**, about a ten-minute drive from Hodges Gardens, follow US 171 north and watch for the turnoff sign. Surrounded by a pine forest and off the beaten path, this hamlet could challenge Garrison Keillor's own Lake Wobegon for the title "The Town That Time Forgot." But therein lies its charm—a quaint and quiet place in today's frenetic world.

When the Louisiana Long Leaf Lumber Company (also known as Four-L) located here in 1899 to harvest the nearby pine forest, it built Fisher as a base of operations. The town grew into a bustling place with red-dirt streets where mules hauled loads of logs. Fisher was built entirely of local lumber, including board sidewalks.

Although Fisher's sawmill days ended in 1966 when new owners bought the mill and sold the company houses, you can still see white picket fences, pine cottages, a post office, and an opera house where people stood in line to see movies that cost a dime. There's also an old commissary where folks once shopped, standing awhile on the store's long front porch to chat with neighbors. Antiques are now on sale here.

The Fisher Heritage Foundation has received grants to restore the commissary, depot, and opera house. Village residents are working to preserve the lumber town's past, and Fisher has been placed on the National Register of Historic Places. Other sites include a caboose painted red with canary yellow trim, an office building, and the Old Fisher Church.

Visitors can step back into the village's history at Christmas, when the entire village glows with lights, and each May, when Fisher celebrates its heritage with **Sawmill Days,** a festival featuring music, food, entertainment, and a variety of logging and woodworking competitions.

Continuing north on US 171 about 6 miles takes you to **Many** (MAN-ee). Westward lies Toledo Bend country, an outdoor lover's paradise of some 185,000 acres. Famed for its fine bass fishing, this large recreation area offers marinas, public parks, restaurants, boating facilities, and camping. Should you decide to go fishing, **Toledo Bend Lake** promises prolific possibilities. The Sabine Parish Tourist and Recreation Commission (318–256–5880 or 800–358–7802) at 920 Fisher Road will answer your questions and point you in all the right directions on this big lake. Ask them about annual events such as the nearby **Zwolle Tamale Festival.**

Leaving Many, take Route 6 northeast to Natchitoches Parish.

Cane River Country

The lovely town of **Natchitoches** (pronounced *NAK-a-tush*), which sprang up on the Red River, is now located on the Cane River (actually a lake). The town didn't move—the river did. But perhaps that's why the place retains its historical charm. As Louisiana's oldest town, Natchitoches was a thriving steamboat port that showed promise of growing into a major metropolis, second in size only to New Orleans, until destiny, in the guise of a spring flood, deemed otherwise. When the Red River carved a new course, Natchitoches was separated from the main body of water and lost its strategic location as a trade center. The shrunken stream left flowing through the old channel was renamed the Cane River. A dam constructed in 1917 created Cane River Lake, which drifts through the city's heart.

Natchitoches also holds the distinction of being the oldest permanent European settlement in the entire Louisiana Purchase Territory, a vast acreage from which all or parts of fifteen states were carved.

TOP ANNUAL EVENTS IN CENTRAL LOUISIANA

Alexandria/Pineville's Mardi Gras Weekend
Alexandria, weekend before Fat Tuesday
(318) 442–9546 or (800) 551–9546.

Choctaw-Apache Powwow
Ebarb, April or May
(318) 645–2588.

Sawmill Days
Fisher, third weekend in May
(318) 256–2001

Melrose Plantation Arts and Crafts Festival
on the Cane River, Melrose
second weekend in June
(318) 379–0055

Natchitoches-Northwestern Folk Festival
Prather Coliseum, Northwestern State University, third weekend in July
(318) 352–4332

Zwolle Tamale Festival
Many, second weekend in October
(318) 256–3523 or (800) 358–7802

Natchitoches Pilgrimage
Natchitoches, second full weekend in October
(318) 352–6398 or (800) 259–1714

Louisiana Pecan Festival
Colfax, first full weekend in November
(318) 627–5196

Christmas Festival of Lights
Natchitoches, first Saturday in December and all December weekends
(800) 259–1714
www.christmasfestival.com

When French Canadian Louis Juchereau de St. Denis (*de-NEE*) docked here in 1714, he found the Native American Natchitoches (a Caddo tribe) living along the north bank of the Red River. The town takes its name from this tribe, and various translations of the word include "place of chinquapin eaters," "chestnut eaters," and "pawpaw eaters." St. Denis chose this spot to found Natchitoches, which evolved from a trading post with both the Native Americans (the French exchanged guns, knives, and trinkets for furs, bear oil, salt, and such) and the Spanish. To thwart Spanish advances **Fort St. Jean Baptiste** (318–357–3101) was established here in 1716. Located at 155 Jefferson Street, the fort boasts a new entrance and attractive and inviting museum. The site is open daily from 9:00 A.M. to 5:00 P.M. Modest admission.

losadaes

Natchitoches was once an outpost on the frontier. **Los Adaes,** near Robeline and Many on Louisiana Highway 6 at Highway 485, is where a mission was built by the Spanish in 1717 and a fort was established in 1721 to guard this section of the Camino Real (royal road).

Until 1773 this was the capital of the Spanish Province of Texas. Los Adaes today is a state historic site where visitors will find reconstructions of buildings and evidence of archaeological explorations of the setting. Los Adaes is located at 6354 Highway 485, Robeline; (318) 472–9449 or (888) 677–5378.

You can see a replica of the old French fort with its walls of sharpened logs on the riverfront. The compound, which contains the commandant's house, a small warehouse, a chapel, barracks, and three huts, is not far from the American Cemetery (where some historians surmise St. Denis and his wife are buried).

If you happen to drive through Natchitoches during December, you'll see why it's called the City of Lights. Some 170,000 multicolored lights glow along the downtown riverbank during the Christmas Festival of Lights, an annual event that attracts thousands of sightseers. The movie *Steel Magnolias,* which was filmed in Natchitoches, features some night scenes showing this glittering spectacle. You may want to take a Steel Magnolias tour to see some of the locations used in the movie. For more information and a local map, stop by the Natchitoches Parish Tourist Commission (318–352–8072 or 800–259–1714) at 781 Front Street.

Along the town's picturesque brick-paved Front Street, you'll pass many antebellum structures in the original downtown area. At the 1843 **Hughes Building,** be sure to notice the courtyard with its ornate spiral staircase of cast iron.

To continue your exploration you can park down by the riverside, just below Front Street, to see the **Roque House.** Located on the bank of Cane River Lake, the Roque *(rock)* House dates from the 1790s. Originally built as a residence at nearby Isle Brevelle, the French colonial structure of hand-hewn cypress was moved to its present site during the 1960s. The restored wood-shingled cottage is especially noted for its *bousillage (BOO-see-ahj)* construction. *Bousillage,* which was used in a number of the state's French colonial buildings, was made by boiling Spanish moss and combining it with mud and hair scraped from animal hides. When packed between wooden wall posts, the procedure was known as *bousillage entre poteaux.* Covered with plaster (sometimes made with lime and deer hair), this mixture provided good insulation.

Natchitoches offers a number of other attractions such as the **Old Court-house** and the **Immaculate Conception Catholic Church,** both located on Second and Church Streets, and also the **Trinity Parish Church** at Second and Trudeau Streets.

Don't leave Natchitoches without stopping by **Lasyone's Meat Pie Kitchen** (318–352–3353), located at 622 Second Street. Meat pies, the featured specialty, resemble fried fruit pies except for the filling. For these tasty items, the staff uses a combination of pork and ground beef with onions and spices. The slowly cooked meat is later thickened with a roux (flour sautéed in oil as a thickening agent) and chilled overnight. At serving time a dollop of the mixture is dropped on a circle of dough; after the crust is folded over and crimped on the edges, the pie is ready to fry.

A former grocer, Jamel Lasyone (lassie-OWN) started the business in 1967. Angela Lasyone and Tina Lasyone continue to carry on family tradition at this restaurant, established by their father.

Order a meat pie with dirty rice (the name given to the dark-stained version cooked with chicken giblets) and a green salad. For dessert you'll want to

Roque House

A Savory Specialty

Mrs. Charles E. Cloutier's recipe for these tasty meat pies first appeared in the *Cane River Cuisine* cookbook. Now you can enjoy this Natchitoches specialty in your own kitchen.

Natchitoches Meat Pie

Filling:

1½ pounds ground beef

1½ pounds ground pork

1 cup chopped green onions, tops and bottoms

1 tablespoon salt

1 teaspoon coarse ground black pepper

1 teaspoon coarse ground red pepper

½ teaspoon cayenne pepper

⅓ cup all-purpose flour

Crust:

2 cups self-rising flour

⅓ heaping cup solid shortening

1 egg, beaten

¾ cup milk

Combine ground beef, pork, onions, and seasonings in large Dutch oven. Cook over medium heat, stirring often until meat loses its red color. Do not overcook meat. Remove from heat and cool to room temperature. Drain off all excess grease. Sift ⅓ cup of flour over meat mixture, stirring until well combined.

Sift remaining 2 cups of flour and cut shortening into flour. Add beaten egg and milk. Form dough into ball. Roll about ⅓ of dough at a time on a lightly floured surface and cut into 5- to 5½-inch circles. Separate circles with waxed paper.

To assemble: Place heaping tablespoon of filling on one side of circle. With fingertips, dampen edge of circle containing meat, then fold top over meat and crimp with fork dipped in water. With fork, prick twice on top.

To fry: Cook until golden brown at 350° F in deep-fat fryer.

These meat pies freeze beautifully if enclosed in plastic sandwich bags. When frying frozen meat pies, do not thaw before frying. Cocktail meat pies may be made the same way, using a biscuit cutter and 1 teaspoon of meat filling.

try another house specialty, Cane River cream pie. The restaurant offers a complete menu and features daily luncheon specials, such as red beans and rice with sausage, veal cutlets, catfish, or chicken breast. Prices are economical. Hours are Monday through Saturday from 7:00 A.M. to 3:30 P.M. You can also order meat pies at www.lasyones.com.

Allow some time for driving through the fertile plantation country surrounding Natchitoches, where you'll see pecan groves and fields of soybeans and cotton. You'll also want to visit one or more of the many nearby plantation homes for which Cane River Country is famous, but be sure to call before you go because operating hours change.

Don't miss **Melrose Plantation** (318–379–0055), 2 miles east of Route 1 at the junction of Routes 493 and 119. Your guide will tell you the legend of the remarkable Marie Thérèse Coincoin, a freed slave who obtained a land grant from the Spanish colonial authorities and, with the help of her sons, established and operated what is now Melrose Plantation.

You'll see the Yucca House, Marie Thérèse's original two-room cypress-timbered home built in 1796, and the African House, supposedly the only original Congo-like architecture still standing in the United States. Other plantation buildings include the white clapboard Big House built in 1833 by Marie Thérèse's grandson, the Weaving House, the Bindery, Ghana House, and the Writer's Cabin. Also on the grounds is the cabin home of former Melrose cook Clementine Hunter, whose colorful and charming murals cover the upstairs walls of the African House.

At one time Melrose was one of the country's largest pecan orchards. John Henry and his wife, fondly known as Miss Cammie, restored the plantation's buildings and turned Melrose into a renowned retreat for artists and writers. Among the many writers who accepted their hospitality were François Mignon, Erskine Caldwell, Lyle Saxon, and Caroline Dormon.

Melrose, which closes on Christmas and New Year's Day, is open daily from noon to 4:00 P.M, and the last tour starts at 3:00 P.M. Admission is charged.

Afterward, continue to **Magnolia Plantation Home** (318–379–2221) at 5487 Highway 119 in the town of Natchez near Derry. Surrounded by stately oaks and magnolias (which inspired the home's name), the large manor house replaces one built in the 1830s. During the Civil War, General Nathaniel Banks's Union forces burned the original home. The family restored it in 1896, using the same foundation and floor plan with fourteen fireplaces and twenty-seven rooms,

scrapbook heaven

Cammie Henry, longtime owner of Melrose, was renowned for her extensive collection of clippings and scrapbooks on Louisiana history. Everything is now in the Cammie Henry Collection at the Watson Library at Northwestern State University in Natchitoches. To learn more about "Miss Cammie" and her collections, tap into www.nsula.edu.

including a Catholic chapel still used for Mass. Throughout the house, you'll see Louisiana-crafted and Southern Empire furnishings such as the parlor's square grand piano made of rosewood.

A working plantation of 2,192 acres, Magnolia has been in the same family since 1753, when Jean Baptiste LeComte II acquired it through an original French land grant. The property also features several dependencies and a massive mule-drawn cotton press. Once known for its racing stables, this National Bicentennial Farm is open for tours daily except Sunday from 1:00 to 4:00 P.M.; the last tour starts at 3:30 P.M. Admission is charged.

Approximately 25 miles south of Natchitoches, just off Route 1 on Route 495, you'll find the **Kate Chopin House** (318–379–2233), home of the **Bayou Folk Museum.** This building, which dates from the early 1800s, is located on Main Street in the charming village of Cloutierville (*KLOOCH-er-vil*). The only place to park is on the narrow street in front of the museum; local traffic, however, tends to be light.

Constructed of slave-made brick, cypress mortised with square wooden pegs, and *bousillage,* the raised cottage–style structure contains four fireplaces that share a single chimney. An exterior staircase leads to the second floor, which served as the living area.

Author Kate Chopin lived in this house with her husband and six children from 1879 until 1884. In the downstairs entrance room, you'll see a showcase featuring an original edition of *Bayou Folk,* a collection of Chopin's short stories about Creole life in which she uses Cane River Country as a setting. Portraits of the author and her family, along with a number of their possessions, are also on display at this National Historic Landmark.

Other rooms feature various collections of jewelry, china, glass, sewing machines, school desks, early phonographs, oak iceboxes, Civil War firearms, and antique furniture. On the upstairs rear porch, you'll see an unusual old sharpshooter coffin.

The museum complex also contains a blacksmith shop; a mule-operated sugarcane mill; and a country doctor's office, furnished with medical equipment and instruments once used by plantation doctors. Except for New Year's Day,

Chopin on Screen

Kate Chopin, who wrote in the late 1800s, was an author out of favor for years, but she has been rediscovered and championed as an ahead-of-her-time feminist writer. One fan was actress Kelly McGillis, who managed to coproduce and star in a cinema version of Chopin's surprisingly modern novel about adultery, *The Awakening,* in 1992. The movie version had to be called *Grand Isle* because the film *Awakenings,* starring Robin Williams and based on the book by Dr. Oliver Sacks, had come out in 1990.

Grand Isle's costuming and set design are properly accurate, as are the well-photographed locations. As a bonus, lots of Louisiana actors found work in the project. The film, while not otherwise remarkable, is a nice compliment to a Louisiana author and is available on videotape.

Easter, Thanksgiving, and Christmas, the Kate Chopin House is open from 10:00 A.M. to 5:00 P.M. Monday through Saturday and 1:00 to 5:00 P.M. on Sunday. The last tour starts at 4:00 P.M. Admission is charged.

If time permits, drive south along Route 1, where you'll see acres of pecan groves. Several pecan processing plants dot the roadside in this area. In season you can stop and buy whole or shelled pecans, roasted pecans, candies made with pecans, and other nutty delights.

Afterward you can either drive on to Alexandria, the state's crossroads, or head north of Natchitoches to take in some interesting sites in that direction.

Taking the northern option, you can retrace your route to Natchitoches or get on U.S. Highway 71 north for a visit to ***Briarwood*** (318–576–3379) at 216 Dormon Road in the northwest corner of Natchitoches Parish. This wonderful wooded area, some 19 miles north of Campti, is located just off Route 9, north of Readhimer and 2 miles south of Saline. (Saline is especially noted for its fine watermelons, so you may want to stop and buy one if you pass this way during summer months.) Briarwood, a wild garden definitely off the beaten path, will especially delight botanists and bird-watchers. A rustic sign suspended over a wooden gate marks the entrance to this 154-acre nature preserve, once the home of Caroline Dormon, America's first woman to be employed in forestry.

corduroy roads

At Briarwood the vegetation is not the only authentic Louisiana object underfoot. On the grounds is a segment of what was a "corduroy road." These old carriage roads were made of logs laid sideways along the roadbed, providing nineteenth-century riders with a jolting journey.

A pioneer conservationist, Dormon played a major role in establishing Louisiana's Kisatchie National Forest, which extends over seven parishes and covers 600,000 acres. Also known internationally for her work as a naturalist, Dormon described and painted rare native species of plants. Her books *Flowers Native to the Deep South* and *Wild Flowers of Louisiana* are both botany classics.

Briarwood boasts Louisiana's largest collection of plants native to the Southeast, where spring might bring spectacular shows of pink dogwoods, white pompons, crabapples, pale pink native azaleas, and mottled-green trilliums. The nature preserve is also home to a woodland iris garden and six different species of pitcher plants.

Briarwood's curators Jessie and Richard Johnson, who knew "Miss Carrie" personally, will welcome you to this serene retreat, which can be explored on foot or aboard the "stealth cart." Richard, who calls Briarwood a "place of renewal, a balm for the soul," will show you Miss Carrie's former log cabin home, deep in the woods. Now a museum, the house contains furniture, household items, and original illustrations from one of the naturalist's books. Be sure to spend a few minutes looking through the scrapbooks, where you'll see some of Miss Carrie's correspondence. One note to a friend reads: "That everlastin' bird book is out at last! I'm bound to say I think it's a darlin'—even if I am its mama!"

Surrounding the cabin you'll see many giant trees, including a longleaf pine possibly three centuries old, known as Grandpappy. Nearby are tulip and sourwood trees, big-leafed magnolias, and native sasanquas—fall-blooming camellias with delicate blossoms and handsome dark foliage.

A trail winds past a pond and through tall pines, mountain laurel, and wild ginger to a one-room cabin on a gentle knoll even farther back in the forest. The simply furnished log house, called Three Pines Cabin, served as Miss Carrie's retreat for writing and painting when too many visitors found their way to Briarwood. "This was her hideaway," Jessie says, "when the world beat a path to her door."

Even though Briarwood does not advertise, some 2,000 visitors discover it each year. The nature preserve is open to the public every weekend in March, April, May, August, and November. Hours are from 9:00 A.M. to 5:00 P.M. on Saturday and from noon to 5:00 P.M. on Sunday. Tours at other times may be arranged by appointment. Admission is charged.

Scenic River Region

After exploring and savoring Briarwood, head for neighboring Winn Parish, the home of Winnfield and the birthplace of Huey P. Long, O. K. Allen, and Earl K. Long—all former governors of Louisiana. Both Routes 126 and 156 east will take you to Highway 167, where you'll turn south to reach Winnfield (less than an hour's drive from Briarwood).

Downtown, you'll see a statue of Huey Long on the courthouse lawn. Nearby, the *Louisiana Political Museum and Hall of Fame* (318–628–5928), housed in a ca. 1908 train depot at 499 East Main Street, offers a look at the lives and times of Louisiana's prominent politicians. You'll see life-size wax figures of brothers Huey P. and Earl K. Long. Other exhibits include photos, campaign memorabilia, and audio and video excerpts from political speeches and public appearances. The museum is usually open Monday through Friday from 9:00 A.M. to 5:00 P.M. and Saturday by appointment. Free admission.

A pleasant place to stay overnight is *Southern Colonial Bed and Breakfast* (318–628–6087), located at 801 East Main Street, Winnfield. The towering two-story house dates from about 1908, and owners Kathy and Bob Noyes will welcome you to their home, which features an inviting front porch and seven fireplaces. The Noyes family occupies the downstairs portion. The second floor, reserved for overnight visitors, features a common parlor and large guest rooms with some interesting antiques. Amenities include cable television, phones, coffee, and wake-up alarms. Guests can enjoy refreshments on the balcony or on the large porch, shaded by an ancient oak tree. Mornings start with a traditional Southern breakfast. Standard rates.

A short stroll from the Noyes's home, you'll find the ***Earl K. Long State Commemorative Area.*** Established in honor of Louisiana's first three-term governor, the one-acre park features a symmetrical design and lovely landscaping. An 8-foot bronze statue, dedicated on July 4, 1963, stands as a memorial to Earl Kemp Long, younger brother of Huey Long. A hedged circular sidewalk leads to a pavilion, a pleasant spot for a picnic.

From Winnfield, take US 167 south via Pineville to Alexandria.

Crossroads

Arriving in Pineville, you'll cross the Red River via the O. K. Allen Bridge to reach Alexandria. Known as a crossroads city, ***Alexandria*** marks the state's geographic center. The parish seat of Rapides (*ra-PEEDS*), Alexandria lost most of its buildings and records in 1864 when the Yankees set fire to the city during the Civil War. Another disaster occurred with the flood of 1866. The Red River separates Alexandria from its sister city, Pineville.

Soon after your arrival, stop by ***Kent House*** (318–487–5998) at 3601 Bayou Rapides Road, Alexandria. Believed to be Central Louisiana's oldest existing building (one of a few area structures to survive the Civil War), the home was completed in 1800. Kent House, which stands on brick pillars, exemplifies the classic Louisiana style of French and Spanish colonial architecture. An elevated construction protected buildings from floods and dampness.

Now restored, the house was moved to its present location from the original site, 2 blocks away. Kent House serves as a museum where visitors may see eight rooms filled with Empire, Sheraton, and Federal furniture, authentic documents dealing with land transfers, and many interesting decorative items.

The four-acre complex also contains slave quarters, a notched-log carriage house, a barn, a blacksmith shop, a sugar mill, and gardens. You'll see a detached kitchen and milk house along with a collection of early nineteenth-century cooking utensils. From October through April open-hearth cooking demonstrations are given each Wednesday between 9:00 A.M. and noon. Prepared foods might include corn bread, chicken, corn soup, lima beans, and cakes. Admission. Kent House is open from 9:00 A.M. to 5:00 P.M. every day

I Ate Alligator at Tunk's Cypress Inn

If you want the world to know you dined on alligator, you can get a bumper sticker announcing the fact at **Tunk's Cypress Inn** (318–487–4014). Also, you can choose from a fried version or Tunk's special Alligator Parmesan. For these menu items, the staff uses farm-raised alligators from Lafayette. Located about 10 miles west of Alexandria at 9507 Highway 28 West, the large rustic restaurant overlooks Kincaid Lake.

Entering, you'll see a mounted 10-foot, 6-inch alligator against a swamplike setting. When I visited, he was all decked out in Mardi Gras regalia. Besides alligator, owners Jimbo and Sandy Thiels offer crawfish, oysters, seafood, catfish, steaks, heart-healthy choices, and more—all prepared Tunk's own special way. Start with a cup of award-winning Miss Mayme's Seafood Gumbo followed by, depending on the season, a crawfish platter. Snapper Sandy, another of Tunk's signature items, features snapper fillets topped with lump crabmeat, shrimp, and crawfish in a creamy sauce then baked and served in a paper bag. (Jimbo shared this special recipe, one of Sandy's creations, so you can enjoy this scrumptious specialty at home.)

Restaurant hours run Tuesday through Saturday from 5:00 to 10:00 P.M. Downstairs, you can enjoy live music at the Oyster Bar, Tuesday through Saturday, from 4:00 to "whenever." Visit www.tunkscypressinn.com.

Snapper Sandy

For cream sauce:

2 tablespoons butter

3 tablespoons flour

Half-and-half (enough to make ⅓ cup of smooth thick sauce)

½ cup Velveeta or other cheese, shredded

Heat butter to 350 degrees. Add flour and whisk to blend. Stir until flour taste is gone, but do not brown. Add half-and-half slowly, continuing to stir. Cook a few minutes until a smooth consistency is reached. Blend in cheese then set mixture aside.

2 snapper fillets

Butter

Seasoning (of your choice)

Crawfish tails, cooked

Shrimp, cooked

Lump crabmeat

Green onion tops, chopped

Butter and season two snapper fillets. Place skin side down in paper bag. Place cooked crawfish tails, cooked shrimp, and lump crabmeat on top of fillets. (Amount depends on size of fillets.)

Spoon cream sauce over fillets. Sprinkle on a few chopped green onion tops. Close bag. Place in metal pan and slide into preheated 400-degree oven. Cook for 20 minutes or until fish is done. Cut away top of bag and serve. Yields 1 serving. (Multiply by number of diners.)

except Sunday, when the house is open by appointment only. Admission is charged. Check out the property at www.kenthouse.org.

Don't miss the ***Alexandria Museum of Art*** (318–443–3458) at 933 Main Street, Alexandria. The museum occupies the original Rapides Bank building, which dates from 1898, the first major building to appear after twin disasters of fire and flood in the 1860s. The facility features a fine collection of modern and contemporary works as well as Louisiana folk arts, traveling exhibits, and a gift shop. The museum, which also sponsors educational and interpretive programs, is open Tuesday through Friday from 10:00 A.M. to 5:00 P.M. Saturday hours are from 10:00 A.M. to 4:00 P.M. The admission fee is nominal.

Continue to nearby ***River Oaks Square Arts Center*** (318–473–2670) at 1330 Main Street, Alexandria. This lovely Queen Anne–style house was given to the city by the Bolton family to be used for the arts. Adjacent to the home stands a new structure housing studios and galleries. About forty local artists now work at the center, and you can watch creativity in action as painters, weavers, and sculptors practice their callings. Browse through individual studios and enjoy Preston Gilchrist's wax encaustic creations, Joseph Pearson's portraits, and Debra Smith Barnes's works in mixed media. In addition to showcasing artists at work, the center sometimes offers classes and workshops in drawing, watercolor, printmaking, sculpture, and collage for both children and adults. River Oaks Square, which features more than twenty exhibits a year, is open from 10:00 A.M. to 4:00 P.M. Tuesday through Friday and 10:00 A.M.

Jerry Lee Has Left the Building . . .

In rock and roll's earliest days, Elvis's biggest rival for the top performer crown was Jerry Lee Lewis, the rambunctious piano player who composed "Great Balls of Fire" and shocked his fans when he married his thirteen-year-old second cousin.

Jerry Lee grew up in Ferriday, Louisiana (northeast of Alexandria via Louisiana Highway 28 and U.S. Highway 84). He came from an interesting family. Two other cousins were Mickey Gilley (no Texas music fan can ignore him) and that tearful evangelist, Jimmy Swaggart.

Ferriday's musical legacy of black delta blues and juke joints coupled with white fundamentalist hymns is responsible for Jerry Lee's sound. If you want to hear more, Ferriday hosts the **Delta Music Festival** each spring.

For more information contact the Delta Music Museum, 218 Louisiana Avenue, Ferriday 71334; (318) 757–9999. Hours are 9:00 A.M. to 4:00 P.M., Monday through Friday. Call for Saturday hours. Free admission.

We Want Beads!

Unless you've done it, it's hard to imagine the thrill of catching a string of beads flung in your direction by Mardi Gras revelers on passing floats. It's absolutely heady—the more you snatch, the more you want. And the number of necklaces you wear reveals the level of your greed (though many of the athletically inclined pass their loot on to others whose catching skills have not evolved to such a high level).

Nearby, a man not only gets beads—the strand lands around his neck. Now that's what I call precision pitching. Between passing floats, kids play around with a basketball, doing tricks on the sidelines. The excitement is contagious, and you get totally caught up in the carnival atmosphere with uplifted arms as far as you can see.

Standing beside me, a woman instructs her two granddaughters: "It's not '*give* me something—it's *throw* me something, mister or please.' Wave your arms and yell, or you won't get anything." The girls follow her advice as festive floats pass with masked riders tossing shiny beads, plastic cups, doubloons, candy, and other treats. Then comes a beauty queen, seated atop a convertible. "Oh, don't waste your breath on her," my parade neighbor says. "She can't throw this far, but she's certainly got that pageant wave down pat."

For a fun-filled, family-oriented *Mardi Gras* celebration, including a chance to catch those beads, head to the Alexandria/Pineville area in Louisiana's Crossroads. Now in its second decade, this festival features a full weekend of entertainment. Friday night arrivals can enjoy specialties from the area's best restaurants at booths set up in the Alexandria Riverfront Center. Saturday events include a children's parade, a 5K run, and another run for fun. Parades on both Saturday and Sunday start with policemen on motorcycles, their sirens going full blast, performing figure eights. Then come the marching bands and flamboyant floats. The annual Krewe Parade draws some 150,000 attendees from as far away as East Texas, South Louisiana, and Mississippi, and an evening post-parade party follows at Convention Hall. For more information, call (318) 442–9546 or (800) 551–9546, or check out www.louisianafromhere.com.

to 2:00 P.M. on Saturday. Besides browsing, you can also buy unique works of art. Take a look at www.riveroaksartscenter.com. Modest admission.

A few steps behind River Oaks Square, you'll find the **Arna Bontemps African-American Museum and Cultural Arts Center** (318–473–4692) at 1327 Third Street, Alexandria. Bontemps, a member of the Harlem Renaissance, wrote novels, poetry, plays, histories, folklore collections, biographies, and children's literature. Housed in the ca. 1890 home where Bontemps was born in 1902, the museum contains the author's typewriter, books, letters, and memorabilia such as photographs of Louis Armstrong, Sidney Poitier, and other entertainers and arts figures. In addition to preserving a literary legacy, Bontemps's childhood home serves as a setting for traveling exhibits, area art displays, and writing classes for local youngsters. The center also showcases the Hall of Fame collection originally kept at Louisana State University's Alexandria branch. Except for major holidays, hours are Tuesday through Friday from 10:00 A.M. to 4:00 P.M. and Saturday from 10:00 A.M. to 2:00 P.M. A nominal donation is appreciated.

Challenge awaits at ***OakWing Golf Club*** (318–561–0260). Located at 2345 Vandenburg Drive, 1 mile off Interstate 49, the Jim Lipe–designed course features tree-lined fairways and undulating greens along with a series of Scottish links–style holes that require your attention. But you can take the guesswork out of your game because the golf carts come equipped with global positioning systems that let you know exactly how far you are from the pin.

This course ranks as a prime example of how a property can be recycled. Now England Industrial Airpark, the airport area had its beginning as an emergency airstrip to Esler Field Airport. In 1939, the Army Air Corps leased it to use as a training facility for B-17 and later B-29 crews during World War II. The site served as home for the Twenty-third Fighter Wing, the successor to the Flying Tigers of Claire Chennault in China.

In 1946, the base was gradually turned over to the city of Alexandria to be used as a municipal airport, but with the outbreak of hostilities, it was reactivated as Alexandria Air Force Base and assigned to the Tactical Air Command. Then, in 1955, the property became England Air Force Base until another base closing in 1992. It now serves as Alexandria International Airport.

Along with the airport and related facilities came a nine-hole base golf course, the nucleus of today's OakWing Golf Club. While playing a round, you can enjoy the setting with lakes, bayous, and wildlife, and even dip into some history. You'll see an old cemetery and a cluster of five mounted military aircraft from World War II through the Gulf War at Heritage Park, which honors the Flying Tigers.

OakWing Golf Club made the cut as one of the state's nine courses included in the Audubon Golf Trail, named for renowned naturalist and artist John James Audubon.

ANOTHER ATTRACTION WORTH SEEING

Alexandria Zoological Park
3016 Masonic Drive, Alexandria
(318) 473–1143
This pleasant zoo features a miniature train to ride and more than 500 animals. In the award-winning Habitat exhibit, which showcases the state's wildlife, architecture, industry, and culture, you'll see alligators, otters, snapping turtles, and more. Open daily, closed Thanksgiving, Christmas, and New Year's. Small admission fee.

Ya-Yas

What other state could possibly serve as a setting for *Divine Secrets of the Ya-Ya Sisterhood*? Alexandria native Rebecca Wells uses central Louisiana as a backdrop for her Southern novel based on a group of friends who remain close through the years and through life's changing circumstances. In Alexandria, you can experience the charm and southern hospitality of Louisiana's Crossroads as you visit sites that inspired Wells's best seller.

After an energetic game of golf, consider treating yourself to a rejuvenating session at **The Nest** (318–443–3322), about twenty minutes from downtown Alexandria. Located at 8645 Highway 165 South in Woodworth, the spa/retreat offers services for both men and women ranging from Swedish, deep tissue, and hot-stone massages to detoxifying body wraps and mineral whirlpool treatments. Best of all, the 252-acre setting induces a state of serenity in itself. This future Nature Conservancy property features grounds studded with sculptures, including many by Russell Whiting, along with interesting architecture and stunning flora and fauna. Call for information on overnight retreats.

Afterward, head back downtown and cross the Jackson Street Bridge to Pineville's Main Street. You'll soon see a cemetery on the left and then **Mount Olivet Chapel.** Built in 1854, the church was dedicated by Bishop Leonidas Polk, who later "buckled sword over gown" to become a Confederate general. The picturesque chapel survived the Civil War, probably because it served as a headquarters for the Union Army.

The Gothic Revival structure, which features some Tiffany windows, was designed by Richard Upjohn, the architect of New York's Trinity Church. Except for its oak floor, the chapel is constructed entirely of native pinewood. Take some time to explore the surrounding cemetery with tombstone dates as early as 1824 still discernible. For a cemetery tour or information about the chapel, call Elaine Hicks at (318) 473–8787.

Military buffs may want to visit the **Alexandria National Cemetery** at 209 Shamrock Avenue, also in Pineville. This cemetery, an art gallery in stone, contains graves from the Civil War, Spanish-American War, and both World Wars.

Central Louisiana's role in supporting the nation's armed forces goes back a long way. In Pineville, the **Louisiana Maneuvers & Military Museum** (318–641–5733) depicts the history of the region's commitment with Maneuvers-era arms, uniforms, and equipment at Camp Beauregard. This facility honors soldiers and civilians of the Louisiana Maneuvers. On the grounds, you'll see a Sherman tank, Patton tank, F-100 Super Saber aircraft, and more.

The re-created World War II barracks museum, which even includes a latrine "living room," houses sergeants' quarters and illustrates how the troops were bunked—head to foot—to help prevent spread of contagious diseases.

Exhibits showcase main players in the Maneuvers—Generals Marshall, Eisenhower, Patton, and Bradley. You'll see a rare and battered Japanese war flag from a ship in Hiroshima Harbor when the atomic bomb was dropped. Other displays of uniforms, and photographs of women at work doing "men's jobs," interpret the female contribution to the war effort.

Upstairs, a home front display shows a family living room with period furnishings, sweetheart pillows, ration cards, and blue stars (in service) and gold stars (killed in service), which were placed on the windows of family dwellings.

Currently a Louisiana Army and Air National Guard training facility, the camp served as an induction center during World War II. Have a photo ID ready as you approach the post. The museum, which closes for lunch from 11:00 A.M. to noon, is open Monday through Friday from 9:00 A.M. to 5:00 P.M. Call ahead for a tour. Free admission.

Dip into Nostalgia at Lea's Lunchroom

Established in 1928, Lea's Lunchroom in Lecompte attracts the locals as well as visitors from all over the world. Lea's has been featured on numerous TV shows (including the long-running late-night *The Tonight Show Starring Johnny Carson*) and in magazines, newspapers, and tour guides throughout the country. Toby Traylor, grandson of the late Mr. Lea Johnson who founded this popular restaurant, now serves as manager. Here he shares the recipe for a perennial favorite:

Chicken and Dumplings

1 stewing chicken	2 teaspoons baking powder
1½ to 2 teaspoons salt	1 teaspoon salt
1 onion, chopped	1/3 cup shortening
1 red bell pepper, chopped	1/2 cup milk
2 cups flour	

Cut up chicken; place in deep pot and barely cover with water. Add salt and simmer until meat is tender.

Debone chicken and set aside, reserving the broth. Add chopped onion and bell pepper to broth, and cook down until soft.

Sift together the flour, baking powder, and salt; cut in shortening. Add milk to make a stiff dough. (Note: If you don't want to make your own dough, use biscuit mix). Roll out to ¼-inch thickness on floured board. Cut into 1-inch squares, and sprinkle with flour. Drop into briskly boiling chicken stock. Cover tightly and simmer for about 40 minutes. Add meat last and serve. Yields 6 to 8 servings.

Cotton: Then and Now

While in this area, consider an eastward excursion to *Frogmore Plantation and Gins* (318–757–2453), where owners Lynette and George Tanner offer a contrast between the old and the new. "Even if you grew up on a cotton plantation, you're going to learn history and trivia at Frogmore that no one else tells. For instance, most of us eat cotton every day," says Lynette. Find out more at 11054 Highway 84 in Frogmore near the Mississippi border. This 1,800-acre working cotton plantation features eighteen antebellum structures, including authentically furnished slave row cabins dating from 1810. Besides touring the buildings, you'll see a film on cotton's role in history, an 1884 antique steam gin, and today's computerized version. You may also get a chance to pick cotton here. Call ahead for hours, which vary by season. Admission. Visit www.frogmoreplantation.com for tour information and special events. From time to time, Lynette schedules gospel music tours.

After visiting Pineville take US 71 south to Lecompte, about 12 miles south of Alexandria. Here you'll find *Lea's Lunchroom* (318–776–5178), a country-style cafe that dishes up hearty Southern cooking. Lea Johnson established this popular eatery in 1928.

The staff believes in fast service and objects to written menus because "they take too much time." At Lea's the server recites the menu, which might feature red beans and sausage with rice and crackling corn bread or a choice of fried fish, beef tips, or ham along with turnip greens and sweet potatoes. Prices are economical. Milk is served in chilled glasses, and you can have a demitasse of coffee after your meal. The restaurant is famous for its hams baked in dough and homemade pies made from secret family recipes. The staff makes about 65,000 pies a year, including apple, pecan, banana cream, cherry, blueberry, blackberry, lemon, chocolate, and coconut. In fact, the Louisiana senate named LeCompte the Pie Capital of the state as a tribute to Lea's seven-plus decades of service.

The restaurant also offers a large selection of regional cookbooks and purchases much of its produce from local growers. Lea's is closed on Monday and opens at 7:00 A.M. on other days. Closing time is 5:00 P.M. Take a look at www.leaslunchroom.com and drool.

Lecompte (*le-COUNT*) was named after an 1850s record-breaking racehorse from a local plantation. Before a sign painter inadvertently inserted a *P*, the place was Lecomte. While in town stop by the *Old Lecompte High School* (318–776–9520), which dates from 1924. Local citizens recently waged a campaign to resurrect their old school—where shouts of students and chiming class bells had not been heard for more than two decades—and won an award from the state for their success story. Now a community center, the large building houses a museum, dining room, public library, meeting rooms, gymnasium, and auditorium.

The remarkable thing about this project is that it was entirely a community effort. All money came from private donations, and local people volunteered their talents to renovate the structure. The building's distinctive historical features, including the auditorium's ornate plasterwork and balcony railing, have been preserved. The end result is a fine multipurpose facility that holds a treasury of memories for generations of former students. A museum, with several rooms, focuses on two centuries of Louisiana history. Visiting hours are Tuesday through Friday from 9:00 A.M. to 5:00 P.M., and Saturday from 9:00 A.M. to 1:00 P.M. Modest admission. Visit www.oldlecomptehighschool.com.

Before leaving this area you may want to drive through the surrounding countryside. Some 300 nurseries are located in the nearby Lecompte–Forest Hill area. Along **Nursery Row** you'll find landscaping bargains in a variety of shrubs, trees, and plants, including ornamental and exotic plants. Although the nurseries supply commercial markets, most will accommodate drop-in retail customers.

Continue to nearby **Bunkie,** where you'll find the **Courtney Gallery of Art** (318–346–9966) at 602 Walnut Street near the Pershing Highway intersection, 1 block off Main Street. Look for a white picket fence fronting a Victorian home. The gallery occupies the Pope House, built in 1900. After a sojourn in Georgia, Juanita Courtney returned to her hometown and opened an art gallery. A professional painter for some thirty years, Juanita's subject matter ranges from landscapes, house portraits, zydeco musicians, and still lifes to barnyard animals, wild animals, people, and pet portraits. Her original oils and watercolors, along with a large selection of prints, wooden door-panel hangings of scenes from yesteryear, and antique wood engravings from vintage newspapers and magazines may be purchased here.

The gallery also carries an assortment of gifts such as pottery, sculpture, and decorative decoys. Unless Juanita is away exhibiting her work at an art show, you can visit during business hours of 9:00 A.M. to 5:00 P.M. Monday through Friday and 9:00 A.M. to 3:00 P.M. Saturday.

Located at 200 West Magnolia Drive, the historic **Bailey Hotel** (866–346–7111) makes a convenient base for venturing beyond Bunkie to nearby attractions in Central Louisiana. Constructed in 1907, the hotel underwent a three-year renovation, reopening in 2001. Listed on the National Register of Historic Places, the property also belongs to the prestigious Historic Hotels of America. The Magnolia Room specializes in Cajun cuisine.

Zanga's, the hotel lounge, offers spirited entertainment where guests might hear everything from jazz and contemporary to authentic Avoyelles Parish music. The lounge takes its name from an early guest. According to an ad in a 1925 issue of the local newspaper: "Professor Zanga will be staying in room 39 at the Bailey Hotel. A Soothsayer and Clairvoyant, Professor Zanga will find your lost articles, minerals, and tell your future." Hotel rates range from standard to moderate. For more information, tap into www.baileyhotel.com.

After exploring Bunkie, consider a trip to the town of *Marksville*. About a mile or so from a 1,000-acre Indian reservation, you'll find the *Marksville State Historic Site* (318–253–8954 or 888–253–8954) at 837 Martin Luther King Drive, Marksville. Marksville's Indian civilization flourished here some 2,000 years ago, and museum exhibits interpret that culture. Situated on a bluff overlooking Old River, the Marksville site encompasses six prehistoric Indian mounds as well as encircling earthworks ranging from 4 to 6 feet tall. Except for Thanksgiving, Christmas, and New Year's Day, the site is open daily from 9:00 A.M. to 5:00 P.M.

Places to Stay in Central Louisiana

WOODLAND AND WATER

Landmark Hotel of Leesville
3080 Colony Boulevard
Leesville
(337) 239–7571 or
(800) 246–6926

CANE RIVER COUNTRY

Best Western of Natchitoches
I–49 and Highway 6
Natchitoches
(318) 352–6655 or
(800) 528–1234

Fleur de Lis Bed & Breakfast Inn
336 Second Street
Natchitoches
(318) 352–6621 or
(800) 489–6621

Hampton Inn
5300 University Parkway
Natchitoches
(318) 354–0010 or
(800) HAMPTON

Holiday Inn Express
5131 Highway 6 West
Natchitoches
(318) 354–9911 or
(800) HOLIDAY

Judge Porter House
321 Second Street
Natchitoches
(318) 352–9206 or
(800) 441–8343

Ramada Inn
7624 Highway 1 Bypass
Natchitoches
(318) 357–8281 or
(888) 252–8281

Tante Huppé Historic Inn
424 Jefferson Street
Natchitoches
(318) 352–5342 or
(800) 482–4276

SCENIC RIVER REGION

Southern Colonial Bed and Breakfast
801 East Main Street
Winnfield
(318) 628–6087

CROSSROADS

Bailey Hotel
200 West Magnolia
Bunkie
(866) 346–7111

Best Western of Alexandria Inn and Suites
2720 West MacArthur Drive
Alexandria
(318) 445–5530 or
(800) 528–1234

Holiday Inn Convention Center
701 Fourth Street
Alexandria
(318) 442–9000

Louisiana Convention Center and Hotel
2301 North MacArthur Drive
Alexandria
(318) 487–8500 or
(877) 487–8500

Paragon Casino Resort
711 Grand Boulevard
Marksville
(318) 253–0777 or
(800) 946–1946
Next to the casino venture
of the Tunica–Biloxi Tribal
Council

**Parc England—
A Boutique Hotel**
1321 Chappie James Avenue
Alexandria
(318) 445–7574

**Ramada Limited
of Alexandria**
742 MacArthur Drive
Alexandria
(318) 448–1611 or
(800) 272–6232

Places to Eat in Central Louisiana

WOODLAND AND WATER

Country Boy Restaurant
105 North Highland Street
Many
(318) 256–3953

CANE RIVER COUNTRY

Just Friends
750 Front Street
Natchitoches
(318) 352–3836

The Landing
530 Front Street
Natchitoches
(318) 352–1579

**Lasyone's Meat Pie
Kitchen and Restaurant**
622 Second Street
Natchitoches
(318) 352–3353

Mama's Oyster House
608 Front Street
Natchitoches
(318) 356–7874

Mariner's
off Louisiana Highway 1
Bypass at Sibley Lake
Natchitoches
(318) 357–1220

FOR MORE INFORMATION

**Alexandria/Pineville Area Convention
and Visitors Bureau**
locations at 707 Main Street
Alexandria 71301
and Alexandria Mall
3437 Masonic Drive
Alexandria 71301
(318) 442–9546 or
(800) 551–9546
www.louisianafromhere.com

Avoyelles Commission of Tourism
208 South Main Street
Marksville 71351
(318) 253–0585 or (800) 833–4195

**Natchitoches Parish Tourist
Commission**
781 Front Street
Natchitoches 71457
(800) 259–1714
www.natchitoches.net

**Sabine Parish Tourist and
Recreation Commission**
920 Fisher Road
Many 71449
(800) 358–7802

**Vernon Parish Tourism and
Recreation Commission**
P.O. Box 349
Leesville 71496
(318) 238–0783 or (800) 349–6287

Winn Parish Tourist Commission
P.O. Box 565
Winfield 71483
(318) 628–4461

Area newspapers include the *Town Talk*
in Alexandria (largest paper in the area,
should have weekly entertainment
listings), the *Sabine Index* in Many, the
Natchitoches Times in Natchitoches, the
Winn Parish Enterprise in Winnfield, the
Record in Bunkie, and the *Weekly News*
in Marksville.

Papa's Bar and Grill
604 Front Street
Natchitoches
(318) 356–5850

CROSSROADS

Bistro on the Bayou
(at England Airpark)
1321 Chappie James
Avenue
Alexandria
(318) 445–7574

Cajun Landing
2728 MacArthur
Alexandria
(318) 487–4912

Critic's Choice
5208 Rue Verdon
Alexandria
(318) 445–1680

415 Murray Street
Alexandria
(318) 442–3333

El Reparo Mexican Restaurant & Grill
550 McArthur Drive
Alexandria
(318) 487–0207

Julia's Mexican Restaurant
2204 Worley Drive
Alexandria
(318) 445–2405

Lea's Lunchroom
1810 Highway 71 South
Lecompte
(318) 776–5178

Lee J's on the Levee
208 Main Street
Pineville
(318) 487–4628

Paradise Catfish Kitchen
4820 Monroe Highway
Pineville
(318) 640–5032

Red River Grill
313 North Washington Street
Marksville
(318) 253–5252

Stalnaker's Restaurant
4320 Stalnaker Road
Pineville
(318) 640–1361

Tunk's Cypress Inn
9507 Highway 28 West
Boyce
(318) 487–4014

Southwest Louisiana

The southwest portion of Louisiana includes coastal marshes with oak ridges along their edges. Inland are found prairie lands. The prairies are cut by several watercourses, including the Calcasieu and the Vermilion Rivers. The low meandering ridges of the prairies are also marked by intermittent, slow-moving streams called coulees. Rice cultivation (which necessitates seasonal irrigation and is often rotated with crawfish farming), along with petroleum, cattle, and seafood industries, makes up a large portion of the regional economy.

Imperial Calcasieu

Forming the heel of the Louisiana boot, the parishes of Cameron, Calcasieu *(KAL-ka-shoe)*, Beauregard, Allen, and Jefferson Davis compose what was once called Imperial Calcasieu.

Made up mostly of marshlands and bayous, Cameron is the state's largest parish and home to Louisiana's outback. Its ***Creole Nature Trail All-American Road*** affords close-up views of the wetlands and wildlife along with myriad birding opportunities. Hurricane Rita delivered a stunning blow to the Creole Nature Trail in September, 2005, so the trail and its flora,

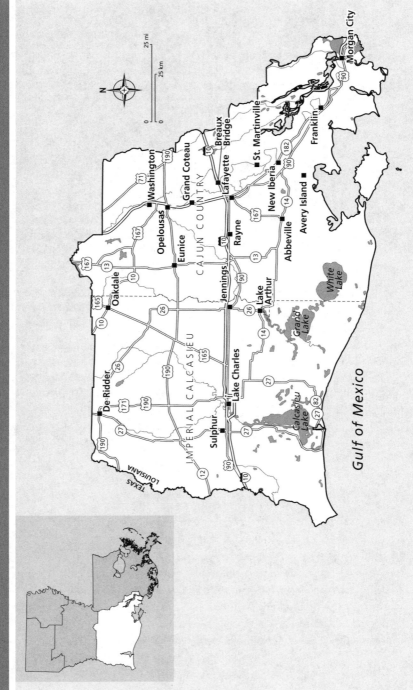

fauna, and facilities are now in a state of recovery. Before planning your visit, review www.creolenaturetrail.org for the latest updates and openings.

As this guidebook goes to press, two major problems remain: debris removal and lack of public restroom facilities. Gasoline and eateries are limited along the trail with none at all available south of Hackberry on State Route 27 and south of the Cameron Prairie National Wildlife Refuge or on State Route 82 from the Texas state line to the Vermilion Parish line.

The Cameron Ferry runs daily from 5:00 A.M. to 9:00 P.M. This fifty-car ferry transports travelers across the Calcasieu Ship Channel. For eastward-bound passengers the trip is free, but those heading west pay a toll of $1.00 per car. If you step to the rail, you might catch a special performance by porpoises, who frequently put on a free show for ferry passengers.

The fishing in Calcasieu Lake will make anglers smile, but accommodations remain few and far between for now. Still, if you're determined to go fishing, birding, or hunting in this area, give Capt'n Sammie Faulk a call at (337) 598–2001 or (337) 540–2050. He knows the territory and can guide you past obstacles.

Railroad buffs might like to start exploring the state's southwestern portion at DeQuincy, reached by taking Route 27 north. Once a rowdy frontier town with eight saloons to serve a transient population of some 200 persons, DeQuincy managed to live down its early reputation after the railroad's arrival, when it began attracting more serious settlers.

Both the *DeQuincy Railroad Museum* (337–786–2823) and the DeQuincy Chamber of Commerce occupy the Kansas City Southern Railroad's original depot at 400 Lake Charles Avenue. Museum exhibits include a 1913 steam locomotive, a coal car, a vintage caboose, and several restored railcars. You'll also see telegraph and railroad equipment, local historical memorabilia such as tick-

GAY'S FAVORITES IN SOUTHWEST LOUISIANA

Acadian Village Lafayette	**Mardi Museum of Imperial Calcasieu** Lake Charles
Atchafalaya Basin near Henderson	**Shadows-on-the-Teche** New Iberia
Avery Island	**Town of Abbeville**
Longfellow-Evangeline State Historic Site St. Martinville	**Town of Washington**
	Vermilionville Lafayette

TOP ANNUAL EVENTS IN SOUTHWEST LOUISIANA

Mardi Gras of Southwest Louisiana
Lake Charles
Fat Tuesday and preceding weekend
(337) 436–9588
www.visitlakecharles.org

Louisiana Railroad Days Festival
DeQuincy Railroad Museum
second weekend in April
(337) 786–8241 or
(337) 786–2823

Festival International de Louisiane
735 Jefferson Street, Lafayette
last weekend in April
(337) 232–8086

Breaux Bridge Crawfish Festival
Breaux Bridge, first full weekend in May
(888) 565–5939
www.bbcrawfish.com

Contraband Days
900 Lakeshore Drive, Lake Charles
first two weeks in May
(337) 436–5508
www.contrabanddays.com

Cajun Food & Music Festival
Burton Coliseum, Lake Charles
mid-July
(337) 436–9588
www.cajunfrenchmusic.org

Shrimp Festival
Main Street, Delcambre, mid-August
(888) 9–IBERIA

The Original Southwest Louisiana Zydeco Music Festival
off Highway 167, Plaisance
last Saturday before Labor Day
(337) 942–2392

Louisiana Shrimp and Petroleum Festival
710 Third Street, Morgan City
Labor Day weekend
(985) 385–0703
www.shrimp-petrofest.org

Frog Festival
Rayne, mid-September
(337) 334–2332

Louisiana Sugar Cane Festivaland Fair
City Park, Parkview Drive, New Iberia
late September
(888) 9–IBERIA

Festivals Acadiens
Lafayette, second weekend in October
(800) 346–1958

International Rice Festival
Crowley, third weekend in October
(337) 783–3067
www.ricefestival.com

ets and timetables dating from the early 1900s, uniforms, and an old mail pouch. You may admire the dispatcher's ability to concentrate as he sits before an antique typewriter absorbed by his work and apparently oblivious to all activity around him . . . until you realize that he's a mannequin. Museum hours Monday through Friday are 9:00 A.M. to 4:00 P.M. Saturday and Sunday hours run from noon to 4:00 P.M. Admission is free, but donations are appreciated.

After leaving DeQuincy take Route 27 south to Sulphur. The ***Brimstone Museum*** (337–527–0357), located at 900 South Huntington Street, Sulphur, is housed in the Southern Pacific Railway Depot. You'll see a wildlife diorama, an antique medical instrument collection, photos of the town during its sulfur-mining heyday, and other exhibits related to the southwestern region.

The museum's focus concerns the history of the American sulfur industry, which started here, thanks to the ingenuity of Herman Frasch. Although it was no secret that sulfur deposits existed in the area, nobody knew how to tap this wealth. Extracting the yellow mineral from its underground home remained in the realm of the impossible until scientist-inventor Frasch solved the problem. He came up with a superheating water process that led to the commercial production of sulfur in the United States. (Prior to 1900 almost all sulfur came from Sicily.) The Brimstone Museum, established in 1976, commemorates Frasch's contribution. Among other things, sulfur is used in making medicines, rayon, fertilizers, insecticides, paper pulp, matches, and gunpowder.

The museum is open Monday through Friday, from 10:00 A.M. to noon and 1:00 to 5:00 P.M. Admission is free.

After browsing through the Brimstone Museum, proceed to the adjacent historic home that houses the *Henning Cultural Center* (337–527–0357). Here, you'll see the work of local artists as well as traveling exhibits from around the country. Hours are 10:00 A.M. to noon and 1:00 to 5:00 P.M. Monday through Friday. Free admission.

After visiting Sulphur, continue to nearby Lake Charles. For a relaxing base in this vicinity, consider making reservations at *A River's Edge Bed and Breakfast* (337–497–1525 or 337–540–3813), only seven minutes from downtown Lake Charles. Located at 2035 Gus Street in Westlake, the property offers a private cottage plus two bedrooms in the main house and a full Southern breakfast.

Savor the serene bayou setting with wildlife and beautiful sunsets from the porch swing, rockers, or patio furniture. Owners Wanda and Billy Traweek encourage guests to enjoy the pool in warm weather months, the fireplace when temperatures turn cool, and Southern hospitality around the calendar. Pampering touches include bedtime treats such as Godiva chocolates and Mardi Gras beads on your pillow. Moderate rates. Preview the property at www.lake charlesbedbreakfast.com.

When you arrive in *Lake Charles,* you may think that the sandy beach studded with palm trees is a mirage. But the artificially created North Beach is indeed real—and the only inland white-sand beach on the entire Gulf Coast. A drive over the Interstate 10 Bridge affords a panoramic view of the beach, which borders the highway.

While driving across the I–10 Bridge, be sure to notice the railing with its design featuring pirate pistols. This area was once *Jean Lafitte*'s stomping ground. The "Gentleman Pirate" was a poetic sort who allegedly stashed some

Hackberry, the Crab Capital of the World

Because hard-shell blue crabs are so plentiful in the Hackberry area, many people enjoy **crabbing,** so you might like to try your luck, too. The basic equipment boils down to two pieces: a net to scoop up the crabs and a bucket to hold them. You can buy crabbing supplies at one of the area bait shops. With net in hand you can walk along a pier and capture any crabs you see on pilings, or you can wade in shallow water and scoop them up before they scurry away. Then there's the string-and-bait method. It entails attaching a one-ounce fishing weight plus a chunk of meat or fish to a string about 20 feet long. Toss the loaded line into the water, preferably near rocks or a dock. When you feel a slight tug, slowly pull the string toward you, keeping the net submerged and as still as possible so that it will look like part of the underwater scenery. As long as it's in the water, the crab will cling to the line. When it gets close enough, sweep it into your net. You have to be swift and synchronized, or the crab will win. After you collect enough crabs to constitute a meal, you can trade your bucket for a cookbook.

of his treasure in nearby watery mazes. To this day Lake Charles still plays host to pirates. Just visit in the spring when the city celebrates Contraband Days, starting with "Lafitte's invasion." The pirate's swashbuckling arrival sets off a jolly two-week round of parades, parties, pageants, boat races, and other festivities. In true buccaneering tradition, one event features the mayor "walking the plank."

Lafitte's loot may be hopelessly hidden, but you'll discover treasure aplenty at the *Cottage Shops,* clustered around Hodges, Alamo, and Common Streets. Some dozen downtown specialty shops offer items ranging from antique armoires and handmade quilts to Cajun upside-down pickles and stained glass.

At 2827 Hodges Street, you'll find *Once in a Blue Moon* (337–491–0520), brimming over with gift items like silver jewelry, wind chimes, candles, and more. Continue to *The Perfect Gift* (337–439–7693) at 2712 Hodges Street for more selections. Among the shop's specialty jewelry, bath items, wines, and gardening accessories, you're sure to discover something that speaks to you.

If you're a coffee lover, don't pass up the *Louisiana Market* (337–439–1617) at 2710 Hodges Street. Owner Judith Romero daily brews up a different flavor from her line of specialty coffees. You'll enjoy sipping coffee as you browse through aisles of authentic Cajun/Creole specialty foods and gifts. From hand-carved ducks to hot pepper jelly, a gift list can be taken care of here in one fell swoop.

To acquaint yourself with the history of Lake Charles, you can visit the *Imperial Calcasieu Museum* (337–439–3797), located at 204 West Sallier

Street. The museum stands on the site of a cabin built by early settler Charles Sallier (*sal-YAY*), for whom the city was named.

Look left as you enter, and you'll see the steering wheel from the paddle wheeler *Borealis Rex*. In earlier days this ship served as the only link between Lake Charles and Cameron, located on Calcasieu Lake's southern side. Each Wednesday a crowd gathered to welcome the steamer bringing mail, freight, and passengers.

Along the museum's right aisle, you'll pass a furnished parlor, kitchen, and bedroom, all depicting scenes from yesteryear.

A collection of personalized shaving mugs adds to the decor in the museum's Gay Nineties barbershop, and a re-created country store nearby features nostalgic merchandise. A mannequin pharmacist stands ready to dispense remedies in his apothecary, an original section from a downtown drugstore. You'll see a physician's travel kit and a glass-cased display of bottles in a rainbow of colors. Be sure to notice the ornate set of ironstone apothecary jars made in France during the early sixteenth century.

A Civil War flag from the Battle of Mobile Bay is on display in the War Room. You'll also see a uniform worn by General Claire Chennault, who led the famed Flying Tigers. This exhibit includes Mrs. Chennault's wedding gown and going-away costume, books, and various items of historical significance.

A Geneva Bible, an Edison phonograph, and a stereopticon are all treasures you won't want to overlook. The museum features a fine collection of bird and animal prints by John James Audubon as well as excerpts from the diary he kept while working in Louisiana. There's an exhibit of Lafitte memorabilia with a copy of the privateer's journal, published more than a century after his death. (Maybe it contains a clue as to where he concealed his contraband.) Admission fee is modest. Be sure to take in the current offerings in the nearby ***Gibson-Barham Gallery,*** which features ever-changing exhibits of both contemporary and traditional work. In

hurricane audreymemorial

On June 27, 1957, Hurricane Audrey hit Cameron Parish, leaving 525 dead. There is a monument in front of Our Lady Star of the Sea Church, 4 miles east of Cameron on Highway 82.

the gift shop, you'll find some unique handcrafted items. View www.imperial calcasieumuseum.org for the current schedule.

Don't leave without stepping out to the museum's backyard for a view of the venerable ***Sallier Oak.*** Some tree experts estimate this magnificent live oak to be more than 300 years old. Whether or not the tree has weathered three centuries, it carries its age well, and its credentials include membership in the Live

Oak Society. With branches dipping almost to the ground, this inviting oak would fulfill any child's tree-climbing fantasies.

Although the Sallier Oak may be visited at any time, the museum's hours are Tuesday through Saturday from 10:00 A.M. to 5:00 P.M.

A walking or driving tour of the city's historic **Charpentier Historic District** takes you through some twenty square blocks of homes dating from the Victorian era. Because many of the houses in this area were constructed before professional architects arrived on the scene, they express the individuality of their various builders. Area carpenters created their own patterns by changing rooflines, porch placements, and other exterior features. Sometimes they combined traditional design elements in new ways. A typical house constructed of native cypress and longleaf yellow pine might feature an odd number of columns with a bay on one side and a porch on the other. This distinctive look now commands an architectural category all its own—Lake Charles style.

The Southwest Louisiana Convention and Visitors Bureau produces an illustrated brochure that outlines a walking-driving route through the historic district. You can request one by calling (337) 436–9588 or (800) 456–7952.

Better yet, you can stay overnight in one of the following lovely historic homes in the Lake Charles Charpentier (French for "carpenter") Historic District. At 504 Pujo Street, you'll see **Aunt Ruby's Bed & Breakfast** (337– 430–0603), actually the city's first boardinghouse. Now owned by the proprietor of Pujo Street Café (only two blocks away), Aunt Ruby's offers six rooms with charming period furnishings. This ca. 1911 home provides private baths, private phone lines, cable TV, a meeting room, and full breakfast. Moderate rates. Visit www.auntrubys.com.

Also located in the heart of this National Register district, you'll find the nineteenth-century **Eddy House Bed and Breakfast** (337–436–3980) at 722 Pujo Street. At this lovely two-story Queen Anne Revival home, two of the four guest rooms feature verandas. To learn more about this ca. 1893 house built by Henry H. Eddy (one of five brothers from Vinton, Iowa, who settled in Lake Charles), see www.eddyhouse.info. Moderate rates.

The historic hospitality continues at **C. A.'s House Bed and Breakfast** (337–439–6672 or 866–439–6672), where guests can choose from large suites in the main house, adjacent guest house, or carriage house (where pets are allowed). Located at 624 Ford Street, the home dates to 1900 and offers luxury accommodations plus a gourmet breakfast served in the dining room. Owner/innkeeper Tanis Robinson named the home for her uncle, the late C. A. King II, who renovated the house and lived here for two decades. Moderate to deluxe. Take a look at www.cas-house.com.

If you have offspring in tow, consider stopping by the ***Children's Museum*** (337–433–9420) while in this area. It's located at 327 Broad Street, Lake Charles. Youngsters can indulge their curiosity and creative instincts through various participatory programs. They can don uniforms and pretend to fight fires or broadcast their own news from a television-studio setting.

Changing exhibits explore areas of natural and physical science, history, art, crafts, and geography. Except for major holidays, hours are 10:00 A.M. to 5:00 P.M. Monday through Saturday. Admission; kids under three get in free. Learn more at www.child-museum.org.

Traveling east from Lake Charles, most drivers take I–10. Route 14, however, runs south of the interstate (more in a meandering fashion than parallel) and offers some scenic vistas denied interstate travelers (albeit periodic road signs caution motorists about speeding on a substandard highway). If you do opt for Route 14, keep in mind that it takes longer, but you might see such striking vistas as entire fields white with egrets.

Persons driving through this part of the state on I–10 risk possible "arrest" if they fail to take the ***Jennings*** exit. Typical case: Mr. L., his wife, and their two children were traveling along said route when stopped by the local sheriff. Mr. L. was not speeding or breaking any other laws. His crime? Not stopping in Jennings. Once a year the local chamber of commerce "arrests" an out-of-state driver for not stopping in Jennings. The party is charged, tried, and sentenced. Any plea-bargaining attempts by a court-appointed attorney are thrown out by presiding judges. The guilty party is sentenced to enjoy a meal before driving away with a load of gifts (plus a tank of gas) from area merchants. Also, he or she must promise to stop in Jennings if passing that way again.

Some travelers bypass highways entirely and simply fly in. An airport adjacent to the interstate attracts all sorts of "fly people"—from Cessna owners to Stearman pilots—who migrate to Jennings during a designated weekend for the annual end-of-the-season fly-in. Pilots practice formation flying in pairs and in groups because the airport allows "free flight" if sessions are performed by seasoned veterans. Pilots can taxi right up to the door of the local Holiday Inn. (From cockpit to motel room might mean a hop, skip, and jump of some 50 yards.)

croprotation

When the people of Lake Charles wanted to do something with the land that used to serve as the town poor farm (where people went in the days before government aid), they put McNeese State University's campus on it.

Mardi Gras is Contagious

Momus, king of Mardi Gras, stepped from his royal yacht at the foot of Pujo Street in Lake Charles at 4:00 P.M. on Tuesday, February 21, 1882. He boarded a chariot waiting on shore, and the parade began. So it was in the beginning when some 2,000 people lined the parade route. Today's Mardi Gras parades attract some 150,000 spectators annually.

"Mardi Gras is contagious," said Dr. Lee J. Monlezun, who with his wife Anne, a dance instructor, spread the infection by opening up festivities to everyone almost three decades ago. Now, the couple serves in an emeritus role by helping participants prepare for the big parade and preliminary events like pageants, costume balls, and the Cinderella night of Mardi Gras. The Royal Gala features a colorful promenade of more than forty-two krewes (social clubs) in glittering costumes. Thousands of residents and visitors watch kings and queens, dukes and duchesses, captains, courtesans, and jesters in an evening of merrymaking at the Lake Charles Civic Center Coliseum.

If your visit to Lake Charles does not coincide with this special season, then head to the *Mardi Gras Museum of Imperial Calcasieu* (337–430–0043) at 809 Kirby Street. Here, in the east wing of historic Central School, it's always Carnival time, and you'll marvel at the memorabilia and spectacular costumes spilling over into six rooms. You'll hear fascinating anecdotes while viewing ornate regalia, which includes elaborate beaded gowns with stunning trains. Intricate workmanship and countless hours go into their construction. From costume designs to finished creations, Mardi Gras preparations continue around the calendar. Museum hours are Tuesday through Friday from 1:00 to 5:00 P.M. Modest admission.

Whether your visit in Jennings results from coercion or choice, all sorts of delights await you off the beaten path. Start with the *Louisiana Oil and Gas Park,* just north of town (and visible from I–10). Louisiana's first oil well produced "black gold" on September 21, 1901, just 5 miles northeast of town in a rice field that belonged to farmer Jules Clement. The park, which commemorates that significant event, contains a replica of the small wooden oil rig used to drill the first well. Next to the derrick stands an early Acadian-style house where the visitor information center is located.

An ideal place to take a driving break, the public recreation area includes a jogging trail, picnic facilities, playground equipment, a lake, and flocks of ducks and geese that act as a welcoming committee. You also can see *Château des Cocodries* (800–264–5521), a live alligator exhibit.

Select a table and spread a picnic, but save some sandwich crusts for the ducks—they consider it their duty to dispose of any leftovers. Maybe the ducks should be thanked for the trophy designating Jennings as Louisiana's cleanest

Replica of an Acadian House at Louisiana Oil and Gas Park

city. After winning the Cleanest City Award three years in a row, Jennings received the trophy for its permanent collection.

Jennings celebrated its first century in 1988. The town was named for a railroad contractor, Jennings McComb. When the railroad came through this section in 1880, McComb erected most of the depots, so railroad officials honored him by giving his first name to the unpopulated area around one of the depots. (A town in Mississippi had already claimed his last name.) Sure enough, the blank spot on the prairie began to attract settlers, mostly from the Midwest. Farmers did not have to first clear the land of trees—there were none. Homesteaders received extra land for planting trees on their property. They also planted crops they had raised in their home states of Iowa, Illinois, Indiana, and Missouri, and began to experiment with rice-farming techniques. By 1894 more than a thousand acres of rice grew on the Cajun prairie surrounding Jennings.

Later a number of Yankees who had fought in the area during the Civil War returned to settle here. The local cemetery contains quite a few more graves for the Blue than the Gray. Consequently Jennings came to be known as a "northern town on Southern soil."

Don't leave Jennings without visiting the ***Zigler Art Museum*** (337–824–0114), acclaimed for its outstanding fine arts collection representing five centuries of European and American art. To get there from the park, take Route 26 south (going under the interstate) until you reach Clara Street, where you'll turn left. At 411 Clara Street, you'll see the museum, a white-columned structure with colonial styling. Two gallery wings were added to the former home of Ruth and Fred Zigler to create this facility.

The three central galleries host ever-changing exhibits of works by both state and national artists. The west wing houses the museum's permanent collection and features such artists as Rembrandt, Whistler, VanDyke, Durer, Pissaro, and Constable. The museum's Louisiana artists collection includes the works of Ellsworth Woodward, Knute Heldner, A. J. Drysdale, Robert Rucker, Muriel Butler, William Tolliver, and others.

Realistic dioramas depicting the state's southwestern wildlife fill the east wing. The museum features a facsimile of John James Audubon's *Birds of America,* an edition that was duplicated from original plates in the National Audubon Society folio. Don't overlook the wonderful wildfowl wood carvings.

Closed on Monday and holidays, the Zigler Art Museum is open Tuesday through Saturday from 9:00 A.M. to 5:00 P.M. and on Sunday from 1:00 to 4:00 P.M. Admission is modest.

Continue to the end of Clara Street, which runs into Cary Avenue. Next, turn on Second Street and go to State Street. At 710 North State Street stands ***Our Lady Help of Christians Catholic Church,*** one of the town's historic buildings. Step inside for a view of the windows in glowing stained glass, made in Germany. In designing the church, Father Joseph Peeters, a native of Belgium, was inspired by Notre Dame in Paris. You'll recognize some of the great Gothic cathedral's characteristics, such as the three arched entrances, in this smaller, plainer version. Constructed of homemade concrete blocks that were cast on the building site, the church was dedicated in 1916 after a building period of several years.

A short walk takes you to the ***Marian Prayer Park,*** located adjacent to the church on the rectory's south side. From here you'll do a bit of backtracking. While retracing your drive, you might want to take a ride along Cary Avenue for a look at the lovely old homes. Architectural features, reflecting a midwestern influence, include turrets, balconies, porches, and gables accented with gingerbread woodwork and fish-scale shingles.

Vive la Louisiane

In Lafayette there are large parades celebrating **Mardi Gras,** rather like the New Orleans version. In the country you will find the *Courir du Mardi Gras* or Mardi Gras Run, which is a wild trail ride by costumed horseback riders (sometimes with homemade masks of screen wire) who go from house to house collecting ("stealing") chickens and supplies for a giant gumbo. The riders are well fueled, the routes (complete with pickup trucks, beer, and a band) and the gumbo are all planned, and there is a big *fais-do-do,* or dance, at the end. You will find this sort of event either on Mardi Gras Day or during the weekend immediately preceding it in Mamou, Iota, Church Point, and Eunice. A good place to call for information would be the Jean Lafitte Park site in Eunice (337–457–7700).

Take a sentimental journey to the **W. H. Tupper General Merchandise Museum** (337–821–5532) at 311 North Main Street, Jennings. The museum's stock came from a store built near Elton in 1910 by Mary and W. H. Tupper for their farm workers. Although the store closed in 1949, the contents remained intact—frozen in time for four decades. The store's original inventory consisted of toys, cosmetics, dishes, drugs, cooking utensils, seeds, fans, jewelry, denim overalls, and other items that bring back memories.

You'll also see a large selection of baskets made by members of the Chitimacha and Coushatta tribes. The Coushattas live 3 miles northwest of Elton on the northern edge of the parish. Museum hours are Monday through Friday from 9:30 A.M. to 5:00 P.M. Admission is modest.

Also sharing the Tupper building, the **Telephone Pioneer Museum of Louisiana** features displays of phones from past to present with exhibits going back to switchboards and party lines. The Children's Telephone Museum, a new addition, offers an educational experience. Learn more at www.tuppermuseum.com.

Before leaving the area, stroll along the brick sidewalks of nearby **Founder's Park** with its fountains, landscaped patios, wrought-iron benches and chairs, and antique clock. This public park features a large hand-painted mural depicting the history of Jennings.

Afterward, stop by **Boudin King** (337–824–6593), located at 906 West Division Street in a residential district. No trip to this area would be complete without sampling boudin (*boo-dan*). The state legislature passed an act declaring Jennings the Boudin Capital of the Universe, and you would be hard-pressed to find a better place for trying this specialty. The late restaurant owner Ellis Cormier, whose customers called him the Boudin King, defined his boudin as a mixture of pork, spices, and long-grain rice. Louisiana French people have been partial to boudin for more than two centuries, and Cormier's Acadian recipe passed down in the family for generations. His widow, June, continues the family enterprise. Parsley, peppers, green onions, and rice (cooked separately) are added to the prime pork. The resulting mixture is stuffed into a sausage casing, then steamed and served warm.

A great appetizer, boudin comes in links, both mild and hot. If you can't decide which to try, you may sample each. Start with mild and work your way up to hot (my favorite).

When June and Ellis Cormier turned their neighborhood grocery store into a restaurant featuring boudin, local folks predicted a short run for the establishment because the Cormiers decided not to serve alcohol. Customers joked that it took both "a pound of boudin and a six-pack of beer to make a seven-course Cajun dinner." That was in 1974, and if you stop by the Boudin King today, you'll probably have to stand in line.

OTHER ATTRACTIONS WORTH SEEING

Cypremort Point State Park
306 Beach Lane, Franklin
(337) 867–4510 or (888) 867–4510
Man-made beach in the marshland on the shores of Vermilion Bay.

Cypress Island Preserve
Off Louisiana Highway 353 between Lafayette and Breaux Bridge. Go to Lake Martin and look for the Nature Conservancy signs. Park at the yellow gates on the levee. You can see virgin cypress swamp; old-growth, live-oak ridges (chenieres); and a huge rookery of birds, including white ibis.

Delta Downs
2717 Delta Downs Drive, Vinton
(800) 589–7441
This track offers Thoroughbred and quarter-horse races from January into August. Quarter-horse racing is quick and the betting is lively. Even the food is pretty good in the clubhouse—try the gumbo. A good place to wear your Wranglers and your old Tony Lama boots.

The Jeanerette Museum
500 East Main Street, Jeanerette
(337) 276–4408
Sugarcane history with wildlife and Mardi Gras thrown in.

Sam Houston Jones State Park
107 Southerland Road, Lake Charles
(337) 855–2665 or (888) 677–7264
At the confluence of three rivers, this woodsy park offers boating, hiking trails, camping, and even cabins for rent (call far in advance).

Although boudin gets star billing here, the menu offers other items such as chicken-and-sausage gumbo, fried crawfish, catfish, chicken, and red beans and rice with smoked sausage. You also can buy hogshead cheese, a sort of pâté especially good when spread on crackers.

Prices are economical to moderate. Boudin King, which closes on Sunday, operates from 8:00 A.M. to 8:00 P.M. Monday through Thursday and until 8:30 P.M. on Friday and Saturday.

Before leaving Jefferson Davis Parish, take Route 26 down to Lake Arthur, 9 miles south of Jennings. For some picturesque scenery, drive along the edge of the lake, lined with lovely old homes. Cypress trees, with swaying Spanish moss trailing from their branches, stand knee-deep in Lake Arthur. In this laid-back resort area, you can fish, hunt, or watch the cranes, egrets, herons, and other birds.

Lake Arthur Park offers a bandstand, pavilions, picnic facilities, and an enclosed swimming area. Throughout the year the town stages events at the park. The park is also the setting for a star-spangled Fourth of July Celebration and a Christmas Festival with thousands of lights. For more information on Lake Arthur events, call the Town Hall at (337) 774–2211.

After enjoying Lake Arthur Park, drive back to Route 26 and travel north until the road intersects U.S. Highway 90. You'll then go east, passing by acres of rice fields on your way to Crowley, the Rice Center of America.

Cajun Country

As home of the International Rice Festival, ***Crowley*** promises plenty of good food along with rice-eating contests, fiddling and accordion competitions, parades, a street fair, a livestock show, and other events.

While you're in Crowley, go by the courthouse square. Starting on Main Street you can drive through the downtown historic district, which features some 8 blocks of lovely Victorian homes. From here take US 90 east to reach Rayne, about 7 miles from Crowley and 13 miles west of Lafayette.

If you didn't realize that ***Rayne*** is the Frog Capital of the World, you will before you depart. The first clue might be big colorful murals on the sides of old buildings—all depicting frogs in one fashion or another. On your driving tour be sure to notice the interesting aboveground cemetery.

Blue Stories

At *Crystal Rice Plantation* (337–783–6417) you'll find the *Blue Rose Museum,* located at 6428 Airport Road in Crowley. The museum's name came from a variety of rice that was developed locally. Rice is the main crop in this area, and the Blue Rose Museum covers the development of the rice industry. (Also on the premises, you can tour a rice farm and see crawfish ponds and an antique automobile collection.) Admission. Find out more about the site's tours (by appointment only) at www.crystalrice.com.

The fictionalized version of the search for a hybrid rice (which the Blue Rose Museum commemorates) is told in the late Frances Parkinson Keyes's 1956 novel *Blue Camellia.* Keyes, a New Englander who lived from 1896 to 1970, spent years in Louisiana churning out big-selling historical novels. Her research is good, and her stories are usually long, family sagas. If you like romance novels or historical fiction, you'll enjoy her books.

River Road covers the sugar industry; *Crescent Carnival* describes New Orleans old-line Mardi Gras krewes (the carnival organizations that sponsor balls and parades), and dishes out generations-old gossip. Look for Keyes's books in your public library—they are mostly out of print.

Mark Twain's jumping frog of Calaveras County would have been in his element here, happy among his peers. This town is filled not only with bona fide frogs but also with pictures of frogs, statues of frogs, literature about frogs, and even frog factories. What do frog factories export? Frog legs for restaurant menus and specimens for scientific purposes, of course. Besides being the center of Louisiana's frog industry, Rayne also ranks as one of the world's largest shippers of frogs.

For fifty-one weeks of the year, Rayne could be considered off the beaten path. During Labor Day weekend, however, the world beats a path to its door for a fun-filled Frog Festival, which features fireworks, frog-cooking contests, frog derbies, and frog beauty contests.

Soon after arriving in town, search out ***Chef Roy's Frog City Cafe*** (337–334–7913) at 1131 Church Point Highway, a quarter of a mile north of I–10, exit 87. Here, you'll find even more frogs—both in the cafe's frog boutique and on the menu.

Chef Roy Lyons, former owner, has instructed chefs in Canada, Mexico, France, Belgium, Turkey, Holland, the Netherlands, and elsewhere on the preparation of Cajun cuisine. In fact, Chef Roy sold his cafe to concentrate on his travels. "We haven't changed a thing," said the new owners Robert Credeur and Chef Benoit Morel.

Start with an appetizer of seafood gumbo or a crab cake, grilled and served with crawfish cream sauce. Blackened chicken salad features mixed greens, juicy blackened chicken strips, and the chef's fig vinaigrette dressing. Popular entrees include shrimp or crawfish enchiladas, seafood platters, and Catfish Willie, grilled and topped with crawfish herb cream sauce. And yes, you can get a fried frog leg platter or a combination with frog leg étouffée. As for dessert, popular choices include peach bread pudding with rum sauce, crème brûlée, or the turtle specialty combining chocolate cake and vanilla ice cream served in a pool of caramel.

The cafe opens daily at 11:00 A.M. and closes at 9:00 P.M. Monday through Thursday, 10:00 P.M. Friday and Saturday, and 2:00 P.M. on Sunday. Prices are moderate.

After leaving Rayne, return to Crowley and take State Route 13 north. Consider a short trip on the ***Acadiana Trail*** (also U.S. Highway 190), which runs through a number of interesting towns such as ***Eunice,*** the state's crawfish-processing center. Depending on the season you'll see acres of rice growing or thousands of crawfish traps in this area where fields do double duty. Now a major agricultural industry, crawfish farming utilizes flooded rice fields during winter and early spring.

Complement your trip to Cajun country by taking in a performance at the *Liberty Center for the Performing Arts* on the corner of South Second Street and Park Avenue in downtown Eunice. Every Saturday night from 6:00 to 7:30 P.M., *Rendezvous des Cajuns,* a live radio show, features a lineup of musicians and entertainers, with Barry Jean Ancelet serving as master of ceremonies. Ancelet announces each act in both Cajun French and English. Don't miss the outstanding exhibits at neighboring *Jean Lafitte National Historical Park and Preserve/Prairie Acadian Cultural Center* (337–457–7700), open Tuesday through Friday (except Christmas Day) from 8:00 A.M. to 5:00 P.M. and until 6:00 P.M. Saturday.

After visiting Eunice, head north to Ville Platte. While passing through Ville Platte, plan to stop by *Floyd's Record Shop* (337–363–2138) at 434 East Main Street (Highway 167), where you'll find not only film, photographic supplies, and regional books but a comprehensive inventory of traditional Cajun music with recordings by artists dating from the 1930s. If Floyd Soileau (pronounced *swallow*) is available, he can give you the history of the sounds he helped preserve by recording these musicians. The retail business, which recently celebrated its fiftieth anniversary, is open Monday through Saturday from 8:30 A.M. to 5:00 P.M. Check out www.floydsrecordshop.com.

For dining, try the *Jungle Club* (337–363–9103) on Highway 167 West (1636 West Main Street), famous for its boiled crawfish trays (in season). This specialty comes in mild, hot, and super-hot choices. Although the crawfish selections including étouffée and bisque remain favorites, the restaurant offers softshell crabs, alligator, and other outstanding dishes such as its award-winning gumbo. The Jungle Club opens for dinner beginning at 5:30 P.M. Monday through Saturday. Prices are moderate.

About 6 miles north of Ville Platte, you'll find *Chicot State Park* (888–677–2442) at 3469 Chicot State Park Road. With 6,500 acres of rolling hills and a 2,000-acre lake, the park offers plenty of recreation opportunities. Modest admission. Just beyond, you can visit *Louisiana State Arboretum* (888–677–6100 or 337–363–6289) with inviting nature trails and footbridges interspersed among labeled specimens of native plants. Rambling through the forest and across hills, ravines, and creeks, you'll see birds, deer, and local flora such as pine, oak, magnolia, beech, dogwood, and papaw. The arboretum is open daily from 9:00 A.M. to 5:00 P.M.; admission is free.

Afterward, continue to *Washington,* one of the state's oldest permanent settlements. Located on Bayou Courtableau, Washington once bustled as a steamboat town, and you can glimpse a bit of local history at *Steamboat Warehouse* (337–826–7227) at 525 North Main Street, Washington, and enjoy

theloneprairie

In Eunice, back by the old railroad tracks, there is a preserved area of prairie that encompasses several city blocks. Although Louisiana once had miles of prairie, civilization and the plow removed most of the typical deep-rooted grasses and fragile wildflowers that form the typical prairie ecosystem. Here, where some untouched land was found, grasses and plants that are original to this soil have been replanted and a true prairie has been growing. Future plans call for an interpretive center, but the sweet smell of prairie grasses is already here. Ask for directions at the Jean Lafitte Park offices; (337) 457–8499.

a good meal at the same time. The large brick warehouse, built between 1819 and 1823 and restored as a restaurant in 1976, specializes in steaks and seafood. After dipping into Catfish Lizzy topped with crawfish étouffée, or a rib-eye, take time to look at lading bills and other documents displayed here. An 1870 shipment, for instance, included candles, claret, coffee, tea, table salt, pickles, apples, and nails. Except for Christmas Day and New Year's Day, the restaurant is open Tuesday through Thursday from 5:00 to 9:30, Friday and Saturday to 10:30 P.M., and on Sunday from 11:00 A.M. to 2:00 P.M. Two cottages on the restaurant's grounds are available for overnight guests. For more information, tap into www.steamboatwarehouse.com.

Many of Washington's historic homes, plantations, and buildings were constructed between 1780 and 1835, and some are open for tours or as bed-and-breakfasts. For more information, contact the Washington Museum and Tourist Center at (337) 826–3627. The museum is open Monday through Friday from 8:00 A.M. to 4:00 P.M. and on weekends from 9:00 A.M. to 4:00 P.M. For more information, visit www.washingtonla.com or www.townofwashingtonla.org.

After exploring Washington, head south to *Opelousas.* On US 190 East, you'll find the tourist information center (337–948–6263). You'll see exhibits on Acadian culture along with old documents, photographs, farm equipment, and firearms.

Another interesting display showcases Jim Bowie's contributions. During his boyhood Bowie lived in Opelousas. After serving for a while in the Louisiana legislature, Bowie moved to Texas, where he fought and died at the Alamo. While legend credits him with the invention of the bowie knife, some historians contend that this is not a fact, although Bowie may have contributed to the knife's design. The center is open daily from 8:00 A.M. until 4:00 P.M., and there's no admission charge.

The *Opelousas Museum and Interpretive Center* (337–948–2589) at 315 North Main Street, Opelousas, presents a fascinating overview of local culture back to prehistoric times. The area can be described as "a melting pot or cultural gumbo" because the settlers came from many ethnic backgrounds.

Named for a Native American tribe that occupied the site earlier, Opelousas became a bayou trading post for French and Indian interchange in 1720. This fertile area also attracted the Spanish around the same time. Displays in the main exhibit room spotlight the people—their agriculture, home and family, business and professions, music, and food.

Among other things, the town pays tribute to the sweet potato's cousin, the yam, with an annual Yambilee Festival the last weekend in October. Spring and fall Folklife Festivals focus on the "olden days." A *Zydeco Festival* is staged in nearby Plaisance each September, and you'll see a presentation on zydeco (*ZI-da-ko*), which might be described as a musical merger of such sounds as rhythm and blues, jazz, rock and roll, gospel, and Cajun music. Opelousas, the birthplace of this unique style, was the home of "Zydeco King," the late Clifton Chenier. Also, before leaving the main room, be sure to notice the exhibits on Mardi Gras and the 1914 Dunbar kidnapping case.

Another section contains the Geraldine Smith Welch doll collection. You'll see more than 400 dolls, grouped in categories from antiques and miniatures to pop culture.

The center also houses the Louisiana Video Collection Library, a valuable resource for delving into state history, and a section on the Civil War when Opelousas served as the state's capital for a brief period. You can visit the center (which is fully wheelchair accessible) Monday through Saturday between 9:00 A.M. and 5:00 P.M. Admission is free, but donations are accepted.

Before leaving town, stop by the *Palace Cafe* (337–942–2142) at 135 West Landry Street (Highway 190 West), where owner Tina D. Elder carries on tradition in the family business started in 1927. Try the fried chicken salad, Grecian salad, or house specialty—baked eggplant stuffed with crab. Top off your meal with the restaurant's famous baklava, a Greek pastry made with pecan butter and honey. Prices are moderate. The cafe is open Monday through Saturday from 6:00 A.M. to 9:00 P.M.

Afterward, head toward *Chrétien Point Plantation* (337–662–7050 or 800–880–7050), located at 665 Chrétien Point Road in the town of Sunset about 12 miles north of Lafayette. From Opelousas get on Interstate 49 South. Take the exit for Sunset/Grand Coteau and drive through Sunset. This puts you on Route 93 South. After 3.8 miles you'll see Highway 356. Turn right, go 1 block, then take another right. Go 1 mile and Chrétien Point Plantation will be on your left.

Built by Hypolite Chrétien II in 1831, this grand Greek Revival house features both a window and a staircase that served as models for those in Tara during the filming of *Gone with the Wind*. The mansion stands on land that was a wedding gift from Chrétien's father, a rich cotton planter and close friend of the pirate Jean Lafitte, who frequently visited this plantation.

When Hypolite II died soon after moving into the mansion, his wife Félic- ité took over the reins and ran the large farming operation. On a mansion tour, your guide will tell you more stories about Félicité, a liberated woman who smoked cigars and played poker—supposedly her aptitude for gambling dou- bled the plantation's size to 10,000 acres. Local lore also holds that she shot a man (perhaps a pirate from Lafitte's crew) on the stairs when he broke in and refused to halt. Bloodstains, which partially show from beneath the carpet run- ner, remain on the steps.

Although the house survived the Civil War's ravage, the plantation's out- buildings were destroyed. Later, after the farm failed and dilapidation set in, the mansion served as a barn where animals roamed and hay was kept. Owners Kristine and Kelly Nations recently completed a year-long historic restoration of the mansion and expanded the gift shop. Except for major holidays or spe- cial events, house tours are offered Monday through Friday from 1:00 to 5:00 P.M. and Saturday and Sunday from 11:00 A.M. to 5:00 P.M. The day's last tour starts at 4:00 P.M., and it's best to call ahead. Admission. Preview the property at www.chretienpoint.com.

Visitors may also stay overnight here in the mansion itself and enjoy a full plantation breakfast and use the pool and tennis courts. Bed-and-breakfast guests get a mansion tour and are welcomed with mint juleps on the gallery. Rates are moderate to deluxe.

As you drive through this part of the country, tune in to local radio sta- tions, where you'll hear the unique sounds of Cajun music and dialect. Some- times the news is broadcast in French and sometimes in English.

For a special treat, take Route 93 (designated a Louisiana State Scenic Byway) and go back across I–49 to the little town of **Grand Coteau.** This was the center for early-nineteenth–century religious education in Acadian Louisiana, with both males and females being accommodated. **St. Charles College,** now a Jesuit seminary, began in 1837 and serves as a center for religious retreats.

The Academy of the Sacred Heart (337–662–5275), 1821 Academy Road, began in 1821 and is still operated by the Religious of the Sacred Heart, known worldwide for their elite girls' schools. The convent and grounds are open for tours Monday through Friday by appointment only. There is a fee. The main school building was erected in 1831; fluted iron columns support its 300-foot- long galleries. Stroll in the pleasant gardens, and be sure to notice the century- old camellia plants.

The convent also has strong Catholic religious associations: One of the mir- acles attributed to St. John Berchmans at his canonization occurred here when a young postulant was miraculously cured.

On a secular note, the village of Grand Coteau has undergone a recent flowering as a good place for visitors to spend time: You can shop diligently, eat well, and browse through antiques shops along the way.

Oldest of the upscale stores is *The Kitchen Shop* (337–662–3500), 296 East Martin Luther King, which offers interesting cookware and gadgets—and scrumptious lunches, delicious desserts, and so much more. Step next door to *Pistache* (337–662–3599) at 294 East Martin Luther King Drive, for some unique jewelry and clothing designs.

Stop by *Catahoula's Restaurant* (888–547–BARK), Highway 93, 0.5 mile off I–49 in Grand Coteau. This restaurant, which overlooks the grounds of St. Charles College, features "new Louisiana cooking," and your visit is destined to be a culinary experience (according to *Gourmet Magazine)*. Open Friday and Sunday for lunch or brunch from 11:00 A.M. to 2:00 P.M., Tuesday through Thursday from 5:00 to 9:00 P.M., and Friday and Saturday from 5:00 to 10:00 P.M. for dinner.

Continue south to reach *Lafayette,* the hub city of Acadiana. The Acadiana area, which comprises nearly one-third of Louisiana's sixty-four parishes, was settled by French Acadians who were ousted from Nova Scotia and New Brunswick by the British in 1755. Forced to leave their homes and property, families were broken up and sent to various destinations. Many eventually made their way to South Louisiana, where Acadians came to be known as "Cajuns."

Make the *Jean Lafitte National Historical Park and Preserve/Acadian Cultural Center* (337–232–0789) at 501 Fisher Road one of your first sight-seeing stops. A free thirty-five-minute film chronicles the Cajun experience, tracing the exile from Nova Scotia to settlement in the state's Southern landscape of bayous, swamps, and prairies. Another sixteen-minute film revisits the Atchafalaya Basin. Exhibits highlight Acadiana's contemporary culture. Except for Mardi Gras and Christmas Day, the park is open 8:00 A.M. to 5:00 P.M. daily.

During the 1770s a large number of Acadians settled in Lafayette (then called Vermilionville because of the nearby bayou's reddish color). In 1884 the town was renamed to honor Lafayette, the French general of American Revolutionary War fame. Now *Vermilionville* (337–233–4077 or 866–992–2968) has been reincarnated as a twenty-three-acre living-history attraction focusing on Cajun and Creole culture. Located at 300 Fisher Road across from the airport, the complex features entertainment, craft demonstrations, and an operating farm typical of those in the eighteenth century. Also, a cooking school staff demonstrates Creole and Cajun methods of food preparation.

Geese strut about, and costumed storytellers, musicians, and craftspeople re-create the folklife of bayou settlers from 1765 to 1890. As Acadian descendants, many staffers switch easily from speaking English to Cajun French. A hand-pulled ferry takes you across Petit Bayou to Fausse Pointe, where you'll

Before the Storm

Thousands of stories surfaced in the wake of hurricanes Katrina and Rita. Here's one from Karen Primeaux of Lafayette, who opened her heart and her home to people—including strangers—displaced by Hurricane Katrina. She shares this firsthand account of those few hours before the storm:

> Thousands of cars entered the contra flow heading out of New Orleans and the Gulf Coast towns, some with a specific destination, but many more without. I nervously called everyone I knew in these areas offering them shelter from the storm. At one point, the count heading to our home was twenty-two. But twenty-five or so other friends and family members were unreachable, which added to my delirium.
>
> As my friend raided the local stores for water and other supplies, I began cooking large amounts of food for our guests while continuously trying to reach my loved ones. My son prepared the house while another friend loaded up ice chests with fresh ice as the phone rang off the hook. I began organizing sleeping arrangements with my mother and sisters for the large influx of guests arriving. We worked out a plan to divide the guests among our homes. My mother, who has the largest home, managed to find room for her brother and his family of twelve, which included his wife, children, and grandchildren.
>
> For the next twelve hours, our guests started arriving by the carloads with clothing, pets, photo albums, and important documents. Everyone was prepared to be away from home for only a couple of days; no one expected what was about to unfold. No one expected anything more than a typical small hurricane party with a bowl of gumbo, lively conversation, hot coffee, and the Weather Channel blaring in the background. No one expected their lives to be forever changed, their souls emptied like Lake Ponchartrain and their hopes diminished by the winds of Katrina.
>
> As the weeks passed, the guests began to leave—one carload at a time, just as they had arrived. Some went home to find minor damage, others to find they had lost everything, and all of them to find only incomplete pieces of the world they had once known.
>
> That week still lingers in our spirits, and we desperately reach for sanity and survival in a moment of history, which changed the face of our state and the entire Gulf Coast. It was a place of unique culture, fun, and spirit before the storm, and with a breath from nature, it had been reduced to distrust, rubble, and broken spirits. As the Gulf Coast struggles to rebuild, we are reminded about the importance of preparedness and the necessity for strangers to always be kind.

meet Broussard family members such as Camille and Eliza. The couple speak and behave as people did in the 1840s and may inquire about your strange apparatus called a camera, your attire, or some unfamiliar expression. Except major holidays, Vermilionville is open Tuesday through Sunday from 10:00 A.M. to 4:00 P.M. Admissions stop at 3:00 P.M. There is an admission fee. Visit www.vermilionville.org for more background.

For dinner, search out *Evangeline Seafood and Steakhouse* (337–233–2658), a family restaurant at 2633 Southeast Evangeline Thruway that dishes up Cajun specialties. Popular entrees include seafood platters and crawfish, crab, and shrimp dinners. A dish called the Evangeline features broiled tilapia or flounder with shrimp-mushroom stuffing and crab cream sauce topping. Prices are moderate.

Basically French country cooking, Cajun cooking utilizes fresh indigenous ingredients such as rice, peppers, herbs, game, and fish—notably the ubiquitous crustacean called crawfish—and Lafayette boasts some great places to sample traditional specialties.

For classic Cajun and Creole cuisine, stop by *Cafe Vermilionville* (337–237–0100), housed in a ca. 1818 Acadian inn at 1304 West Pinhook Road. For lunch, try the bronzed shrimp and artichoke salad or crab cakes Vermilion. Dinner selections might include such specialties as smoked salmon and tasso, pecan tilapia, or tuna steak topped with seared foie gras.

Because music plays a primary role in Acadiana's culture, you might enjoy "two-stepping" to the sounds of Cajun triangles, fiddles, and accordions at one of the local Cajun dance hall/restaurants. Both *Randol's Restaurant and Cajun Dancehall* (800–YO–CAJUN) at 2320 Kaliste Saloom Road and *Prejean's Restaurant* (337–896–3247) at 3480 I–49 North specialize in Cajun cooking and feature live music.

Save plenty of time to explore downtown Lafayette, and consider starting your tour at the *Acadiana Center for the Arts* (337–233–7060). Located at 101 West Vermilion Street, this multifaceted arts and cultural facility features worldwide traveling exhibits and the work of local artists. Many artists maintain studios in the Lafayette area, and you can spend a couple of days gallery hopping. The center's hours are Tuesday through Friday from 10:00 A.M. to 5:00 P.M. If a special exhibition is in progress, the facility also opens on Saturday from 10:00 A.M. to 6:00 P.M. Admission. Check out upcoming events at www.acadiana artscouncil.org.

Afterward, head to nearby Jefferson Street. While strolling around, be sure to look for the fascinating outdoor murals painted by Robert Dafford. One intriguing creation, "'Til All That's Left Is a Postcard," can be viewed at 407 Jefferson Street.

In the heart of downtown, *Jefferson Street Market* (337–233–2589) houses an interesting collection of sixty-five specialty shops and a fine arts gallery showcasing the works of regional, national, and international artists. Located at 538 Jefferson Street, the complex carries fine French antiques, cypress wares and furnishings, and design accessories. Look for the work of Bonnie Camos, Tony Mose, and Bruce Odell. Hours are Monday through Friday from 10:00 A.M. to 5:00 P.M. and Saturday from 10:00 A.M. to 5:30 P.M.

Other great downtown stops include *Teche Drugs & Gifts* (337–235–4578), which spreads from 501 to 511 Jefferson Street and offers much more than sundries and gifts, and *Sans Souci Fine Crafts Gallery* (337–266–7999) at 219 East Vermilion Street. Here, you'll find creations by Louisiana Crafts Guild members in both traditional and contemporary pottery, blown glass, wood and metal sculptures, jewelry, furniture, and more.

The *Lafayette Natural History Museum & Planetarium* (337–291–5544) offers educational fun at 433 Jefferson Street. You'll view interesting exhibitions, a state-of-the-art planetarium, discovery room, and museum store. Kids especially find it intriguing to investigate a crime scene in the forensic lab. Museum hours are Tuesday through Friday from 9:00 A.M. to 5:00 P.M., Saturday from 10:00 A.M. to 6:00 P.M., and Sunday from 1:00 to 6:00 P.M. Admission.

Don't miss the *Lafayette Museum–Alexander Mouton House* (337–234–2208) at 1122 Lafayette Street. The home of Louisiana's first Democratic governor, this antebellum town house contains antiques, Civil War relics, and historic documents. Go upstairs and see the lavish hand-beaded Mardi Gras costumes and other glittering regalia. The museum's hours are Tuesday through Saturday 9:00 A.M. to 4:30 P.M. and Sunday 1:00 to 4:00 P.M. Admission is modest.

A walking tour from this point will take you past some of the city's landmark buildings, including the *Cathedral of St. John the Evangelist,* an interesting structure of German-Romanesque design.

Either University Avenue or St. Mary Avenue, both of which turn off Lafayette Street, will lead you to the University of Louisiana at Lafayette. Look for a parking place somewhere near the student union, then head for the tall cypress trees. Right in the middle of campus, you'll see an honest-to-goodness swamp studded with cypress trees trailing their streamers of Spanish moss. Called *Cypress Lake,* the natural swamp (about the size of a city block) comes complete with native vegetation, waterfowl, migratory birds, fish, and even alligators.

ils sont parti!

In south Louisiana even the horses might speak French. At the start of each race at Evangeline Downs, the announcer does not shout "They're off!" but rather "Ils sont parti!"

Because this is a miniature swamp, you get a sense of the mysteries such an environment conceals—without the threat of danger. Visitors are welcome to stroll along the water's edge and feed the ducks. Small signs placed at intervals in the murky water invite you to PLEASE FEED THE FISH and inform you that this is an alligator habitat. (You're not supposed to feed the alligators, but if you toss half a hot dog to the fish and it's intercepted by an alligator, it's best to let him have his way.)

While on campus, be sure to visit the ***Paul and Lulu Hilliard University Art Museum*** (337–291–5544), a handsome reflecting structure at 710 East St. Mary Boulevard. After taking in the current exhibitions, you can check out the great titles at the James W. Bean Bookstore on the second floor. Museum hours are Tuesday through Saturday from 10:00 A.M. to 5:00 P.M. To see a schedule of current and upcoming events, click on www.louisiana.edu/uam. Admission.

Don't miss the ***Odell Pottery Studio*** (337–268–4007) at 625B Garfield Street. World champion and three-time United States Pottery Olympics Champion Bruce Odell started his gold medal collection in 1992, when he traveled to Italy for this international competition.

You might even catch Bruce behind the showroom in a spectacular raku firing session, a heated procedure featuring flashing red hot rainbows of metallic color. Demonstrations take place most days or by appointment. And when you see the inventory of contemporary and traditional fine crafts in clay, glass, metal, and wood, you'll probably find something you can't live without. Visitors are welcome Tuesday through Saturday from 10:00 A.M. to 6:00 P.M.

Night owls will want to take in some lively music and dancing at the ***Blue Moon Saloon*** (337–234–2422 or 877–766–BLUE), a venue for Cajun, country, and zydeco music. Join the honky-tonk troubadours at 215 East Convent Street and kick up your heels. Click on www.bluemoonpresents.com for upcoming performances and information about the in-house hostel, an economical place to hang your hat while visiting Cajun country and in walking distance of both the bus and train stations.

A must-see in Lafayette is ***Acadian Village*** (337–981–2364 or 800–962–9133), located on the southwest edge of town. After leaving the campus take Route 167 south until you reach Ridge Road, where you'll turn right. Next take a left on West Broussard Road. Then you'll follow the signs to Acadian Village. By the time you reach this cluster of buildings situated on a bayou and surrounded by gardens and woodlands, you'll agree it's definitely off the beaten path.

When you step through the gate, you may feel as if someone turned the calendar back about 200 years. With its general store, schoolhouse, chapel, and original steep-roofed houses, the folklife museum replicates a nineteenth-century Acadian settlement.

Acadian Village

Stop at the general store to buy a ticket and pick up a guide sheet describing the individual buildings. Strolling along a brick pathway and crossing wooden footbridges, you'll wend your way in and out of the various vintage structures. Although the blacksmith shop, chapel, and general store are reproductions, all other structures are authentic, most dating from the early 1800s. Transported from various locations throughout Acadiana, they were restored and furnished with native Cajun household items, clothing, photographs, books, and tools. The charming village captures the spirit of early Acadiana, and commercialism is noticeably absent.

The **LeBlanc House,** birthplace of Acadian state senator Dudley J. LeBlanc, contains a display featuring the tonic Hadacol. An early elixir touted to cure all ailments, this vitamin tonic concocted by LeBlanc, fondly known as "Couzan Dud," contained 12 percent alcohol. During the early 1950s George Burns, Bob Hope, Jack Benny, Mickey Rooney, Jimmy Durante, and other entertainers performed in Hadacol caravans, updated versions of the old-time traveling medicine shows.

The **Billeaud House**'s exhibits focus on spinning and weaving. You'll see looms, spinning wheels, and a display of homespun coverlets and clothes. Take a look at the cotton patch, planted behind the cottage. If you packed a picnic, this peaceful setting is the perfect spot to enjoy it as you watch villagers (wearing the traditional clothing of their ancestors) spin wool on a porch or chat by the bayou.

Acadian Village is open daily from 10:00 A.M. to 4:00 P.M. except for major holidays. Admission is charged.

From Lafayette's outskirts it's only a fifteen-minute drive northeast via Route 94 to **Breaux Bridge,** also known as the Crawfish Capital of the World.

If you visit **Mulate's Cajun Restaurant** (337–332–4648 or 800–422–2586) at 325 Mills Avenue (on Route 94) in Breaux Bridge, owner Goldie Comeaux promises you a Cajun *"bon temps!"* Besides a good time, you can also anticipate good food.

The restaurant's support beams came from cypress trees cut more than seventy years ago at the nearby swamp in Henderson. Local festival posters and paintings by Acadian artists line Mulate's walls, and the tables are covered with red-and-white checkered cloths. Most waiters speak both French and English.

Order some stuffed mushrooms or catfish tidbits to nibble on as you soak up some of the atmosphere, best described as lively and informal. While waiting for your entree, you can take Mulate's Cajun quiz: "How to tell a full-blooded, dipped-in-the-bayous Cajun from someone who just wishes he was."

The restaurant offers dozens of fresh seafood dishes including catfish, shrimp, oysters, and frog legs. The dinner of stuffed crabs, also a house specialty, comes with jambalaya, coleslaw, homemade french fries, and garlic bread. If you order the super seafood platter, you can sample stuffed crab, stuffed bell pepper, fried shrimp, catfish, oysters, frog legs, and jambalaya. Prices are moderate.

Authentic "chank-a-chank" music sends everybody, including children, to the dance floor. Parents holding toddlers in their arms waltz round and round or dance the Cajun two-step to the beat of triangles, fiddles, and accordions. The restaurant features live music at lunch on Saturday and Sunday and seven nights a week. Mulate's hours, which vary seasonally, usually run from 11:00 A.M. to 10:00 P.M. daily.

If you visit the Breaux Bridge area during the fall, you can watch sugarcane being harvested and hauled to market. This state produces much of America's sugar. (The sugar you spooned into your morning coffee or cereal may have come from South Louisiana's cane fields.) Harvesting starts in October, before winter's first freeze, and extends through late December. When the cane reaches a height of 9 to 11 feet, it is cut by mechanical harvesters and left in rows on the ground. Then the leaves are burned off, and the cane is loaded on trailers to be taken to nearby mills for processing. In this part of the country, you'll drive along roads strewn with stalks and pass many slow-moving trucks transporting their cargoes of cane from field to mill.

Only a few miles east of Breaux Bridge lies one of this country's great untamed regions, the **Atchafalaya Basin** (that large uncluttered area west of

Spice Up Your Life

Don't leave Breaux Bridge without stopping by **Café des Amis** (337–332–5273) at 140 East Bridge Street. Here you'll enjoy scrumptious specialties such as duck and andouille gumbo and crawfish pie (crawfish or shrimp étouffée served in puff pastry). Get your camera out for this dish, which turns heads from tables all around. Or try the restaurant's terrific signature dish, barbecue shrimp Pont Breaux style. (Look for author James Lee Burke's autograph on the wall.)

Cafe hours are 9:00 A.M. to 9:00 P.M. Wednesday and Thursday, 7:30 A.M. to 9:30 P.M. Friday and Saturday, and 8:00 A.M. to 2:30 P.M. Sunday. You can also enjoy a zydeco breakfast, complete with music and dancing, each Saturday morning from 8:30 to about 11:30 A.M. Pay a visit to www.cafedesamis.com for more information. Moderate prices.

The staff provided one of its special recipes for Syrup Cake, also known as *Gâteau Sirop*. Manager Mary Miller describes this traditional Cajun dessert as "sweet, moist, and spicy with the crunch of roasted pecans."

Syrup Cake (Gâteau Sirop)

2 cups canola oil or peanut oil	4 teaspoons ground cinnamon
2 cups raw sugar	4 teaspoons ground cloves
3½ cups cane syrup	4 teaspoons ground ginger
⅔ cup dark molasses	4 tablespoons vanilla extract
4 teaspoons baking soda	4 cups sifted flour
2 cups boiling water	¾ cup chopped pecans
8 eggs	

Mix oil, sugar, cane syrup, and molasses in a bowl.

In separate container stir baking soda into boiling water. Add to above mixture. Add all other remaining ingredients except pecans. Beat well at medium to high speed with an electric hand mixer, then pour into a stainless-steel full-size baking pan that has been sprayed with a pan spray.

Bake at 350 degrees for about 30 minutes. Test with a toothpick to see if middle is still wet. Turn pan around in oven to ensure even baking. Add chopped pecans on top and continue baking until the cake is done throughout. Serve warm with vanilla or chocolate ice cream. Yields 16 slices.

Baton Rouge on your state map). In this vast wilderness swamp, an overflow area for the Atchafalaya (*a-CHAFF-a-lie-a*) River, you can step back into a pristine world, but don't venture into its depths on your own. If you're game for a guided safari, take Route 347 northeast from Breaux Bridge, then pick up Route 352 to reach Henderson, the gateway to the Atchafalaya Basin. This area features a number of boat tours designed to introduce visitors to the Atchafalaya Basin's mysteries.

Driving through various portions of South Louisiana in the spring, you sometimes see people wading in ditches of water near the roadside. They are **crawfishing**—capturing those tasty little lobster look-alikes. Now that commercially grown crawfish is so readily available, this practice is not as common as it once was. Crawfishing is still great sport, however, and if you feel the urge to engage in this activity (children especially find it fascinating), it's a simple matter to buy some set nets at a local hardware store. Next, find a nearby grocery store and buy some beef spleen, known as "melt." Then search out a deep ditch or swampy area. In this area of the state, you don't have to be a super sleuth to find one. Cut the meat into small pieces, and tie them to the centers of the nets. Spacing the nets several yards apart, place them in the water. After a few minutes grab a stick and start yanking the nets up, and presto!—dinner.

If you prefer someone else to snare and prepare your crawfish, head for Henderson and *Pat's Fisherman's Wharf Restaurant* (337–228–7110), located on Route 352 across the bridge at 1008 Henderson Levee Road. Request to be seated on the porch, and you can look directly down into Bayou Amy.

Restaurant owner Pat Huval helped put Henderson on the map. After buying the restaurant in 1954, he added crawfish to the menu. (At that time, restaurants seldom served crawfish.) The specialty proved so popular that it created a new industry for the town—raising, processing, and selling crawfish.

Here is the place to sample Hank Williams's famed "jambalaya, crawfish pie, and filet gumbo," while a Cajun band provides listening entertainment. Be sure you're hungry because the meal starts with a salad and a cup of delicious gumbo (probably the state's most famous dish and often served with a dollop of rice). When my husband and I visited, the waitress brought gumbo for us, and she gave me some rice but left none for my husband. Returning momentarily, she set down a bowl of rice, saying, "Here is for Papou" (*pa-POO*).

Afterward, a large platter (garnished with two bright red crawfishlike miniature lobsters in armor) containing crawfish étouffée, fried crawfish, *boulette* (a fried crawfish meatball), and hush puppies, arrives.

If you don't want crawfish for dinner, a delicious alternative is Pat Huval's seafood platter, a house specialty featuring a green salad, seafood gumbo, fried shrimp, oysters, catfish, french fries, and hush puppies. "Our food is so fresh," says Huval, "the catfish slept in the river last night." The restaurant is noted for its dirty rice (so called because it's cooked with chopped chicken giblets—not dropped on the floor). In season you can also order turtle soup. Rates are moderate. The restaurant is open Sunday through Thursday from 11:00 A.M. to 10:00 P.M. and until 10:30 P.M. on Friday and Saturday. Check out www.pats fishermanswharf.com.

For your excursion into the Atchafalaya, you can catch a boat tour (airboat and swamp tours are also available) at *McGee's Landing* (337–228–2384). To get there head for 1337 Henderson Levee Road and turn left at the fourth exit. Just past Whiskey River landing, you'll see McGee's.

The ninety-minute tour takes you into a different world—a jungle of plants such as wild hibiscus, lotus, and elephant ears. Lots of trees also grow here— cypress, hackberry, willow, and oak, to name a few. The swamp serves as home to alligators, nutrias, muskrats, minks, opossums, otters, ducks, turkeys, wading birds, and other wildlife. You'll glide under the Swampland Expressway, the 18-mile span on I–10, which opened up Cajun Country to the rest of the world. Building this bridge, once considered impossible because of the basin's boggy bottom, required considerable engineering ingenuity. If you encounter fog when driving on this stretch of interstate over the swamp, please exercise extreme caution. Heavy mists come with the terrain, and being suspended over a swamp magnifies the hazard. Tours are offered daily, starting at 10:00 A.M. If you arrive before or after a tour in progress, you can grab a sandwich or full meal at McGee's Atchafalaya Cafe; hours are 10:00 A.M. to 5:00 P.M. Monday through Thursday, until 10:00 P.M. Friday and Saturday, and until 7:00 P.M. Sunday or 8:00 P.M. during summer. Visit www.mcgees landing.com.

markedroutes

Out from St. Martinville on Louisiana Highway 96 there are small hand-painted wooden shrines, commemorating the fourteen Stations of the Cross, affixed to trees along the highway. Catholics from the church at the Isle L'Abbe community walk this route annually during Lent.

You can see one shrine next to the historic marker at the beginning of *Oak and Pine Alley.* The marker signals the starting point of the fabulous pre–Civil War wedding procession for a bride of the locally prominent Durand family. During her wedding, the bride passed under trees that were decorated for the occasion with gold dust sprinkled on webs spun by imported spiders.

From here head south toward *St. Martinville.* You can either return to Breaux Bridge by way of Route 347, which continues to St. Martinville, or follow Route 31 south from Breaux Bridge. Another option is Route 96, an off-the-beaten-path road by way of Catahoula.

Only a few minutes from downtown St. Martinville in a serene park setting at 1200 North Main Street, you'll find the *Longfellow-Evangeline State Historic Site* (337–394–3754 or 888–677–2900) on the banks of Bayou Teche. (The word *teche,* pronounced "tesh," comes from a Native American word meaning "snake" and refers to the bayou's serpentine path.)

This large complex offers a new museum and visitor center and an Acadian farmstead and facilities for picnicking. The park's main thrust, however, is to preserve and interpret the history of its early French settlers. Many Acadians who were forced by Britain to leave their Canadian "Acadie" in 1755 later made their way to South Louisiana. Henry Wadsworth Longfellow's epic poem *Evangeline,* the symbol of all Acadiana, tells the story of their long struggle to find a new home.

On the ***Olivier Plantation,*** an 1815 Creole raised cottage serves as the park's focal point and contains furnishings typical of that period. This plantation house and its detached kitchen and herb garden, in a setting of ancient live oaks for which Cajun country is famous, present a living history lesson. Stop by the visitor center for a look at the variety of exhibits related to early Acadian and Creole lifestyles. Except for Thanksgiving, Christmas, and New Year's Day, the park is open daily from 9:00 A.M. to 5:00 P.M. Tours take place on the hour with the day's last one starting at 4:00 P.M. Plan to arrive fifteen minutes early to watch the video site introduction. Admission is modest.

Continue to the charming downtown area of "Le Petit Paris," as St. Martinville was once known. The town became a haven for aristocrats escaping the French Revolution's horrors during "the worst of times." Slave rebellions in the Caribbean sent other French planters here, and French Creoles from New Orleans joined them. With a patrician population prone to staging courtly ceremonies, elaborate balls, concerts, and operas, St. Martinville developed into a cultural mecca.

The mother church of the Acadians occupies a place of prominence on the ***St. Martin de Tours Church Square.*** Dating from 1832, the current structure contains some original sections from its 1765 predecessor—an altar, box pews, and a chapel. Inside St. Martin de Tours Catholic Church are a silver and gold sanctuary light and carved marble baptismal font, said to be gifts from Louis

Take the Scenic Route

While driving along Highway 90, watch for the Cade/St. Martinville exit and follow Louisiana Highway 182 to enjoy a picturesque drive. Along the way you'll see an old dance hall that dates back more than forty years, now renamed The Stockyard Saloon, plus inviting golf courses. Other roadside landmarks include Bruce Foods, where authentic Cajun seasoning and food are prepared for distribution, and Camp Pratt, a prisoner-of-war camp for German soldiers during World War II. Spanish Lake, a natural refuge for wildlife and waterfowl, lies adjacent to Camp Pratt. The Jean Lafitte Scenic Byway follows State Route 182 to Highway 14 in New Iberia and then continues to Holmwood.

XVI and Marie Antoinette. Somewhat to the side and rear of the church, you'll see a statue of Evangeline, for which actress Dolores del Rio posed when she portrayed the heroine in an early movie filmed here. Movie cast members later presented the bronze monument to the townspeople.

Le Petit Paris Museum (337–394–7334), constructed in 1861, stands adjacent to the church and contains local arts and crafts, colorful carnival costumes, Mardi Gras memorabilia, and a gift shop. Except for major holidays, the museum is open daily from 9:30 A.M. to 4:30 P.M. To book a tour of the museum and grounds, please call ahead. Modest fee.

maraisand platins

On the southwestern prairies of Louisiana you'll find two distinct types of ponds that are referred to by terms that are French in origin. "Marais" are irregular shaped marshy spots that fill seasonally. "Platins" are on higher ground and are circular. Both occur naturally and are useful to the region's cattle ranchers.

Within easy walking distance (a block or so) from Church Square, you'll see the *Evangeline Oak* on Bayou Teche's bank. Like Evangeline, many Acadian refugees in pursuit of their dreams stepped ashore at this spot. According to legend, Evangeline's boat docked under the large old tree when she arrived from Nova Scotia searching for her lover. Local lore differs from Longfellow's tale, but both stories portray the heartbreak of a forced exodus. Emmeline Labiche (Evangeline's real-life counterpart), after a ten-year search, discovered her true love, Louis Arceneaux (Gabriel in Longfellow's poem), here under the Evangeline Oak, only to learn that he had since married another. (If oak trees could talk, this one might say that another tree actually witnessed the sad scene because *which* live oak is the authentic Evangeline Oak remains a topic of debate. This massive specimen nevertheless serves as a stately symbol.)

The adjacent *Acadian Memorial* (337–394–2258) at 121 South New Market Street, St. Martinville, pays tribute to the memory of individual women, men, and children who came to Louisiana during the 1760s after the harsh exile from their Canadian homeland. A mural portrays the Acadians' arrival, and in several cases, direct descendants posed for this group portrait. The Wall of Names lists some 3,000 refugees identified using early state documents. Visitors can step out back to the garden, which features an eternal flame as its focal point and overlooks Bayou Teche. This facility also serves as a genealogy and media center and is open daily from 10:00 A.M. until 4:00 P.M.

Only a few steps from the memorial and the Evangeline Oak's spreading branches, the *Old Castillo Bed and Breakfast* (337–394–4010 or 800–621–

3017), beckons travelers. Located at 220 Evangeline Boulevard, the galleried two-story brick structure with French doors features large rooms furnished with antiques and reproductions. Some rooms overlook Bayou Teche and the celebrated Evangeline Oak, and others offer a view of St. Martin de Tours Church Square.

Owner Peggy Hulin encourages guests to enjoy beignets or French toast with cafe au lait prepared the traditional way but also offers full American breakfasts. Standard to moderate rates. For a closer look, visit www.old castillo.com.

After exploring "Evangeline country," follow Route 31 south toward New Iberia, into Vermilion Parish. To see why Vermilion Parish has been called the most "Cajun place" on earth, head southwest on State Route 14 to **Delcambre Shrimp Boat Landing.** Known as the Shrimp Capital of Louisiana, the picturesque Acadian town of Delcambre stands with one foot in Vermilion Parish and the other in Iberia Parish.

At the fisherman's wharf you can hear Cajun French spoken and watch the day's catch being unloaded. You can also buy shrimp—fresh, frozen, cleaned, or the do-it-yourself kind—at any of the several seafood shops here and indulge in a shrimp feast at the covered picnic area nearby.

In August Delcambre hosts a four-day shrimp festival, which includes a

Look around You . . .

English architect Christopher Wren's burial marker in St. Paul's Church advises those who seek a monument to "look around you." Likewise, visitors to Abbeville can look around them for "monuments" to the work of contemporary Louisiana architect A. Hays Town.

Town, who has achieved fame for his architectural restorations, began his work here in Southwest Louisiana.

For instance, St. Mary Magdalen Church is a restoration for which Town can claim credit. Among the thousands of homes he has restored, you'll find some along the river here in Abbeville.

Town works to achieve the look of Louisiana's heritage in his restorations: warm brick, aged wood, pleasant vistas, gentle living spaces. He does so by using recycled building components: wood, shutters, doors, windows, and bricks. Town's patrons collect these items themselves, and it can take years to gather enough for a single home.

So anyone with a Hays Town house has personally put in long hours of effort to assist Town in achieving the level of perfection you'll see in Abbeville.

blessing of the fleet. During shrimping season, generally from April through June and again from August through October, you'll see shrimp boats departing from Delcambre on their way to Vermilion Bay or the Gulf of Mexico. After harvesting their bounty the shrimp trawlers return to home port, their hulls filled with iced-down shrimp to be sorted, packed, and frozen. From this small inland port, millions of pounds of shrimp are shipped annually to both American and international markets.

Afterward, continue west to nearby Erath, a sleepy French village and home of the *Acadian Museum,* also known as Musée Acadien (337– 937–5468 or 337–233–5832). "Probably more French is still spoken in business and on the streets of Erath than anywhere in South Louisiana," says attorney Warren Perrin, who founded the museum and maintains an office here. Housed at 203 South Broadway in the "Old Bank of Erath," exhibits offer both French and English interpretations and focus on the Prairie Bayou Acadians. Some 2,000 artifacts, books, drawings, photos, maps, and models pertaining to Cajun culture back to the Acadian expulsion from Nova Scotia fill three rooms. Although Hurricane Rita interrupted daily operations by dumping eighteen inches of flood water, the museum has reopened with an exciting new exhibit. "We have eight pre-deportation artifacts ca. 1690, excavated by a Nova Scotian named Sara Beanlands from the old Thibodeau Farm, now near Windsor, Nova Scotia," said Perrin. For more background, visit www.acadianmuseum.com. Open Monday through Friday, the museum's hours are 1:00 to 4:00 P.M. Admission is free.

Don't miss *Abbeville,* Vermilion's parish seat. This charming French-flavored town, which served as the setting for several movies, lies west of Erath on Route 14. You'll find the beautiful St. Mary Magdalen Church built in 1910, lovely homes, and outstanding eateries like *Black's Oyster Bar* at 319 Père-Megret and *Dupuy's Oyster Shop* at 108 South Main; both specialize in fresh shellfish.

herecomesthe . . .

Daytime weddings in Abbeville at St. Mary Magdalen Church provide a spectacular entrance for the bride. As the last of the wedding party, the bride and her father come in from outside the church, with the door being held open so that light streams into the dim interior and forms a halo around her.

At the wedding reception (perhaps just down the street at *Magdalen Place,* a recently restored building on the town square) you'll witness an old Cajun custom as the occasional guest pins money to the bride's veil for the privilege of a dance.

Never Too Late for an Apology

In 1755, the British forced French Acadians to leave their homes in Nova Scotia. In 2003, the Queen of England signed a Royal Proclamation addressing this injustice to an entire culture. How did this expression of royal regret come about? Louisiana attorney Warren A. Perrin embarked on a long crusade for an apology from the British Crown regarding the Acadian deportations. Here's what he has to say about the matter:

"Without the support of the two million Acadians in the world, the apology would not have been possible. My goal was to make the effort one of reconciliation rather than confrontation, and results speak for themselves: the Proclamation has become a rallying point of both the Acadians and the descendants of the settlers who took over their lands after the diaspora. Further, it is on display in the church at Grande Pre in Nova Scotia, acknowledged to be the most-visited and revered place for Acadians in the world today."

Look for Perrin's historical biography, *Acadian Redemption: From* Beausoleil *Broussard to the Queen's Royal Proclamation,* available at bookstores, the Acadian Museum in Erath, and online at www.acadianmuseum.com (where you can also read the Queen's Proclamation). The Louisiana Press Women's Association chose it as Best History Book for 2004.

The town is also home to the ***Abbey Players,*** a local theater group that, in the words of resident Gerard Sellers, a documentary filmmaker, location scout, and performer himself, has a reputation for presenting polished performances and producing professional actors. You'll find the ***Abbey Theater,*** which is on the National Register of Historic Places, at the corner of Lafayette and State Streets. For information on performances, call the Abbeville Tourist Center at (337) 898–4264, or the Abbey Players at (337) 893–2442.

Steen's Syrup Mill, located at Abbeville, is one of the nation's largest open-kettle syrup mills. Here, from mid-October through December, you can smell the sweet boiling cane syrup as raw sugarcane is converted into an amber-colored substance almost as thick as taffy. For more information on the area, call the Vermilion Parish Tourist Commission at (337) 893–2491.

Abbeville also is home to the ***Depot at Magdalen Place*** (337–740–2112), with two restored cabooses nearby (one is wooden with a cupola, the other is steel with a bay window). You will also find a museum with local artifacts (ask about alligator products) and an assortment of regional gifts for sale. Also ask here about taking a walking tour with a local costumed tour guide—or use a handy brochure to guide yourself. Hours run 10:00 A.M. to 5:00 P.M. Tuesday through Friday and 10:00 A.M. to 3:00 P.M. Saturday.

Afterward, return to Delcambre and take Route 675 to Jefferson Island, about 10 miles west of New Iberia. Jefferson Island, the setting for **Rip Van Winkle Gardens Bed and Breakfast** (337) 359–8525, sits atop a salt dome (the tip of a huge mountain of salt forced to the surface from deep within the earth). Located at 5505 Rip Van Winkle Road, the site boasts a rich history, which guests will enjoy delving into.

You approach the property along a 2-mile drive lined with live oak trees. And you'll check in at the opulent home that stage actor Joseph Jefferson designed and had built in 1870. Guests can stroll through twenty-five acres of lovely landscaped gardens.

Jefferson, one of America's most famous nineteenth-century actors, made a name for himself portraying Rip Van Winkle. He bought Jefferson Island to use as a winter retreat and hired French craftsmen from New Orleans to build the unique house with its elements of Moorish, Victorian, gingerbread, and Steamboat Gothic architecture.

It is said that Jefferson Island was one of pirate Jean Lafitte's hideouts, and the three pots of gold and silver coins discovered here in 1923 lend credibility to the rumor; the Lafitte Oaks mark the spot where the treasure was found.

Wandering about, you can enjoy views of peaceful Lake Peigneur. Tranquility, however, has not always been part of the picture. In 1980, a freak mining disaster violently rearranged the island's geography when a drilling rig punctured the salt dome under Lake Peigneur. The resulting maelstrom swallowed up the lake's contents—crewboats, barges, and all. Visitors can view a ten-minute film on this strange episode and take a house and garden tour. Admission. Visit the site via www.ripvanwinklegardens.com. Moderate to deluxe rates.

From Jefferson Island, continue on Route 675 into New Iberia. The Spanish-influenced town takes its name from Europe's Iberian peninsula. Many of James Lee Burke's novels take place in this setting, which he calls "one of the most beautiful places in America." For a map detailing a walking/driving tour of sites that figure prominently in several of Burke's famed Dave Robicheaux novels, stop by the Iberia Parish Convention and Visitors Bureau at 2513 Highway 14. Also, check out www.cityofnewiberia.com for more information on the local scene.

Don't miss **Shadows-on-the-Teche** (337–369–6446 or 877–200–4924), a white-pillared plantation house located at 317 East Main Street. Start your tour at the new Shadows Visitors Center, located directly across the street from the mansion, and view the orientation video.

Statuary, camellias, wisteria, magnolia trees, and magnificent live oaks festooned with Spanish moss form a serene backdrop for Shadows-on-the-Teche.

The mansion's name was inspired by the interplay of lights and darks across the lawn, created by sunlight filtering through the trees.

Built in 1834 for sugar planter David Weeks, the manor house stands on Bayou Teche's bank. (You don't see the bayou until you step into the backyard.) Slaves collected mud from the bayou's banks to make the house's coral-colored bricks. All the Shadows' main rooms open onto galleries, and there is no central hall. An exterior flight of stairs in front of the house, concealed by a lattice, leads to the second floor.

When William Weeks Hall (the original owner's great-grandson) took over the mansion during the early 1920s, he found it in an advanced state of deterioration. An artist, Hall lived in Paris before relocating to New Iberia to accept his lifetime challenge of restoring the Shadows to its former grandeur. Throwing himself into the restoration project, he also threw open his doors to extend Southern hospitality to such celebrities as Mae West, Henry Miller, W. C. Fields, and H. L. Mencken. In the studio you'll see a door covered with signatures scribbled by Hall's houseguests—Cecil B. DeMille, Arleigh Burke, Tex Ritter, Walt Disney (along with his alter ego, Mickey Mouse), and others. Hall's friends referred to him as "the last of the Southern gentlemen."

Hall, who died in 1958, willed Shadows-on-the-Teche to the National Trust for Historic Preservation. When researchers discovered the mansion's original inventory of furnishings filed in an adjoining parish, they used it as a mandate to furnish the house as authentically as possible. The mansion's accessories include everything from indigo-dyed trousers and pier tables to finger bowls and foot warmers.

Except for major holidays, the mansion is open Monday through Saturday from 9:00 A.M. to 4:30 P.M. Sunday hours are noon to 4:30 P.M. Admission is charged.

Directly across the street at 314 East Main, you'll see the lovely flower-filled gardens of *leRosier Country Inn Bed & Breakfast* (337–367–5306 or 888–804–ROSE). The property features a handsome, restored 1870 home and, behind it, a replicated Acadian raised cottage. The owners furnished the inn with antiques and floral prints, which echo the place's name. A vintage rosebush that refused to die—even when covered by the iron fence's concrete foundation— inspired the inn's name. That former lone survivor now keeps company with many varieties of antique roses.

Guests can start the day with a gourmet country breakfast. Check out www.lerosier.com for more information. Moderate rates. Also, the inn houses *The Main Street Grill,* which features upscale Southern cooking and a full bar. The restaurant is open for lunch Tuesday through Friday from 11:00 A.M. until

2:00 P.M. and for fine dining on Friday and Saturday from 5:00 until 9:00 P.M. Moderate to expensive.

Take an after-dinner stroll to the nearby Iberia Bank and see the spotlighted statue of **Hadrian**, the only full-length rendering that dates from the Roman emperor's lifetime. (Someone at leRosier will point you in the right direction.) Created by an unknown Roman sculptor around A.D. 130, the statue of white marble stands 7 feet tall and weighs about 3,000 pounds. After departing Italy, the statue commanded a post at an English castle prior to its arrival in New Iberia.

During your visit, plan to stop by **Lagniappe Too Cafe** (337–365–9419) for lunch. Located nearby at 204 East Main Street, this delightful little restaurant lives up to its name. *Lagniappe* translates to "a little something extra," which is exactly what you get at this eatery, owned by Elaine and Al Landry.

No matter which entree you select, you can't go wrong. I had the mirliton (a type of tropical squash) stuffed with shrimp and beef, and it was delicious. There's also an eggplant version; each comes with a salad, vegetables, and special Lagniappe bread rounds. Another popular item is the shrimp and avocado salad. Don't forgo dessert here. If you miss Tante Mouth's W. B. ("World's Best") Bread Pudding with hot rum sauce, you'll leave hating yourself. Al's original art, a feast for your eyes, lines the walls. Some works are serious and others whimsical.

Lagniappe Too serves lunch Monday through Friday and is open from 10:00 A.M. until 2:00 P.M. The cafe also serves dinner on Friday and Saturday from 6:00 to 9:00 P.M.

The **Estorge-Norton House** (337–365–7603), a charming three-story structure of cypress that dates from about 1912, offers bed-and-breakfast accommodations. Located at 446 East Main Street in the heart of New Iberia's historic district, the home makes an ideal place to headquarter while taking in the local attractions, which should definitely include a walking tour of the historic district.

On the second floor a variety of accommodations is offered. An apartment on the third floor sleeps four. Guests can enjoy a full breakfast in the sunroom or dining room. Maybe a Creole specialty, grits and grillades, will be on the menu. Standard to moderate rates. For more information, visit www.bbhost .com/estorgenortonhouse.

At 309 Ann Street, you'll find the **Konriko Rice Mill and Company Store** (337–364–7242 or 800–551–3245), offering tasty treats and an interesting tour. Sip a cup of coffee while you watch a twenty-minute slide presentation on Cajun culture and the history of rice harvesting and milling. Afterward you can tour America's oldest working rice mill and browse in the Konriko Company Store (a replica of an actual company store). You might be given a rice cake to munch on and a sample of artichoke rice or other Konriko specialty. The store, which carries local foods, craft items, and gifts, is open Monday through Saturday from 9:00 A.M. until 5:00 P.M. Modest tour charge. See www.conradricemill.com.

Before leaving town, plan an outing to **Antique Rose Ville** (337–367–3000) at 2007 Freyou Road, where you'll find a ca. 1830 antebellum cottage with a backdrop of lovely gardens. Guests can stroll the grounds, smell the roses, and enjoy a meal or high tea. Call first for a reservation. You can view the property at www.antiqueroseville.com.

From New Iberia it's only about 6 miles south on Route 329 to **Avery Island** (800–634–9599). Chances are your kitchen cabinet already contains the island's famous export, Tabasco sauce. The red sauce comes in a small bottle for a very good reason: It is meant to be used sparingly, unless Cajun blood runs in your veins.

Not only is the sauce hot, but so is the temperature (most of the time) on this lush island, the home of the **McIlhenny Tabasco Factory.** An introductory movie explains how Tabasco peppers are grown, aged, and made into the fiery sauce. The peppers are pulverized, put into oak barrels, and covered with a thick layer of salt (which is mined in tunnels beneath the island's surface) for three years of fermentation. You can observe the bottling process from behind a glass window. You'll also receive a miniature bottle of the celebrated hot pepper sauce to take back home (the ⅛-ounce size is in such demand by restaurants that orders cannot be filled fast enough). Hours are 9:00 A.M. to 4:00 P.M. daily. Free admission. Afterward, stop by the Tabasco Country Store and try some sweet and spicy or jalapeño ice cream. (No, I'm not kidding; they're putting hot peppers in ice cream.). Tap into www.tabasco.com for some great recipes, history, or a shopping spree. Tabasco lovers can now order the original sauce or habanero, green pepper, chipolte, or garlic pepper flavors by the gallon.

While here, take time to explore the island's 250-acre bird and animal sanctuary, **Jungle Gardens** (either by car or on foot). If you packed a lunch, head for the picnic tables under massive bearded live oak trees. You'll be entertained by prancing peacocks and nesting egrets against a backdrop of exotic vegetation from all over the world. Wasi orange trees, Chinese bamboo, South American papaya trees, and Egyptian papyrus all grow here as well as a profusion of other trees, shrubs, and blooming plants. Don't miss the ancient statue of Buddha, originally commissioned for a Chinese temple, sitting atop a lotus throne in a glass pagoda overlooking a lagoon.

Another must in this wildlife paradise is **Bird City,** one of the country's largest egret rookeries. During the latter part of the nineteenth century when the great demand for feathers to adorn women's hats almost led to the egret's extinction, conservationist Edward Avery McIlhenny (son of Tabasco's creator,

Edmund McIlhenny) caught seven young egrets and raised them in a flying cage that he built on the island. The snowy egrets were later released to fly south for the winter, but they returned to Avery Island the next spring. Their descendants continue the practice—to the tune of some 20,000 birds each year.

Proceed on your safari with caution. Alligators slither all around. (How close they get is up to you.) They love to be tossed marshmallows (a practice frowned on by the management). To alligators, marshmallows look like egret eggs, and they gobble up both with gusto. Jungle Gardens (337–369–6243) can be visited seven days a week; hours are from 9:00 A.M. to 5:00 P.M. Admission is charged.

While in this area, consider a visit to *Franklin.* A lovely town founded in 1808, Franklin features several plantation homes as well as the nearby *Chitimacha Tribal Museum* (337–923–4830) in Charenton. Here, you'll see authentic clothing, dugouts, and other exhibits pertaining to the tribe's history. Hours run Tuesday through Saturday from 9:00 A.M. to 4:30 P.M. Admission is free.

Settled mainly by the English, the town (said to be the only one in the state that sided with the North during the Civil War) was named for Benjamin Franklin.

Located at 3296 East Oaklawn Drive, off Irish Bend Road, *Oaklawn Manor* (337–828–0434) makes an interesting stop. The home was built in 1837 by Judge Alexander Porter, an Irish merchant who founded the state's Whig Party and also served as a United States senator.

Once the center of a large sugar plantation, the three-story Greek Revival house, which faces Bayou Teche, is splendidly furnished and contains many European antiques and extensive collections of Audubon prints and hand-carved game birds of Louisiana. The house's bricks were made from clay on the premises. Magnificent live oaks and lovely gardens provide a perfect setting for the mansion, now owned by former Louisiana governor Mike Foster.

You'll see an aviary, a gift from Warner Brothers following the filming of a movie here. Be sure to visit the mansion's original milk and butter house on the grounds.

Except for major holidays, Oaklawn is open daily (even on Monday, when many area plantations close) from 10:00 A.M. to 4:00 P.M. Admission is charged.

Continuing south on US 90 takes you to *Morgan City,* a commercial fishing center and home of the *Louisiana Shrimp & Petroleum Festival.* This annual Labor Day weekend celebration features a Blessing of the Fleet ceremony on Berwick Bay and a water parade of shrimp boats, pleasure craft, and the king's and queen's big vessels. With much music and merriment, the boats bearing royalty meet and greet in a bow-to-bow "kiss" (a feat requiring skillful navigation), and the king and queen lean forward from their respective decks for the traditional champagne toast. Along with shrimp eating, other events include a Cajun cook-off, a gala street parade, fireworks, arts and crafts, and children's activities. In the downtown Historic District, festival-goers can enjoy music under the oaks at *Lawrence Park.*

Before leaving Morgan City, consider taking a guided walking tour through the *Swamp Gardens* (985–384–3343) at 725 Myrtle Street, Morgan City, and visiting a cypress home called *Cypress Manor and Mardi Gras Museum* (985–380–4651) at 715 Second Street, Morgan City. Tours take place Tuesday through Saturday from 10:00 A.M. to 4:30 P.M. and Sunday from 1:00 to 5:00 P.M.

About 3 miles north of town on Route 70 at Lake Palourde, you'll find *Brownell Memorial Park* (985–384–2283), a pleasant place to take a driving break. The Brownell Carillon Tower houses sixty-one bronze bells, which chime on the hour and half hour. The park offers picnicking facilities and is open Wedneday through Sunday from 9:00 A.M. to 4:00 P.M. Admission is free.

If you continue traveling southeast on US 90, you'll arrive in Houma, a perfect place to begin exploring the toe portion of Louisiana's boot.

Places to Stay in Southwest Louisiana

IMPERIAL CALCASIEU

Aunt Ruby's Bed & Breakfast
504 Pujo Street
Lake Charles
(337) 430–0603

Best Western Richmond Suites Hotel
2600 Moeling Street
Lake Charles
(337) 433–5213 or
(800) 643–2582

C. A.'s House Bed and Breakfast
624 Ford Street
Lake Charles
(337) 439–6672 or (866) 439–6672
www.cas-house.com

Days Inn Lake Charles
1212 North Lakeshore Drive
Lake Charles
(337) 433–9461 or
(888) 436–2580

Eddy House Bed and Breakfast
722 Pujo Street
Lake Charles
(337) 436–3980
www.eddyhouse.info

Hampton Inn Sulphur
210 Henning Drive
Sulphur
(337) 527–0000 or
(800) 426–7866

Inn on the Bayou
1101 West Prien Lake Road
Lake Charles
(337) 474–5151 or
(800) 642–2968

Microtel Inn
2619 South Ruth Street
Sulphur
(337) 477–4230 or
(888) 771–7171
www.microtelinn.com

A River's Edge Bed and Breakfast
2035 Gus Street
Westlake (Lake Charles)
(337) 497–1525 or (337) 540–3813
www.lakecharlesbed breakfast.com

CAJUN COUNTRY

Best Western Hotel Acadiana
1801 West Pinhook Road
Lafayette
(337) 233–8120 or
(800) 937–8386

Chrétien Point Plantation
665 Chrétien Point Road
Sunset
(337) 662–7050 or
(800) 880–7050
www.chretienpoint.com

Comfort Inn Opelousas
4165 I–49 South
Service Road
Opelousas
(337) 948–9500

Days Inn Crowley
9571 Egan Highway
Crowley
(337) 783–2378 or
(800) 940–0003

Days Inn Lafayette
1620 North University
Lafayette
(337) 237–8880 or
(800) 329–7466

Estorge-Norton House
446 East Main Street
New Iberia
(337) 365–7603

Hilton Garden Inn Lafayette/Cajundome
2350 West Congress Street
Lafayette
(337) 291–1977

Hilton Lafayette
1521 West Pinhook Road
Lafayette
(337) 235–6111 or
(800) 33–CAJUN

Holiday Inn Lafayette
2032 N. E. Evangeline
Thruway
Lafayette
(337) 233–6815 or
(800) 942–4868

La Quinta Inn
2100 Northeast Evangeline
Thruway
Lafayette
(337) 233–5610 or
(800) 531–5900

leRosier Country Inn Bed & Breakfast
314 East Main Street
New Iberia
(337) 367–5306

Old Castillo Bed and Breakfast
220 Evangeline Boulevard
St. Martinville
(337) 394–4010 or
(800) 621–3017

Rip Van Winkle Gardens Bed and Breakfast
5505 Rip Van Winkle
Garden Road
(Jefferson Island) New Iberia
(337) 359–8525

Places to Eat in Southwest Louisiana

IMPERIAL CALCASIEU

Big Daddy's
1737 West Sale Road
Lake Charles
(337) 477–9033

Boudin King
906 West Division Street
Jennings
(337) 824–6593

Le Café at L'Auberge du Lac Hotel & Casino
777 Avenue L'Auberge
Lake Charles
(337) 395–7777 or (866)
580–7444

Louisiana Café at the Lakefront Hotel
507 North Lakeshore Drive
Lake Charles
(337) 437–1695

Luna's Bar and Grill
719 Ryan Street
Lake Charles
(337) 494–5862

Pujo Street Café
901 Ryan Street
Lake Charles
(337) 439–2054
www.pujostreet.com

Seafood Palace
2218 Enterprise Boulevard
Lake Charles
(337) 433–9293

Steamboat Bill's
732 Martin Luther King Drive
Lake Charles
(337) 494–1700

Steamboat Bill's on the Lake
1004 North Lakeshore Drive
Lake Charles
(337) 494–1070

CAJUN COUNTRY

Antique Rose Ville Tea Room
2007 Freyou Road
New Iberia
(337) 367–3000
www.antiqueroseville.com

Black's Oyster Bar
319 Père-Megret
Abbeville
(337) 893–4266

Blue Dog Café
1211 West Pinhook Road
Lafayette
(337) 237–0005

Bon Creole
1409 East St. Peter Street
New Iberia
(337) 367–6181

Cafe des Amis
140 East Bridge Street
Breaux Bridge
(337) 332–5273

Cafe Vermilionville
1304 West Pinhook Road
Lafayette
(337) 237–0100

Charley G's
3809 Ambassador Caffery
Parkway
Lafayette
(337) 981–0108

Chef Roy's Frog City Cafe
1131 Church Point Highway
Rayne
(337) 334–7913

Clambeaugh's
111 North Main Street
St. Martinville
(337) 394–3949

Clementine Dining & Spirits
113 East Main Street
New Iberia
(337) 560–1007

Don's Seafood and Steak House
301 East Vermilion Street
Lafayette
(337) 235–3551

Dupuy's Oyster Shop
108 South Main
Abbeville
(337) 893–2336

Evangeline Seafood and Steakhouse
2633 Southeast
Evangeline Thruway
Lafayette
(337) 233–2658

Judice Inn Restaurant
3134 Johnston Street
Lafayette
(337) 984–5614

Jungle Club
1636 West Main Street
Ville Platte
(337) 363–9103

LaFonda Restaurant
3809 Johnston Street
Lafayette
(337) 984–5630

Lagniappe Too Cafe
204 East Main Street
New Iberia
(337) 365–9419

Little River Inn
833 East Main Street
New Iberia
(337) 367–7466

Mulate's Cajun Restaurant
325 Mills Avenue
Breaux Bridge
(337) 332–4648 or
(800) 422–2586

Palace Cafe
135 West Landry Street
Opelousas
(337) 942–2142

Pat's Fisherman's Wharf Restaurant
1008 Henderson
Levee Road
Henderson
(337) 228–7110

Poche's
3015-A Main Highway
Breaux Bridge
(337) 332–2108

Poor Boy's Riverside Inn
240 Tubing Road
Lafayette
(337) 235–8559

Possum's Restaurant
1007 Little Oak Drive
St. Martinville
(337) 394–3233

Prejean's Restaurant
3480 I–49 North
Lafayette
(337) 896–3247

Randol's Restaurant and Cajun Dancehall
2320 Kaliste Saloon Road
Lafayette
(800) YO–CAJUN

Rice Palace
2015 North Cherokee Drive
Crowley
(337) 783–3001

Steamboat Warehouse
525 North Main Street
Washington
(337) 826–7227

Victor's Cafeteria
109 East Main Street
New Iberia
(337) 369–9924
(Dave Robicheaux's hangout)

FOR MORE INFORMATION

Acadia Parish Convention and Visitors Commission
401 Tower Road
Crowley 70526
(337) 783–2108

Allen Parish Tourist Commission
8904 Highway 165
Oberlin 70655
(337) 639–4868 or (888) 639–4868

Beauregard Parish Tourist Commission
104 West Port Street
Box 1174, DeRidder 70634
(800) 738–5534

Breaux Bridge Bayou Teche Visitor Center
314 East Bridge Street
Breaux Bridge 70517
(337) 332–8500

Cajun Coast Visitors & Convention Bureau
112 Main Street
Patterson 70392
(800) 256–2931

Cameron Parish Tourist Commission
P.O. Box 388
Cameron 70631
(337) 775–5222
www.cameronparish.net

Iberia Parish Convention & Visitors Bureau
2513 Highway 14
New Iberia 70560
(337) 365–1540 or (888) 9–IBERIA
www.iberiatravel.com

Jefferson Davis Parish Tourist Commission
Louisiana Oil and Gas Park
100 Rue de l'Acadie
P.O. Box 1208, Jennings 70546
(800) 264–5521
www.jeffdavis.org

Lafayette Convention and Visitors Commission
1400 Evangeline Thruway
P.O. Box 52066, Lafayette 70505
(800) 346–1958
www.lafayettetravel.com

Southwest Louisiana Lake Charles Convention and Visitors Bureau
1205 North Lakeshore Drive
Lake Charles; 70601
(800) 456–7952
www.visitlakecharles.org

St. Landry Parish Tourist Commission
131 West Bellevue Street
Opelousas 70570
P.O. Box 1415
Opelousas 70571–1415
(337) 948–8004 or (877) 948–8004

St. Martinville Parish Tourist Information Center
215 Evangeline Boulevard
P.O. Box 379
St. Martinville 70582
(337) 394–2233

Area newspapers include the *Daily Advertiser* and *Times of Acadiana* in Lafayette. Both will have entertainment listings. The weekly *Times of Acadiana* will be trendier and also covers Cajun music venues well. Other local newspapers are the *Lake Charles American Press* in Lake Charles (which has a very good Web site: www.americanpress .com), the *Breaux Bridge Banner* in Breaux Bridge, the *Cameron Parish Pilot* in Cameron, the *Crowley Post Signal* in Crowley, and the *Daily World* in Opelousas.

Put your radio on in Cajun country—in Ville Platte you can catch the music show from Fred's on Saturday morning from 9:00 to 11:00 on KVPI at 1250 AM. KRVS at 88.7 FM in Lafayette will have Cajun music on the early show every morning and zydeco on Sunday. You will also hear newscasts in French on AM stations throughout the area from time to time. Also, if you want to really hear the local accent, just listen to the TV spots in Lafayette.

Southeast Louisiana

Southeast Louisiana—the toe of the boot—boasts incredibly diverse landscapes to charm any traveler. And there have been many visitors, from the early Europeans who marveled at the almost bank-to-bank alligators in the rivers to the stars of the 1967 film *Easy Rider* on their high-flying quest for the perfect Mardi Gras.

North of Lake Pontchartrain lie the piney Florida Parishes, where local heritage is more likely English than French. This area was not part of the 1803 Louisiana Purchase but was a section of Spanish, then English, west Florida, hence the name.

Plantation homes can be found along the River Road between New Orleans and the Feliciana Parishes (the "happy land" of the painter John James Audubon) east of the capital city Baton Rouge, itself a town of great charm.

The heart of Southeast Louisiana is, of course, New Orleans. The Crescent City, founded on a "beautiful crescent" of the river by French Canadians in 1718, remains a great and unique destination for tourists. (Katrina could not change that.)

The area below New Orleans is marked by waterways, fishing and shrimping industries, and the oil business—and small communities known for fun-filled festivals and good times.

MISSISSIPPI
LOUISIANA

THE FELICIANAS

Jackson

FRENCH
CREOLE
COUNTRY

New Roads

Bogalusa

TURF AND SWAMP

"RED STICK"

Hammond

Baton Rouge

Lake
Maurepas

Lake
Pontchartrain

Slidell

PLANTATION
COUNTRY

CRESCENT CITY
REALM

New Orleans

BAYS AND
BAYOUS

Thibodaux

Houma

SWAMPLAND

Port Sulphur

Venice

Mississippi R.

Gulf of Mexico

N

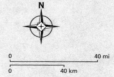

0   40 mi
0   40 km

Swampland

Entering Terrebonne (*TER-a-bone*) Parish from the west, take State Route 182 to reach Houma (*HOME-uh*). Between Morgan City and Houma, this road follows Bayou Black. Driving along, you'll notice portions of the dark water covered by a bright green film. This substance, known as duckweed, may look like slime to you, but to ducks, it's dinner. A close examination of the plant reveals a mass of tiny four-petaled flowers. One of the world's smallest flowering plants, duckweed makes a tasty salad for ducks and geese. As part of America's WETLAND Birding Trail, Terrebonne Parish boasts five birding sites, including the Mandalay Wildlife Refuge and the Pointe-Aux-Chien Wildlife Management Area.

Because of its many waterways, **Houma** is sometimes called the Venice of America. Its navigable bayous and canals serve as streets for shrimp boats and various vessels that glide by the town's backyards. The parish was established in 1834 on the banks of Bayou Terrebonne (which means "good earth"), and more than half of it is water. Houma is named for a Native American tribe that settled here during the early eighteenth century. Later Cajun settlers arrived and were joined by English, German, and Irish families.

Houma rebounded rapidly from the heavy-duty flooding, wind damage, and power outages resulting from hurricanes Katrina and Rita. In fact, positioned as the town was between the areas of the two storms' impact, Houma

GAY'S FAVORITES IN SOUTHEAST LOUISIANA

A Cajun Man's Swamp Cruise
Houma

Chauvin Sculpture Garden
Cahuvin

Delta Queen Steamboat Company Cruise
New Orleans

Feliciana Cellars Winery
Jackson

French Quarter
New Orleans

Garden District
New Orleans

Grand Isle State Park
Grand Isle

Laura, A Creole Plantation
Vacherie

Louisiana State University
Baton Rouge

Ponchatoula Country Market
Ponchatoula

Rural Life Museum and Windrush Gardens
Baton Rouge

Town of Jean Lafitte

Town of St. Francisville

served as a base for helicopter pilots all over the state as they carried on rescue missions in the desperate post-hurricane days.

A delightful way to acquaint yourself with the local flora and fauna is to take a swamp cruise, and the region offers several choices. For a swamp tour with a unique slant, try *A Cajun Man's Swamp Cruise* (985–868–4625), headquartered on State Route 182, about 15 miles west of Houma and 20 miles east of Morgan City at Bob's Bayou Black Marina.

Black Guidry, a French-speaking Cajun singer who dishes up music with his commentary and tour, serves as captain for this trek into a beguiling wilderness. "Folks, if you want to know something, ask me," he says. "If I don't know the answer, I'll tell you a lie, and you won't know the difference." It's obvious that he knows this lush area well, and he often checks his crab traps along the way.

Black will take you through a surrealistic world of cypress trees with swaying Spanish moss. You'll see elephant ears, palmettos, muscadine (wild grape) vines, and pretty purple water hyacinths (which rob the water of oxygen and are extremely difficult to control). Black will point out bulrush, which provides nesting areas for snowy egrets, black-crowned night herons, and other birds. You'll probably see cormorants, ibis, blue herons, ducks, cranes, red-tailed hawks, and perhaps bald eagles and pelicans. You may also spot nutrias (fur-

The Story of Our Vanishing Coast Begins Here

Houma native Melanie Melancon urges everyone to join the effort to save our wetlands, now in jeopardy. Here is what she has to say about this critical issue:

To prevent another catastrophe, Louisiana's wetlands must be restored; not just the levees. The wetlands and barrier islands once served as a shield from the impact of hurricane winds and storm surge. This shield is no longer there and is still disappearing at a rate of the size of a football field every 30 minutes. To tell the story of where it all began and to witness the vanishing wetlands firsthand, Houma offers an experience blended with rich history, breathtaking and sometimes stunning scenery, and a thriving culture.

Houma, the heart of America's wetland, is losing the largest concentration of wetlands in Louisiana. Along with the disappearing wetlands, a rare culture and an important economy are threatened into extinction. The music, food, coastlines, wildlife, fish, and game, that make Louisiana a unique and original state are in desperate need of America's attention and support. This land where Louisianans built their livelihood, raised their families, and provided a crucial piece of America 's economic puzzle is poised to disappear entirely.

TOP ANNUAL EVENTS IN SWAMPLAND

Thibodaux Fireman's Fair
Thibodaux, first weekend in May
(877) 537–5800

**International Grand Isle
Tarpon Rodeo**
Grand Isle, last full weekend in July
(985) 787–2997
www.tarponrodeo.org

Cajun Heritage Festival
205 West Seventy-Ninth Street
Cut Off
second weekend in September
(877) 537–5800

Voice of the Wetlands Festival
Houma, mid-October
(800) 688–2732

French Food Festival
307 East Fifth Street
Larose, late October
(985) 693–7355

bearing members of the rodent family), otters, turtles, snakes, alligators, and other creatures that populate this eerie realm.

Black's "pet" alligators recognize the sound of his boat and come when he calls (unless they're hibernating). Papa Gator, who is 14 feet long, and other members of his family may put in an appearance.

After the boat tour Black will play his guitar and sing for you. A gifted musician, he composes songs and appears on national television. Maybe he'll sing "Crawfish, Crawdads, Mudbugs, and Other Things" (from one of his albums) or a Hank Williams favorite like "Jambalaya," whose famous line "Son of a gun, we're gonna have big fun on the Bayou!" takes on added relevance in this setting.

During the musical session Black will show you his Cajun accordion made from part of a wooden chest, diaper pins, and other materials of opportunity. Cajuns are noted for their resourcefulness; they are also known for their friendliness, zest for life, strong family ties, and cooking skills. "Most Cajun men cook," says Black's wife, Sondra, "and are *good* cooks."

The swamp cruise, narrated in either French or English, takes about two hours and costs $20 per adult and $10 per child (ages three through twelve). Kids younger than three get free rides. Telephone ahead because tour times vary, and reservations are required. Click on www.cajunman.com for more background.

If you're game for another tour, visit ***Wildlife Gardens*** (985–575–3676) at 5306 North Bayou Black Drive in Gibson. North Bayou Black Drive runs parallel to State Route 182. Owned by Betty Provost and her husband, Vernon Eschete, the preserve is populated with some 500 animals from South

Voice of the Wetlands

Lending his talent and energy to bring awareness to Louisiana's coastal and cultural erosion, two-time Grammy nominated musician Tab Benoit from Houma formed Voice of the Wetlands in 2003. An annual VOW festival, the only event in Louisiana to address the loss of the state's coast and culture, takes place in Houma during mid-October. Look for Tab's musical releases including *Voice of the Wetlands* with Dr. John, Tab Benoit, Cyril Neville, George Porter Jr., Anders Osborne, Big Chief Monk Boudreaux, Houma native Waylon Thibodaux, and other artists. Learn more at www.voiceofthewetlands.com.

Louisiana. The family pets range from nutrias, bobcats, raccoons, and deer to ducks and black swans. The natural swamp setting in Gibson is also home to great horned owls, pheasants, exotic chickens, alligators, and alligator loggerhead turtles.

Here, depending on the season, you can give bread to the white-tailed deer, perhaps scratch their velveteen horns, and watch their fawns being bottle-fed. Watch out for Clarence, a 90-pound alligator loggerhead turtle. The family also operates an alligator farm, and visitors can touch the babies and observe the different stages of alligator growth.

On a guided tour, you'll see an authentic trapper's cabin with furnishings. A gift shop on the premises sells native crafts. Except for Sunday and major holidays, tours are given daily from 9:00 A.M. to 3:00 P.M. Admission is charged.

Betty also offers bed-and-breakfast. "Guests can stay in one of our four little rustic cabins nestled in the swamp," she says. Moderate rates.

After your encounter with the local wildlife, continue on State Route 182 east to Houma. While there, take time to drive along Route 311 on the city's western outskirts to see several lovely plantation homes situated along Little Bayou Black.

Stop by ***Southdown Plantation House*** (985–851–0154), located about 3 miles southwest of town on the corner of Route 311 and St. Charles Street at 1208 Museum Drive, Houma. This grandiose pink Victorian mansion, trimmed in green, also serves as the Terrebonne Museum. Inside the twelve-room structure, you'll see a colorful Mardi Gras exhibit. Be sure to notice the hall doorways with inserts of stained glass in a sugarcane motif. There is also an exhibit on the Houmas Indians, with handicrafts and photographs.

Other interesting exhibits focus on local history and the state's native peoples. You'll also see a re-creation of the Washington, D.C., office of the late Allen J. Ellender from Houma, who served almost thirty-six years in the U.S.

Senate. Autographed pictures of familiar political personalities line the wall. Senator Ellender's colleagues acknowledged him as the Senate's master chef, and his original gumbo recipe is still prepared in the U.S. Senate dining room. You can pick up a brochure featuring some of Senator Ellender's Creole recipes such as gumbo, shrimp Creole, jambalaya, oyster stew, and pralines.

Guided tours take about one hour, and the day's last tour starts at 3:00 P.M. Except for holidays, Southdown is open Tuesday through Saturday 10:00 A.M. to 4:00 P.M. Admission. Visit www.southdownmuseum.org.

While in Houma, consider headquartering at **Grand Bayou Noir** (985–873–5849 or 985–804–0303), the home of Judge Timothy Ellender and his wife, Debra. In a setting of stately oak trees at 1143 Bayou Black Drive, the handsome white Georgian-style home dates to 1936 and fronts Big Bayou Black. The lush grounds feature four acres of cultivated plants including fifteen citrus varieties and twenty-eight species of banana trees along with a vegetable and herb garden.

In addition to guest rooms in the main house, accommodations include a suite in the adjacent guest wing with a private balcony and entrance. Like the late U.S. Senator Ellender (his uncle), the judge knows his way around the kitchen, and so does his son. Guests can anticipate a gourmet breakfast, served in the main dining room. Starting with a fruit medley, the meal might feature bananas Foster pancakes with smoked bacon plus an egg dish laced with crawfish and garnished with a sky vine blossom and sprig of dill from the property. Actually, most breakfasts here utilize ingredients gathered fresh from the backyard. Moderate. Check out www.grandbayounoir.com.

While in Houma, don't miss **Bayou Terrebonne Waterlife Museum** (985–580–7200) at 7910 West Park Avenue. Start your visit by watching the

Getting Grounded

In Southeast Louisiana there are rich powdered loess soil and some remaining mixed hardwood bottomland forest in the area just east of Baton Rouge in the Feliciana Parishes.

Just north, or east of the Mississippi River, the shallow and brackish Lake Pontchartrain is the largest of a chain of lakes leading into the Gulf of Mexico. North of Lake Pontchartrain the land rises to the sandy soil region of the piney woods.

The land along the Mississippi on the West Bank and nearing the Gulf of Mexico on the East Bank is cut by slow-flowing bayous winding through swamps and marshes. Highland occurs on natural levees along watercourses and on old shoreline ridges called cheniers for the oak trees (des chenes) growing there.

Hot Weather Tip

Keep your bathing suits and a towel in the car to be ready for a quick dip. North of Lake Pontchartrain, ice-water creeks with local swimming holes can be found—ask at a busy filling station, especially if you see inner tubes hanging around. Pushepatappa Creek, north of Bogalusa near Varnado, and Big Creek, outside Amite off Highway 16, are both local favorites. Or check out a "tubing" company—you rent a tube, float down a river, and the service picks you up. Try near Franklinton on Highway 25 from Folsom.

You might also find swimming opportunities on the beach at Grand Isle or around False River. Only swim where it is allowed—Louisiana has serious water pollution problems, and you don't want to take a risk.

eight-minute video presentation, which provides an orientation to the facility. Interactive exhibits showcase the area's close link with the seafood and water-transportation industries and spotlight the plight of the vanishing wetlands. Hours are Tuesday through Friday from 10:00 A.M. to 5:00 P.M. and Saturday from noon to 4:00 P.M. If you visit on Tuesday or Thursday from 5:30 to 7:00 P.M., you'll hear some toe-tapping Cajun music. Modest admission. Learn more at www.houmaterrebonne.org.

Before leaving town, you'll want to take in some Cajun music and dancing. At *The Jolly Inn* (985–872–6114), located in a former warehouse at 1507 Barrow Street, every out-of-towner gets an honorary Cajun certificate entitling him "to all privileges, duties, and honors of those who love the lifestyle of the Acadian people and culture." One requirement is to be able to dance at least one step of the Cajun two-step. If you don't know how, the locals will gladly share their expertise.

When dinnertime rolls around, you can dig into a boiled seafood dinner or platter of steaming crawfish at *1921 Seafood Restaurant* (985–868–7098) at 1522 Barrow Street, just across the street from The Jolly Inn. (It may be my imagination, but the crawfish look bigger in Houma than most other places—maybe because they are not farmed here but trawled from the local bayous.) Restaurant hours run 5:00 to 10:00 P.M. daily except on Friday when the place opens at 11:00 A.M.

Heading south on State Route 56 will take you to *Cocodrie*, a popular spot with anglers and only about thirty-five minutes from Houma. On the way, you'll pass through Chauvin, home of an extraordinary sculpture garden. To see this collection of more than one hundred concrete sculptures, which ranks among the world's top three finest examples of folk art, turn left on State Route 58 at the traffic light intersection onto Sarah Bridge and cross Bayou Petit Caillou.

Then take a right at the first street to 5337 Bayouside Drive. You'll see Nicholls State University Art Studio on the left and the Sculpture Garden on your right.

The **Chauvin Sculpture Garden** spills over with the incredible creations of reclusive artist Kenny Hill. Hardly anything is known about Hill other than he was a bricklayer by trade and spent about a decade filling this small piece of property with his profound and unique body of work.

Angels and other amazing creatures painted in vivid Cajun colors testify to the artist's obvious struggle with good and evil. This implementation of his vision, loaded with Biblical and political allegory, reflects such torment that it can prove painful to see. Most of all, you want to know more about the man who could create all this, then disappear. Hill reportedly declared his work a story of salvation, saying, "It's about living and life and everything I've learned." The Sculpture Garden is open from dawn to dusk. Admission is free, but donations are accepted and used to maintain this remarkable collection.

Across the road, you can visit the **NSU Art Studio** (958–594–2546) and view its permanent collection by local artists. Hours are 1:00 to 4:00 P.M. every Monday, Wednesday, and Friday, or by appointment. For more information, call the NSU Division of Art at (985) 448–4597. Nicholls State University is located in nearby Thibodaux.

Afterward, follow State Route 56 to Cocodrie. At **Coco Marina** (985–594–6626 or 800–648–2626), Johnny Glover promises good fishing year-round at his facility on the Gulf of Mexico's fruitful fringes. Here you can charter a boat (the marina currently operates ten boats, ranging from 25 to 38 feet in size) for fishing expeditions. A day's catch might include black drum, redfish, speckled trout, sheepshead, cobia, red snapper, flounder, and mackerel. The marina has recorded daily catches of more than twenty-six different species, and a typical weekend haul might bring in a sampling of ten to fifteen species.

Celebrate your catch at the **Island Oasis Bar** while enjoying a wetlands sunset. Afterward, you can dine at the **Lighthouse Restaurant,** which offers

Feeling Crabby?

One of the simplest outdoor pastimes Louisiana folks enjoy is crabbing. Any hardware store or bait shop can supply you with white twine and crab nets.

Tie an old chicken neck (crabs like smelly food) into the center of a net and lower it into salt or brackish water from a pier. Have ready a wooden bushel basket with top to hold your scuttling crabs. A set of tongs to pick them out of the net saves fingers.

Buy some crab-boil mix (a bag of spices; Zatarain's brand is good). Boil a huge pot of water, steep the mix plus salt and lemon, and add crabs. Twenty minutes later you have a free feast (not counting your net and seasoning costs).

seafood specialties. Or you can feast on your own catch in the privacy of your condo. The complex offers accommodations from motel units to studio apartments, and all buildings stand on 12- to 14-foot pilings. Except for the months of November through March and major holidays, the marina is open daily. Rates are standard to moderate. Visit cocomarina.com.

While in Cocodrie visit the *Louisiana University Marine Consortium* (LUMCON, 985–851–2800). This working research facility also welcomes tourists for free. You will find exhibits on the environment and some aquarium displays and, best of all, a viewing tower that lets you have a gull's-eye view of the surrounding saltwater marshes. Stroll the boardwalks and see the local birds. Hours are 8:00 A.M. to 4:00 P.M. daily. Learn more at www.lumcon .edu.

Afterward, return to Houma and follow Route 24 east until you reach Route 1 in Lafourche Parish. Then head south on Route 1, which runs parallel with Bayou Lafourche, known locally as the "longest street in the world." This waterway, busy with the traffic of barges, shrimp boats, and a variety of other vessels, extends to the Gulf of Mexico. A number of Cajun fishing communities line the shore.

Slow down when you reach the little town of *Golden Meadow* (actually you should slow down *before* you get here because the speed limit means what it says). Watch for a small shrimp boat, the *Petit Caporal,* moored beside Route 1. Named for Napoleon Bonaparte, the century-old boat serves as a monument to the area's shrimping industry. Driving through the area south of Golden Meadow and all the way down to the coast, you'll see a variety of birds—gulls, terns, shorebirds, and such.

Located on the Gulf of Mexico at the end of Route 1, you'll discover *Grand Isle.* A bridge links the narrow 8-mile barrier island to the mainland. You'll drive past fishing camps, homes built on tall pilings, and other beach properties. Grand Isle is noted for its excellent birding, especially during spring and fall when migrating flocks follow the flyway (the migratory interstate for birds from Canada to Mexico), which crosses the island.

Grand Isle State Park (985–787–2559 or 888–787–2559), at the island's eastern tip, normally offers many seashore recreation opportunities such as fishing, surfing, crabbing, picnicking, and camping. The park took a hard hit from Hurricane Katrina but is now back up and running. The storm wiped out many facilities and demolished several buildings, including the manager's house. Workers spent several months clearing away the debris. "We're not 100 percent operational yet," said a staffer. "Maybe 80 percent." Currently, the park is open for overnight RV camping, but no day use. Before you go, call for an update.

For the Birds

Grand Isle is for the birds—at least just before and after their great migration over the Gulf of Mexico. In early spring, just after a cold snap, the trees of the island are filled with warblers and songbirds taking their ease after their long trek.

Grand Isle is also a site for the Audubon Society Christmas Bird Count, the annual census of birds that takes place all over the United States. The Grand Isle count is always high.

You can see interesting species at any time. Check out the gulls and terns for some western strays. Keep an eye out for scissor-tailed flycatchers (that tail is remarkably long: you can't miss them). You probably won't see an albatross, but one dedicated birder did add one to his life list here.

On the Internet go to www.audubon.org, look for Louisiana in the state lists, then go to the map. You can download a map for birding on Grand Isle, showing which of the small residential streets might lead you to a good venue.

You'll have to return north after you've finished fishing and sunning because Grand Isle is the end of the line.

At Golden Meadow once more, you can vary your route by switching from Route 1 to Route 308 (which also runs parallel to the waterway) on the eastern bank of Bayou Lafourche. Continue driving north toward Thibodaux (*TIB-a-doe*). Two miles before reaching Thibodaux, just off Route 308 on Route 33, you'll find **_Laurel Valley Plantation_** (985–446–7456). Dating from the 1840s, this complex is America's largest surviving sugar plantation. Head first for the General Store and Museum where you'll see a couple of locomotives, old machinery, and a pen filled with chickens, ducks, sheep, and goats. The store carries prints depicting Laurel Valley Plantation as it looked during the nineteenth century, as well as local arts and crafts. You'll also see vintage items: iron pots, churns, crocks, smoothing irons, farm implements, and pirogues. Laurel Valley Village consists of some sixty weathered structures, including a manor house, school, blacksmith shop, and barns. A cane-lined drive takes

Shrimp Boats

you past rows of workers' cabins. Pick up a leaflet at the museum and go exploring on your own. Weather permitting, hours run from 10:00 A.M. to 3:00 P.M. Wednesday through Friday, and 11:00 A.M. to 3:00 P.M. on Saturday and Sunday. For more information on the complex, call the Thibodaux Chamber of Commerce at (985) 446–1187.

After leaving Laurel Valley, drive on into ***Thibodaux*** (about five minutes away) to see the town's fine group of Victorian homes and other interesting buildings such as the courthouse, St. Joseph's Catholic Church, and St. John's Episcopal Church. Dating from 1844, St. John's is the oldest Episcopal church west of the Mississippi River. Nearby ***Nicholls State University*** also features an interesting boat-building facility. After touring Thibodaux take Route 308 north toward Napoleonville.

Plantation Country

About 2 miles south of Napoleonville, a town founded by a former soldier of the Little Corporal, you'll find ***Madewood*** (985–369–7151 or 800–375–7151) at 4250 Highway 308. Dating from the 1840s, this magnificent white-columned Greek Revival mansion features a huge ballroom, handsome walnut staircase, and ornate plasterwork. The home is furnished with period antiques, fine paintings, Oriental rugs, and crystal chandeliers.

"We're the least commercial of the area plantations," says Keith Marshall, "and some of our guests have returned four and five times." He and his wife, Millie, make their lovely plantation home on Bayou Lafourche available for both day tours and overnight lodging. On the grounds you'll see an interesting old cemetery, several plantation outbuildings, and lovely landscaping complete with live oak trees and swaying Spanish moss.

Overnight guests are greeted with wine and cheese. A house tour, an elegant dinner (with candlelight and wine) followed by after-dinner coffee and brandy in the parlor, and a full plantation breakfast are included in the price of a mansion room or the nearby raised bay cottages. Rates are deluxe. With the exceptions of Thanksgiving, Christmas Day, and New Year's Day, Madewood is open daily from 10:00 A.M. to 4:00 P.M. Admission is charged.

Depending on your time frame and interests, you can travel farther east to do some plantation hopping along the ***Great River Road*** (actually composed of several state highways), which parallels both sides of the Mississippi River between New Orleans and Baton Rouge. Along the way you'll see lovely scenery—magnolia, oak, pecan, and willow trees and many of the South's most beautiful plantation homes. Several of the plantation homes are patterned after Greek temples and feature long oak-lined approaches. Many of these magnifi-

OTHER ATTRACTIONS WORTH SEEING IN SWAMPLAND

Annie Miller's Son's Swamp Tours
Bayou Delight Restaurant, Houma
(985) 868–4758 or (800) 341–5441
Before boarding, grab a bite at Bayou
Delight. Locally, this swamp tour has
the usual pleasant patter, as well as
comfortable seats and alligators who
appear on cue. Kids will enjoy this.
Reservations suggested. Visit
www.annie-miller.com.

Edward Douglass White Historic Site
2295 St. Mary Street, Thibodaux
(985) 447–0915
White, U.S. Supreme Court chief justice
from 1910 to 1921, was born in this
raised cottage, now maintained as a
historic site by the state of Louisiana.
Although the home may be closed for
renovation, the grounds remain open
for visitors.

View of Grande Terre Island
From the easternmost tip of Grand Isle
you can see across to the onetime
location of U.S. Army Fort Livingston.

After Jean Lafitte vacated his pirate lair
here in 1814, the military fortified his
old camp.

Wetlands Acadian Cultural Center
Jean Lafitte National Historical
Park and Preserve
314 St. Mary Street, Thibodaux
(985) 448–1375
This multisited national park offers a
glimpse into the life of those Acadians
(Louisiana immigrants from French
Canada, evicted by the conquering
English in the late 1700s) who settled
along the waterways of the state.
Here they trapped, fished, and hunted
while developing their own unique
crafts. The center, which often features
local craftspeople and experts, houses
a theater for video presentations as
well as detailed displays and artifacts.
This is a good place to check up on
what's happening locally: festivals,
performances, even how the fishing is.

cent old mansions offer both tours for daytime visitors and bed-and-breakfast accommodations for overnight guests.

Among the homes you can visit along River Road are **San Francisco,** with its elaborate Steamboat Gothic design, and the impressive Greek Revival–style **Oak Alley,** with its grand canopy of live oaks.

For a rare glimpse into the past, stop by **Laura, a Creole Plantation** (225-265-7690) at 2247 Highway 18 near Vacherie. Located on the west side of the Mississippi River, this multicolored manor house built in 1805 was named for Laura Lacoul, whose memoirs provide firsthand accounts of a thriving, hard-driving sugar and wine importation business managed for eighty-four years by women—no languorous hours spent sipping mint juleps on Laura's verandas.

To make Laura's colorful, sometimes cruel history come alive for visitors, general manager Norman Marmillion and staff tracked down and studied some 5,000 pages of documentation from several states and as far afield as the

Laura, a Creole Plantation

National Archives in Paris. People find Laura captivating "not because of our ancient moss-draped oaks or a few pieces of furniture," Marmillion notes, "but because our stories transport visitors into the fascinating world of Creole Louisiana." Throughout the house and wine cellar, mannequins depict Laura, various family members, and servants. From baby teeth to voodoo charms, Laura's family artifacts, clothing, photo albums, business ledgers, and slave records reinforce accounts of "the good, the bad, and the ugly" shared by staff members.

plantationsin themovies

Louisiana appears on the silver screen with great regularity. Fans of Anne Rice might recognize Destrehan Plantation as the scene for parts of the film *Interview with a Vampire.* The Bette Davis–Olivia deHavilland vehicle *Hush, Hush, Sweet Charlotte* took place at Houmas House. Nearby Ashland (also called Belle Helene) was the setting for *The Beguiled* with Clint Eastwood. Oak Alley appears in *Primary Colors.*

Historians regard Laura as the American home of the Br'er Rabbit stories. "Here in our remaining slave quarters, the centuries-old tales of the West African folk hero [Compair Lapin] were first written down in North America, later to be translated, adapted, and become widely known as the American legend, Br'er Rabbit," Marmillion says. Slaves from Senegal brought the stories to Louisiana during the early 1700s.

Except for major holidays, Laura is open daily from 9:00 A.M. to 5:00 P.M. The day's first tour starts at 9:30 A.M. and the last one at 4:00 P.M. Pay a virtual visit to www.lauraplantation.com. Admission is charged.

Sugar Palace Pleasures

Photo opportunities abound at **Houmas House Plantation and Gardens** (225–473–7841), once known as the "Sugar Palace" because of its extensive sugarcane holdings. Located in Darrow (River Road, Burnside) at 40136 Highway 942, this grand plantation home takes its name from the Houmas tribe who occupied a village here when French explorer LaSalle arrived in 1682. The home boasts fourteen Doric columns and a magnificent three-story spiral staircase. With its spacious rooms and comfortable antiques, this is the plantation most appealing to contemporary tastes in interior design.

Start your visit in the gift shop by viewing a presentation on the property's history. Then meander about the extensive grounds, maintained by ten full-time gardeners. Owner Kevin Kelly has added gorgeous gardens, along with exotic plants, statuary, reflecting ponds, and fountains.

The site is open Monday through Wednesday from 10:00 A.M. until 5:00 P.M. and Thursday through Sunday from 10:00 A.M. until 8:00 P.M. Admission. For more background, see www.houmashouse.com.

While touring Houmas House, you'll want to savor a meal at **Latil's Landing Restaurant** on the premises. *Esquire* magazine (November 2005) named this one of America's Top 20 New Restaurants. Executive chef Jeremy Langois, who enjoys creating traditional Louisiana dishes with unique touches, collects culinary accolades, too. Langois puts a southern spin on crème brûlée. Here's his version of this classic dessert:

Mint Julep Custard Brûlée

2 cups heavy whipping cream

¼ cup bourbon

½ cup blanched fresh mint leaves

2 egg yolks

3 whole eggs

1 cup sugar

Pinch of cinnamon

Pinch of nutmeg

1 cup sugar for brûlée

Scald heavy whipping cream and bourbon. Blanch mint leaves in boiling water for 10 seconds, remove mint leaves and plunge in ice water. Strain and puree leaves with 1 cup of the milk and bourbon mixture. Combine eggs, sugar, cinnamon, and nutmeg in a mixing bowl and add mint puree. Slowly pour the cream and bourbon mixture into the egg mixture, while whisking constantly. Run the mixture through a strainer. Pour into six 6-ounce soufflé cups. Place the soufflé cups in a water bath, and cover with aluminum foil.

Bake at 350 degrees for 30 minutes. Remove from oven, place soufflé bowls on flat pans and immediately refrigerate for 2 hours. Once the custard has cooled, dust the top of each with sugar. Using a blow torch, carefully caramelize the sugar on top of each of the custards until golden brown. Be careful not to blacken the sugar as it will have a bitter taste. Serve with a dollop of slightly sweetened whipped cream. Yields 6 servings.

From Laura, follow the River Road (Highway 18) west to **Donaldsonville.** First settled in 1750, this little city was a thriving port in the nineteenth century and served as the Louisiana state capital in the 1830s. Donaldsonville is now best known as the home base of Chef John Folse.

germancoast

When Louisiana was a young French colony, it was difficult to attract settlers. Finally some German farmers were enticed and given land along the Mississippi River in the 1760s. This area became known as the German Coast. Soon the Germans intermarried with the French-Acadian exiles who arrived a bit later. That is the reason that Schexnayder is a typical "French" Louisiana name. The name Hymel (pronounced *HEE-mel*, or *EE-mel*) probably began as "Himmel." The little community of Des Allemands (usually pronounced *des-AL-muns*) is just inland on the West Bank of the German Coast—the name *des Allemands* is French for "Germans."

Bittersweet Plantation, 404 Claiborne Street, is Folse's property, and his imaginative take on native Louisiana foods (and a good following from television shows and cookbooks) has made this is a popular spot for overnight guests. Call (225) 473–1232 for bed-and-breakfast reservations at Bittersweet Plantation. Overnight guests may also make dinner reservations when booking a room. Deluxe.

Also in Donaldsonville check out **Rossie's Custom Framing and Gallery,** an emporium in an old five-and-dime. Featured is primitive painter Alvin Batiste (view his work at www.alvinbatiste.com). Hours are 8:30 A.M. to 5:00 P.M. Tuesday through Friday, 9:00 A.M. to 5:00 P.M. on Saturday, and from 9:00 A.M. to 3:00 P.M. Sunday. Rossie's is at 510 Railroad Avenue. (Also on Railroad Avenue are the **Railroad Cafe** at 212 Railroad Avenue, with simple po'boys and plate lunches, and the **Grapevine Restaurant** at 211 Railroad Avenue, offering good Cajun cooking.

Check out Donaldsonville's museum, the old B. Lemann department store building, and the Fort Butler historic site—a Union Army fortification where African-American soldiers served in the Civil War. You can continue following the Mississippi west toward White Castle to visit Nottaway Plantation.

Nottoway (225–545–2730) is the biggest plantation house of all. The mansion is located at 30970 River Road (Highway 405).

Nottoway, sometimes called the White Castle, is a splendid interpretation of the Italianate style. The three-story mansion with sixty-four rooms, once the centerpiece of a 7,000-acre plantation, was designed by acclaimed architect Henry Howard. Sugar baron John Hampden Randolph commissioned the house, which was completed in 1859. The 53,000-square-foot home provided plenty of space for the Randolphs' eleven children, staff, and visitors. Cornelia,

OTHER ATTRACTIONS WORTH SEEING IN PLANTATION COUNTRY

Destrehan Plantation
13034 River Road, Destrehan
(985) 764–9315
Built in 1787, this is a fine example of the Louisiana French colonial–style plantation house. Careful restoration is ongoing, supported by a fall festival and other events. Besides a resident ghost, you will also find a nice museum shop for souvenirs.

River Road
From Houmas House, ride up the River Road to view Bocage Plantation (in 2 miles), Hermitage Plantation (3 miles), and Belle Helene or Ashland Plantation (7.5 miles). You can actually get to Baton Rouge (37 more miles) by taking the River Road (part of the way is gravel). You eventually get to the campus of Louisiana State University, and you will pass through the community of Carville, which at one time housed the American treatment center for Hansen's disease (leprosy). Carville is named for the family of James Carville, outspoken political operative.

Sunshine Bridge
Donaldsonville
The Sunshine Bridge over the Mississippi River commemorates the song written by Louisiana governor Jimmie Davis, "You are My Sunshine." Davis was a prolific songwriter and performer who penned such favorites as "That Silver-Haired Daddy of Mine"; "Sunshine" was his greatest hit.

one of the Randolph daughters, wrote a book about life at Nottoway entitled *The White Castle of Louisiana*. You can buy a copy at the gift shop. Nottoway is now owned by Paul Ramsay of Sydney, Australia.

Perhaps the home's ornate interior, the setting for exquisite antiques and art, is best exemplified by the grand White Ballroom. This immense room, with its white marble fireplace and Corinthian columns, is a vision in varying shades of white. With its gleaming floor (covered by three layers of white enamel), vanilla-colored walls, and lofty ceiling, this room made an elegant backdrop for both balls and weddings. Six of the Randolph daughters were married in the White Ballroom, and during the past decade some 500 weddings have also been performed here.

At Nottoway, unlike some mansions, visitors are told they may explore after the tour and go through any door that's not closed. Overnight guests are free to stroll through the mansion after hours between 5:00 and 10:00 P.M.

Dinner may be served either in Randolph Hall, an elegant restaurant on the grounds, or in the mansion's first-floor Magnolia Room (formerly a three-lane bowling alley original to the house).

Overnight guests are served sherry on arrival and can enjoy a full plantation breakfast the following morning.

TOP ANNUAL EVENTS IN PLANTATION COUNTRY

Gonzales Jambalaya Festival
Gonzales, last weekend in May
(225) 647–2937 or (800) 680–3208

Louisiana Catfish Festival
Des Allemands, second weekend
in July
(985) 758–7542

Donaldsonville Sunshine Festival
Louisiana Square
Donaldsonville
late October to early November
(225) 473–4814

Destrehan Plantation Fall Festival
13034 River Road
Destrehan
second full weekend of November
(985) 764–9315

Festival of the Bonfires
P.O. Box 247
Lutcher 70071-0247, December
(800) 367–7852
www.festivalofthebonfires.org

Nottoway is open daily for lunch from 11:00 A.M. to 3:00 P.M. and for dinner from 6:00 to 9:00 P.M. Nottoway closes at 3:00 P.M. on Christmas Eve and reopens on December 26. Otherwise, the mansion can be visited daily from 9:00 A.M. to 5:00 P.M. Admission is charged. Rates are moderate to deluxe. Visit the mansion at www.nottoway.com.

When you leave Nottoway, you will exit near the gift shop. To see the world's smallest church (quite a contrast to the South's largest mansion), turn left when you drive out of Nottoway's parking lot. This puts you on Route 405, also called River Road, which runs in front of the mansion and beside the levee. Proceed toward Bayou Goula and watch for the *Chapel of the Madonna* on the

Political Louisiana

The marble halls of the Louisiana State Capitol (tallest in the country) have heard their share of political gossip. Political aficionados can watch the legislature in action from the galleries and, in the area near the elevators toward the rear of the main floor, speculate on whether the holes in the marble really date from the assassination of Huey Long. Long's statue stands atop his grave, just in front of the capitol. His son, former U.S. Senator Russell Long, posed for the statue.

Also on the capitol grounds is a plaque commemorating Louisianian Zachary Taylor, who was commandant of the U.S. Army barracks here when he was named president in 1848. Supposedly, the letter telling him of his election sat at the post office for several days before Taylor paid the postage due.

left. (My car clocked the distance at 4.3 miles.) A green sign on the road's right side announces: SMALLEST CHURCH IN THE WORLD/MADONNA CHAPEL. Unfortunately there's no place to park except on the roadside in front of the church, but at the time of my visit some members of a utility crew at work nearby assured me that this was quite all right.

You may feel a bit like Gulliver approaching a Lilliputian chapel as you open the gate of the fence surrounding this miniature church, which is about the size of a large closet. Mounted on the wall to the right of the door, you'll see a wooden box, which should contain a key to unlock the front door. If the key is not there, check the top of the door frame or ask at the house next door.

When I visited, several candles were burning, and three straight wooden chairs flanked each side of the altar. I was told that the church was built in 1890 by a devout woman to fulfill a vow she had made during her daughter's critical illness. An annual Mass is held here on August 15. You can sign a register and make a donation if you wish.

After this brief detour return to Route 1 (there's a cut-through near Bayou Goula) and head north toward Baton Rouge. A few miles north you may want to stop in downtown Plaquemine to see the locks, built in 1900, which once provided the only access to waterways west of the Mississippi. **Plaquemine Locks** (no longer in use) linked the navigable Bayou Plaquemine with the Mississippi River. Here you'll see the original lockhouse with exhibits on the river's traffic and history. The facility also features picnic grounds and an observation tower that affords a sweeping view of the Mississippi River. After visiting Plaquemine continue to Baton Rouge, about 15 miles north.

"Red Stick"

According to legend, **Baton Rouge**'s name came from a notation on a map used by French explorer Pierre le Moyne, sieur d'Iberville, and his brother, Jean Baptiste le Moyne, sieur de Bienville, who led an expedition up the Mississippi River in 1699. Iberville spotted a tall cypress pole smeared with animals' blood, which apparently marked the dividing line between the hunting grounds of the Bayou Goula and Houmas Native American tribes who shared this area. When Iberville jotted *"le bâton rouge"* (French for "red stick") on his map, little did he know that he had named what would become Louisiana's capital city.

Baton Rouge offers many attractions, but most of them hardly qualify as off the beaten path, particularly the State Capitol or a major college campus like Louisiana State University. You'll miss some unique places, however, if you bypass them. Many of the city's historic sites are clustered close to the **State Capitol**, which stands on the north side of the downtown area. You can't miss it—it's thirty-four stories high, the tallest state capitol in the United States. The observation tower on the twenty-seventh floor affords a panoramic view of the city. A special project of Governor Huey P. Long, the Capitol was completed in 1932. (Ironically, Long was later shot on the first floor of this building.)

Don't miss the **Old State Capitol,** which Mark Twain called "an atrocity on the Mississippi." Located at 100 North Boulevard in Baton Rouge, this Gothic Revival castle houses Louisiana's Center for Political and Governmental History (225–342–0500). Hours are 10:00 A.M. to 4:00 P.M. Tuesday through Saturday and noon to 4:00 P.M. Sunday. Tours take one hour; modest admission. You may also want to visit the **U.S.S. Kidd** (225–342–1942), a World War II destroyer, located downtown on the riverfront at the foot of Government Street. Except for major holidays, hours are 9:00 A.M. to 5:00 P.M. daily, and admission is charged.

The **Louisiana State University Museum of Art** (225–389–7200), which features a collection of more than 3,500 works of fine and decorative arts, is now housed in the new **Shaw Center for the Arts.** The museum occupies the fifth floor of the Shaw Center, which covers a full city block bordered by North Boulevard, Convention, Third, and Lafayette Streets in the heart of downtown Baton Rouge.

batonrouge stars

Joanne Woodward and critic Rex Reed both attended LSU. Filmmaker Steven Soderburgh, whose *Sex, Lies and Videotape* won a Palm award at the Cannes Film Festival, was also a Baton Rougean.

Located at 100 Lafayette Street across from the Old State Capitol, the handsome Shaw Center serves as a venue for LSU's Laboratory for Creative Arts and Technology, the Manship Theatre, and local Arts Council. Also housed here, the LSU School of Art Gallery features exhibits by LSU faculty members and students.

Before or after your gallery excursion, you can stop by the LSU Museum Store and/or enjoy a snack or meal at PJ's Coffee House and Wine Bar, Capital City Grill, or rooftop Japanese restaurant Tsunami, which affords a sweeping river view.

Check out an overview of the permanent collection, latest offerings, and upcoming exhibits at www.lsumoa.com. LSU Museum of Art hours run Tuesday through Saturday from 10:00 A.M. to 5:00 P.M., Thursday from 10:00 A.M. to 8:00 P.M., and Sunday from 1:00 to 5:00 P.M. The museum closes on Mondays and major holidays. Admission.

After your downtown sight-seeing tour, head toward the city's southwestern corner for a visit to **Louisiana State University.** LSU offers interesting attractions ranging from museums and a live Bengal tiger to Indian mounds

TOP ANNUAL EVENT IN "RED STICK"

Greater Baton Rouge State Fair
730 North Boulevard
Baton Rouge, mid-October
(225) 755–FAIR

and a Greek amphitheater. You'll find the campus 1.5 miles south of downtown Baton Rouge, between Highland Road and Nicholson Drive.

Stop first at the visitor information center, located on the corner of Dalrymple Drive and Highland Road, where you can pick up a parking permit (required Monday through Friday) and a campus map.

While on campus, stop by the *LSU Faculty Club* (225–578–2356) for lunch. Located on Highland Road across from the Parade Ground, the eatery is housed in a handsome Italianate-style structure that dates to 1939. The Faculty Club offers soups, salads, and sandwiches along with seafood, chicken, beef, and pasta entrees and desserts in an attractive setting, enhanced by easy listening music. Popular choices include the shrimp salad, gourmet burger, or glazed crabmeat sandwich on an English muffin with cheese and fruit. Whatever the talented pastry chef prepares will make a fitting finale for your meal. Maybe panna cotta will be featured when you visit. (See sidebar recipe.) Serving hours are Monday through Friday from 11:30 A.M. to 1:30 P.M. Prices are economical to moderate.

Afterward you can visit Memorial Tower, built in 1923 as a monument to Louisianians who died in World War I. Plans are now underway to set up a military museum here.

Take time to stroll to nearby Foster Hall, home of the *Museum of Natural Science,* to see dioramas depicting Louisiana's wildlife. On display are mounted specimens of birds, reptiles, and animals, including LSU's original

Casinos

Since Louisiana legalized gambling, there have been numerous gambling boats docked throughout the state. As is usual in Louisiana, the introduction of legal gambling was all very exciting, very political, and very controversial. If you like the constant electronic clamor of slot machines and you relish sitting in a room without clocks or windows, you're going to enjoy Louisiana casinos. The ones in Baton Rouge are on the Mississippi River (they are boats, but they seldom cruise) in the Catfish Town vicinity of restored, old-wharf-area buildings.

A Dessert for All Seasons

Straight to you from the pastry chef at the LSU Faculty Club comes this luscious dessert recipe. If you subscribe to the theory of eating dessert first because of life's uncertainty then you'll savor the following all-season treat, Panna Cotta with Strawberry–Vin Santo Sauce, and maybe forget all about lunch.

Italian for "cooked cream," Panna Cotta is a light, silky egg custard, sometimes flavored with caramel. It's served cold and is especially good in summer with fresh berries on top or drizzled with chocolate sauce. If perchance there's any custard left over, it's also great for breakfast. The chef compares it to crème brûlée without the caramelized top and suggests starting it one day ahead.

Panna Cotta with Strawberry–Vin Santo Sauce

Panna Cotta:

¼ cup cold water

4 teaspoons unflavored gelatin

4 cups whipping cream

1 cup sugar

1 tablespoon orange blossom honey

¼ teaspoon vanilla extract

1 tablespoon Vin Santo,* Muscat wine, or cream sherry

2 cups pine nuts (9 ounces)

Strawberry–Vin Santo Sauce (see recipe)

Additional pine nuts

Pour ¼ cup water into metal bowl; sprinkle gelatin over it. Let stand until gelatin softens, about 10 minutes. Set bowl in saucepan of simmering water. Stir just until gelatin dissolves, about 1 minute.

Combine cream, sugar, honey, and vanilla in heavy, large saucepan. Bring to a boil, stirring until sugar dissolves. Remove from heat. Add gelatin mixture and Vin Santo; whisk until well blended.

Divide 2 cups pine nuts among ten ¾-cup custard cups. Divide cream mixture among cups. Chill overnight.

Set cups in small bowl of warm water to loosen panna cotta, about 20 seconds each. Run small knife between panna cotta and custard cups. Invert panna cotta onto plates. Spoon Strawberry–Vin Santo sauce over. Sprinkle with additional pine nuts; serve.

Strawberry–Vin Santo Sauce

1 pound fresh strawberries, hulled and quartered (about 4 cups)

½ cup sugar

2 tablespoons Vin Santo*

¼ teaspoon vanilla extract

¼ teaspoon (packed) grated lemon peel

Puree 1 pound strawberries in food processor. Transfer puree to heavy large saucepan. Mix in sugar, Vin Santo, vanilla extract, and grated lemon peel. Simmer over medium-low heat, stirring often, until sauce is reduced to 2 cups, about 15 minutes. Cool. (Sauce can be prepared two days ahead. Cover and refrigerate.) Makes 10 servings.

*An Italian dessert wine available at some liquor stores and specialty foods stores.

Bengal tiger mascot. (You also can visit the current mascot, Mike V, who resides in an environmentally controlled home outside Tiger Stadium—a nearby sign reads GEAUX TIGERS!)

Before leaving campus make a point of seeing the 3,500-seat Greek amphitheater; the avenue of stately oak trees, planted as memorials for LSU alumni killed in World War II; and two intriguing Indian mounds believed to date from 3300 to 3800 B.C.

A short distance northwest of the campus, you'll find **BREC's Magnolia Mound Plantation** (225–343–4955), one of the state's oldest plantations. Once a 900-acre plantation extending from Tiger Stadium to the Mississippi River Bridge and back to Highland Road, it now occupies 16 acres. Even

lsusports

When the legislature is not in session, the best games in Baton Rouge are usually on the Louisiana State University campus. The Tigers field teams in every possible sport, and they do very well in most. Tiger Stadium earns its nickname "Death Valley" for the steep sides and the roaring hometown crowds. The baseball and basketball teams have gained national honors.

The Marching Tiger Band puts on spectacular halftime shows. It is said that the late governor Huey Long, who was a big LSU booster, wanted LSU to have a band big enough to spell out the full name of opponent Virginia Polytechnic Institute on the field. He got it.

though this historic site (owned by the Recreation and Park Commission of East Baton Rouge Parish) is sandwiched between bustling downtown Baton Rouge and LSU, it is more than two centuries removed. In the museum store, a diorama shows the locations of early outbuildings and also the plantation's original boundaries. Located at 2161 Nicholson Drive, the 1791 home serves as a lovely example of French Creole architecture. Surrounded by a grove of live oak and magnolia trees, the house stands on a ridge facing the Mississippi levee.

Magnolia Mound, authentically restored, is made of large cypress timbers joined by wooden pegs and packed with *bousillage*. Be sure to notice the quaint

Alligator Bayou Swamp Tours

Alligator Bayou (225–677–8297 or 888–3–SWAMPS), a wilderness tucked away into Baton Rouge's outskirts at 35019 Alligator Bayou Road, Prairieville, offers boat excursions complete with local flora and fauna. Hours vary by season. Frank Bonifay, Jim Ragland, Serenity, Tattoo, and their animal friends will treat you to an informative session combining history and ecology sprinkled with humor. Reservations required. Call for information on guided swamp tours. For a virtual visit, check out www.alligatorbayou.com.

iron latches and the carved woodwork. In the dining room you'll see an unusual buffet with locked wine compartments and a Napoleon mirror over the mantel. Other interesting furnishings include an overseer's desk in the plantation office, a pianoforte in the parlor, and an old rope bed. According to the museum's guide, the familiar expression "Good night; sleep tight" originated because some old-fashioned beds used rope-supported mattresses that had to be pulled taut periodically. Mattresses made with Spanish moss were used on plantation beds during summer months and were replaced by feather mattresses for winter.

colonialafricans

Recent historical research has revealed that Louisiana has a rich African-connected past. Historian Gwendolyn Midlo Hall's book, *Africans in Colonial Louisiana,* shows that, in the early years of French domination, Africans retained tribal ties, names, and language to a greater extent than realized, especially in this area. The Pointe Coupee district was headquarters for an unsuccessful revolt in 1795—organized not just by African slaves, but also by their white allies, Europeans holding the beliefs of French revolutionaries.

On the grounds you'll see both a kitchen garden and a crop garden and several outbuildings typical of early plantation life—a detached kitchen, a *pigeonnier,* and an overseer's house.

If you visit on Tuesday or Thursday from October through May, you may see bread or biscuits being made and smell chicken roasting. To illustrate the lifestyle of colonial Louisiana, the staff schedules ongoing activities like quilting and open-hearth cooking demonstrations plus three major events each year. Turning the calendar to December, typical holiday activities at Magnolia Mound include candlelight tours with costumed guides, simple period decorations, and a bonfire on the grounds to guide *le pere* Noel. Except for major holidays, hours run from 10:00 A.M. to 4 P.M. Monday through Saturday, and from 1:00 to 4:00 P.M. Sunday. Tours start hourly with the day's last tour at 3:00 P.M. Admission. Visit www.magnoliamound.org.

If you want to step back into the nineteenth century, drive to the junction of Interstate 10 and Essen Lane, where you'll find the entrance to an outdoor complex called ***Rural Life Museum and Windrush Gardens*** (225–765–2437).

The museum's grounds occupy part of a family plantation that Steele Burden and his sister Ione Burden donated to Louisiana State University. The 450-acre tract serves as a setting for the museum as well as an agricultural research station.

The folk museum consists of more than twenty-five old buildings collected from farms and plantations throughout the state. Instead of a "big house" (most farm families could not afford extravagant residences), you'll see a brick-front overseer's cottage with a parlor, dining room, and two bedrooms. The rooms

OTHER ATTRACTIONS WORTH SEEING IN RED STICK

Greater Baton Rouge Zoo
3601 Thomas Road
(225) 775–3877
Spend a pleasant afternoon on the zoo's walkways, then treat yourself to a miniature train ride.

Louisiana Naval War Memorial
305 South River Road
Baton Rouge
(225) 342–1942
In addition to the U.S.S. *Kidd,* the memorial on the riverfront holds the largest collection of ship models in the South. There is a replica of the gun deck of Old Ironsides (the U.S.S. *Constitution*) and the pilothouse of an 1880s steamboat, as well as a restored jet. Be sure to take a look at the Mississippi River while you're there.

Louisiana State Capitol grounds
Near the capitol is a sunken rose garden. The Pentagon Barracks, dating from 1819, once served as dormitories for LSU students back when the school was all-male and had a somewhat military regimentation—one of LSU's nicknames is "The Old War Skule." By 1906 the Pentagon housed female students and today it holds apartments for legislators. Those privileged to stay here can enjoy the Christmas spectacle at the capitol with long strings of colored lights adorning it.

Louisiana State University Campus
Highland Road and Nicholson Drive, Baton Rouge
The old part of the campus invites strolling, especially in spring when the azaleas are in bloom. This campus has been rated one of the ten most attractive in the country, and the warm red tile roofs and stuccoed loggias of the Italianate complex of core campus buildings has an inviting atmosphere. The campanile chimes the hours.

are furnished with authentic utilitarian pieces. Nearby stands a kitchen, detached from the main house because of the danger of fire.

A row of slave cabins and other rustic buildings paint a picture of austerity. In the sick house, the plantation's infirmary, you'll see rope beds, a tooth extractor (ca. 1800), and a shock treatment machine from the 1850s (which generated mild electrical charges for treating arthritis, nervous twitches, and other ailments).

You can also visit a commissary, smokehouse, schoolhouse, blacksmith's shop, gristmill, cane grinder, and sugarhouse. Other structures include a country church, pioneer's cabin, corncrib, potato house, shotgun house, Acadian house, and dogtrot house. The museum's big barn contains hundreds of items, including a voodoo exhibit, a 1905 Edison phonograph, plantation bells, bathtubs, irons, oxcarts, trade beads, an African birthing chair, and pirogues.

Call ahead for a one- to two-hour guided tour for ten or more persons. The museum is open from 8:30 A.M. to 5:00 P.M. daily. Admission is charged. Visit the Web site at http://rurallife.lsu.edu.

The Wandering River

The reason there is a Pointe Coupee (or "cut point") is that the Mississippi River, in its ceaseless fight to make a beeline to the Gulf, lopped off a turn and created a lake here. Think of the river as a garden hose whipping around on the grass. The force of water is seldom a steady pulse. Also consider the varying composition of the river's bed and its banks—some areas more firm than others, with soil constantly washing away. You can then begin to understand the quandary of the U.S. Army Corps of Engineers as it tries to tame this monster.

The most important building near here is the Old River Control Structure, which keeps the Mississippi from moving into the bed of the Atchafalaya and going south to Morgan City instead of proceeding eastward toward New Orleans. In the great flood of 1927, the Atchafalaya River basin was subject to dreadful flooding from the Mississippi.

To see an impressive collection of European antiques and architectural elements, head for **Fireside Antiques** (225–752–9565) at 14007 Perkins Road. Shop hours are Monday through Saturday from 10:00 A.M. to 5:00 P.M. View the inventory at www.firesideantiques.com.

Afterward, follow U.S. Highway 190 west to Livonia and into the French Creole country of Pointe Coupee Parish.

French Creole Country

Don't miss **Joe's "Dreyfus Store" Restaurant** (225–637–2625) at 2741 Maringouin Road West (also State Route 77 South) in Livonia. Bright, noisy, and popular, this jeans-and-Keds kind of place offers creative Creole cuisine in an old general store/pharmacy. The interior features displays of old-fashioned pharmaceutical products and nostalgic items, and Cream of Wheat posters line the walls. Try the marinated crab claws or turtle soup au sherry. Other specialties include crawfish entrees (seasonal), angel hair pasta with shrimp and crabmeat, stuffed eggplant, crab and spinach au gratin, and pork loin. For dessert, order the bread pudding with rum sauce. Prices are moderate. Restaurant hours are Tuesday through Thursday from 11:00 A.M. to 8:30 P.M. Friday and Saturday 11:00 A.M. to 9:30 P.M., and Sunday from 11:00 A.M. to 3:30 P.M. See www.joes-dreyfusstorerestaurant.com for some background.

Afterward, follow State Route 78 north until it intersects State Route 1. You'll take a left here for **New Roads,** stopping first at nearby **Parlange Plantation** (225–638–8410), on State Route 1 just north of the State Route 78 intersection. Overlooking False River, a lovely oxbow lake created when the mighty Mississippi River changed its mind, this galleried West Indies–type home built by the

July 4th Boat Parade
New Roads, July 4
(225) 638–3500

Noel sur la Fausse Riviere
New Roads, first Saturday in December
(225) 638–3500

Marquis Vincent de Ternant dates from 1750. A National Historic Landmark (a status attained by few structures), Parlange is still a working plantation of 2,000 acres and home to descendants of the original family. On a house tour, you'll see eight generations of Parlange and Brandon family possessions, rare antique furnishings, china, and crystal.

The main salon features unusual corner-hung family portraits. The guide will tell you about Virginie (Mme. Pierre Gautreau), who posed for John Singer Sargent's then-startling *Portrait of Madame X* now housed in New York's Metropolitan Museum of Art. A house tour includes the wine cellar, which contains wooden brick molds used in the home's construction, and *pigeonniers* flanking the entrance. Parlange is open daily by appointment from 9:30 A.M. to 4:30 P.M. If possible, schedule your visit one week ahead. Admission is charged.

Continue north to the charming town of New Roads, where you should consider making *Jubilee!* (225–638–8333) your base. Virginia and Ovide De Soto offer bed-and-breakfast with a big serving of warm hospitality in their lovely 1840 Creole cottage on three acres facing the Mississippi River. Located at 11704 Pointe Coupee Road (Highway 420) near the ferry, the home is furnished with antiques, including many unusual accessory pieces. Architectural

Into the Hills

The soil in this region is loess—a rich but powdery mix that tends to form deep gorges. This formed the **Tunica Hills** region near Angola, where the deep ravines around Little Bayou Sara are the haunt of a large number of bird species, some of the last bottomland hardwood forest, and some buried treasure.

The treasure in question was in the form of grave goods of the Tunica-Biloxi Indian tribe. The Native American group lived in this region in the 1700s and traded extensively with the French. Their graves, with contents of precious objects, contained an assortment of French trade goods, ceramics, beads, and metal, as well as handcrafted items. Ownership of the treasures passed from the person who dug them up to Harvard University and finally to the Tunica-Biloxi tribe, who now house the collection in a museum on tribal land near Marksville.

OTHER ATTRACTIONS WORTH SEEING IN FRENCH CREOLE COUNTRY

West Baton Rouge Museum
845 North Jefferson Avenue
Port Allen
(225) 336–2422
A plantation cabin, an 1830 French Creole cottage, and a 1904 sugar mill can all be seen and enjoyed here.

West Baton Rouge Parish Tourist Commission Office
2750 North Westport Drive
Port Allen
(800) 654–9701
Take a break and enjoy a video and some displays on this mostly rural area across the river from Baton Rouge.

features include walk-through windows and eight fireplaces complete with original cypress mantels. The couple's newly added cottage opposite the pool features a double Jacuzzi.

Virginia serves a full country breakfast and will share some of the home's history with you. Ovide (a descendant of Spanish explorer Hernando de Soto) can direct you to some interesting off-the-beaten-path spots. At several nearby points, you can drive up the levee via a single-lane dirt-gravel road for a sweeping view of the river. Amenities include a pool and sometimes calliope music from passing paddle wheelers. Rates are moderate.

After exploring Pointe Coupee Parish, head for the St. Francisville Ferry. Except for the period between midnight and 4:00 A.M., the ferry leaves twice hourly, at a quarter past and a quarter to the hour. While waiting, you'll see people standing around chatting or perhaps Miss Emily or an enterprising youngster going from car to car selling bags of parched peanuts, pralines, or soft drinks. Don't wait too long before sampling this soon-to-vanish mode of transportation from New Roads to St. Francisville. In lieu of a ferry, future travelers will drive across a long single-span bridge connecting the parishes of Pointe Coupee and West Feliciana.

The Felicianas

After crossing the Mississippi River, follow the ferry road (State Route 10, which soon becomes Ferdinand Street) up a hill into *St. Francisville*, a picturesque town in a tranquil setting of live oak, magnolias, and pine trees. A fascinating place to visit, this quaint village in West Feliciana Parish retains its nineteenth-century charm. Many plantation houses, built during the early 1800s, lie tucked away in the surrounding countryside.

About a mile from the ferry, you'll see a sign for *Shadetree Inn* (225–635–6116) on your right. Perched on a hill at the corner of Ferdinand and Royal Streets, Shadetree offers bed-and-breakfast in three romantic hideaways: The Loft, Sun Porch, and Gardener's Cottage, each with its own ambience. Enticements include a treetop deck along with hammock and swings on the grounds—perfect for sipping coffee, reading, and listening to the birds (whose avian ancestors attracted John James Audubon to this area named Feliciana). You'll enjoy strolling the grounds here and may see squirrels, chipmunks, and deer. A cicada chorus also provides evening music. A continental breakfast of juice, coffee, and pastries with an assortment of jams, jellies, and lemon curd awaits. Moderate to deluxe rates. Visit this retreat online at www.shadetreeinn.com.

Even though you'll want to linger at Shadetree, the village begs to be explored and lends itself beautifully to walking.

Clustered along Ferdinand and Royal Streets, you'll pass lovely houses, antique shops, offices, banks, and churches. The National Historic District contains 146 structures.

At 11621 Ferdinand Street, you'll see *Grace Episcopal Church,* an English Gothic–style structure surrounded by a canopy of moss-covered oak trees. Fighting came to a halt for the funeral of Union naval officer John E. Hart during the Civil War. Hart had asked for a Masonic burial, and his fellow Confederate Masons honored the deathbed request. A granite slab in the churchyard cemetery tells his story.

battleonthe bluffs

The State Historic Site at **Port Hudson,** 236 U.S. Highway 61, Jackson (225–654–3775 or 888–677–3400), marks the site of a Civil War battle, one in which African-American troops fighting in the Union Army acquitted themselves well in their first outing. Union troops besieged the Confederate defenders of the high bluffs from May until July 1863, when starvation forced them to surrender.

The site today includes a museum, guided trails, and a picnic area. There are often reenactments with authentically clothed and outfitted soldiers of both sides.

Hours are 9:00 A.M. to 5:00 P.M. daily except for major holidays. Modest admission.

Housed in a 1905 bank building at 9814 Royal Street, you'll find the *Grandmother's Buttons* (225–635–4107) retail shop with unique bracelets, brooches, earrings, cuff links, and watches. You can browse through the *Button Museum,* which features multitudes of intricate buttons in pearl, glass, enamel, brass, cut steel, jet lustre glass, celluloid, horn, and pewter—all with pertinent identification.

When owner Susan Davis stepped into her grandmother's sewing room one afternoon more than a decade ago, she had no notion that the buttons she saw there would change both her life and that of her husband, Donny, a former farmer and wildlife biologist. The button jewelry that Susan crafted in an upstairs bedroom blossomed from a budding supplemental income into a booming business for both of them. The couple subsequently hired a designer and production staff and started showing jewelry at major markets across the country. Prominent stores, museum shops, boutiques, and catalogs now carry the Grandmother's Buttons line nationwide.

"Our museum star is the rare George Washington inaugural button," said Susan. "We're also doing more reproductions now, like perfume buttons." Check out the bountiful possibilities at www.grandmothersbuttons.com.

Next, continue to the **West Feliciana Historical Society Museum** (225–635– 6330), which also houses the town's visitor center, at 11757 Ferdinand Street, for a map detailing a driving-walking tour of St. Francisville. While here take time to see the museum's dioramas, displays of vintage clothing, documents, maps, and other interesting exhibits. The museum is open from 9:00 A.M. to 5:00 P.M. Monday through Saturday. Sunday hours are 9:30 A.M. to 5:00 P.M. Admission to the museum is free.

Continue to the **Myrtles** (225–635–6277), an elegant home located at 7747 U.S. Highway 61, 1 mile north of Route 10. The plantation's name comes from

The State Pen

Want to see an electric chair? The Louisiana State Penitentiary Museum has one, and you can see it from 8:00 A.M. to 4:30 P.M. Tuesday through Friday, and Saturday from 9:00 A.M. to 5:00 P.M. Call (225) 655–2592 for information. The museum is located at **Angola State Penitentiary,** at the end of Highway 66.

Also on view are exhibits of confiscated prisoner-made weapons, the script of the movie *Dead Man Walking* (the protagonist was an Angola resident), and various guns and paraphernalia, including photos of all those who sparked a firsthand acquaintance with the seat in question. Grim but unique.

The penitentiary hosts an interesting biannual event, the Prison Rodeo, held at the prison each Sunday in October plus the third weekend of April.

One of the best-known prisoners ever to reside at Angola was Huddie "Leadbelly" Ledbetter, twelve-string guitarist, Louisiana native, and incomparable blues artist. Leadbelly is best known for his composition "Goodnight Irene." His song was good enough to win him a reprieve from Governor O. K. Allen and get him out of Angola.

For additional background, go to www.angolamuseum.org.

the many crepe myrtles on the grounds. The oldest portion of the house was built around 1796 by General David Bradford, leader of the Whiskey Rebellion in Pennsylvania. Later owners enlarged the Myrtles and added wide verandas trimmed in "iron lace," one of the house's trademarks. Inside, you'll see Italian marble mantels, mirrored doorknobs, and Irish and French crystal chandeliers. The house is also noted for its elaborate interior plasterwork—and its resident ghosts.

Overnight accommodations feature beautifully furnished bedrooms and a continental breakfast. Rates are moderate to deluxe. Except for major holidays, the mansion is open for tours from 9:00 A.M. to 5:00 P.M. daily. Mystery tours are given on Friday and Saturday evenings. Admission is charged.

Varnedoe's Carriage House Restaurant (225–635–2635) offers upscale down-South cuisine on the grounds of the Myrtles Plantation. The staff serves lunch Tuesday through Friday from 11:00 A.M. to 2:00 P.M.; dinner hours run Tuesday through Thursday from 5:00 to 9:00 P.M. and until 10:00 P.M. Friday and Saturday, with Sunday brunch from 10:30 A.M. to 3:00 P.M. For more information on the mansion, check out www.myrtlesplantation.com.

Afterward, continue to ***Butler Greenwood*** (225–635–6312), a plantation located 2.2 miles north of town at 8345 US 61. Watch for a sign on the left marking the tree-canopied drive that leads past a sunken garden and through a parklike setting. Before Hurricane Andrew blew in, says owner Anne Butler, one could not see sky through the arching live oaks—many of which grew from acorns brought from Haiti in 1799 by a planter's family.

A prolific writer whose published works span both fiction and nonfiction, Anne sandwiches in sentences between family responsibilities and guests. Her latest books include *Audubon Plantation Country Cookbook* and *Bayou Plantation Country Cookbook with Photos*.

On a tour of the English–style house, you'll see a formal Victorian parlor with a twelve-piece matched set of Louis XV rosewood furniture upholstered in its original red velvet. A Brussels carpet, French pier mirrors, and floor-to-ceiling windows topped by gilt cornices echo the room's elegance. Other treasures include a Prudent Mallard bed and dresser, oil portraits, and an extensive collection of vintage clothing. House tours are offered daily from 9:00 A.M. to 5:00 P.M. Admission.

Accommodations, which include a continental breakfast, range from the plantation's original detached kitchen of slave-made brick dating from 1796, when Spain ruled the region, and the cook's nineteenth-century cottage to eight cottages set against a lovely backdrop of greenery and a pond where ducks glide and deer come to drink. Rates are moderate to deluxe. Preview the property at www.butlergreenwood.com.

TOP ANNUAL EVENTS IN FELICIANAS

The Audubon Pilgrimage
St. Francisville, third full weekend
in March
(225) 635–6330

**Jackson Assembly Antiques
Festival and Tour**
Jackson, last weekend in March
(225) 634–7155

**Angola Arts and Crafts Show
and Sale**
Angola State Penitentiary
Angola, early April and Sundays in
October
(225) 635–6330

Angola Penitentiary Inmate Rodeo
Angola State Penitentiary
Angola, Sundays in October and one
weekend in April
(225) 635–6330

The Southern Garden Symposium
St. Francisville, October
(225) 635–6330

**The Myrtles Plantation Halloween
Extravaganza**
St. Francisville, October, Halloween night
(225) 635–6330 or (800) 809–0565

Highland Games of Louisiana
Jackson, November
(225) 634–7155
www.highlandgames.com

Christmas in the Country
St. Francisville, first weekend in
December
(225) 635–6330

For serious birders, artist-naturalist Murrell Butler offers bird and nature walks. Currently, his local checklist contains 138 species, and 78 of these nest on his property.

After leaving Butler Greenwood, continue north to nearby ***Catalpa Plantation*** (225–635–3372 or 225–247–4134) at 9508 Old US 61. Here, Mary Thompson carries on a tradition of hospitality that goes back six generations. Mary's late mother, Mamie Fort Thompson gave delightful tours of her ancestral home that she described as "lived in, loved, and used."

Just as Miss Mamie shared personal anecdotes while pointing out various pieces and paintings, such as the Thomas Sully portrait of her grandmother Sarah Turnbull from nearby Rosedown Plantation, so does Mary, who offers guests a sherry in honor of her mother.

Much of the home's china, crystal, and other decorative items came from Rosedown. Some beautiful silver pieces only survived the Civil War because "they were wrapped in burlap and buried beneath the pond," Mary explains, showing visitors through her home filled with exceptional antiques such as a rosewood Mallard parlor set, Playel piano, Sevres whale-oil lamp, crystal cranberry champagne glasses, antique china, porcelain, and a rare vase from the Vatican.

Mary is delighted to offer tours of her family home by appointment. To schedule one, please call between 10:00 A.M. and 4:00 P.M. Admission is charged. Preview the plantation at www.catalpaplantation.com.

Afterward, you may want to visit the **Cottage Plantation** (225–635–3674) at 10528 Cottage Lane. To reach the Cottage continue north on US 61. Watch for a turnoff sign on the right side of the road, then follow the narrow lane that winds through the woods. You'll cross a small wooden bridge just before you reach the plantation complex.

Definitely off the beaten path, the main house is located in an idyllic setting, thick with trees draped in Spanish moss. If you have trouble locating the Cottage, you might be interested in knowing that Andrew Jackson found it when he and his officers stayed here on their way home after the Battle of New Orleans—without today's road signs.

The 1795 galleried two-story cottage contains most of its original furniture. Outbuildings include the original detached kitchen, one-room school, smokehouse, slave cabins, and other dependencies from bygone days.

Except for holidays, the home opens daily for tours from 9:30 A.M. to 4:30 P.M. and offers bed-and-breakfast. Rates are moderate. Visit www.cottageplantation.com to see more.

Consider wandering farther off the beaten path to **Greenwood Plantation** (225–655–4475) at 6838 Highland Road, St. Francisville. Now the home of the Richard Barnes family, this replica of an 1830 Greek Revival mansion rose from its 1960 ashes to reclaim the area within its twenty-eight surviving columns. Beautifully restored to original specifications with a copper roof, period furnishings, and silver doorknobs and hinges, Greenwood Plantation served as the setting for six movies, including *North and South*. Visitors can choose from his-

savvyeating

North of Lake Pontchartrain the menus reflect Southern specialties. Look for barbecue and fried catfish and ask for sweetened iced tea.

One of the enduring restaurant phenomena in the Florida Parishes is the popularity of the all-you-can-eat catfish place. They dot the highways and all offer the same dining experience: seats at communal tables and endless trips to the buffet for an array of fried seafood, side dishes, and desserts, all served with sweet iced tea or cold drinks (beer is sometimes available).

To experience this at its apex, drive up Highway 21 north of Covington to Bush.

The House of Seafood Buffet huddles in a blue cement-block building surrounded by a vast parking lot that quickly fills. For less than $20 you get catfish plus everything from barbecued ribs to alligator with fried okra and some boudin thrown in. Hours are 4:00 to 10:00 P.M. Thursday and Friday, and 3:00 to 10:00 P.M. Saturday.

torical, agricultural, or movie tours. Hours run 9:00 A.M. to 5:00 P.M. daily. Admission is charged. The plantation also offers bed-and-breakfast Moderate rates. View the property at www.greenwoodplantation.com.

Afterward, return to town and *Rosedown Plantation State Historic Site* (225–635–3332 or 888–376–1867) at 12501 Highway 10, St. Francisville. The property's classic Greek Revival mansion dates to 1835 and was built by Martha and Daniel Turnbull, who patterned the plantation's lovely formal gardens after those they visited on their European honeymoon. They were especially inspired by the gardens at Versailles, and their avenues of shrubs and trees, formal parterres, and classical landscapes reflect a seventeenth-century French influence.

You'll enjoy strolling through these gardens of winding paths with vintage plantings and early varieties of azaleas, camellias, rare trees, and ancient live oaks. Ranked among the nation's most significant historic gardens, Rosedown's gardens are especially delightful in spring.

"Rosedown is one of the most complete antebellum sites in the United States," said a staffer. "We have twenty-eight acres of formal gardens, and the house contains 85 to 90 percent of its original furnishings, which is highly unusual for an antebellum site."

Touring the home, you'll see some lovely period pieces including the music room's original piano and a charming nursery filled with family toys.

OTHER ATTRACTIONS WORTH SEEING IN FELICIANA

Afton Villa Gardens
US 61
St. Francisville
(225) 635–6773 or (504) 861–7365
Around the ruins of what had been the Afton Villa Plantation is now a beautiful garden to delight the senses. One of the finest of the Southern gardens, it has been lovingly cared for and restored by its New Orleans owners. Open March through June and October through December 1. Admission.

Audubon Pilgrimage in mid-March
Small Southern towns with a wealth of older homes put on these springtime festivals to showcase their architectural heritage. Flowers are in bloom and

everything sparkles. You will find private homes to tour and your guides will be local volunteers, usually in costume for the event. There is entertainment available in the evening after you've seen one "petticoat table" or one set of "Old Paris china" too many. Call the West Feliciana Parish Tourist Commission at (225) 635–6330 for details.

Casa de Sue Winery & Vineyards
14316 Hatcher Road
Clinton
(225) 683–5937
Tours available (call first) of Louisiana's first licensed winery, open daily except Sunday. See www.casadesuewinery.com.

One Big Fair

At the King Cabin a mess of greens is simmering on the back of a woodstove and a pone of corn bread is in the oven. All's fine at *Mile Branch Settlement* and the rambling community of log buildings, assembled from throughout Washington Parish. It is inhabited by folks in nineteenth-century clothes who cook, make soap, grind corn, fuss over chickens, and in general live a pioneer lifestyle for the four days (Wednesday through Saturday) of the *Washington Parish Free Fair,* held the third week in October.

The largest free country fair in the nation, this annual event brings to Franklinton an enormous number of visitors and depopulates the rest of the parish. There's entertainment on an outdoor stage (amateurs mostly, but with country stars at night) as well as a rodeo, 4-H animals (don't miss the judging of squealing little pigs), and prizes for the best pies, roses, and art. At the Mile Branch Settlement area there is a spelling bee, plus a country store with a big wheel of cheese for slicing, and a log church where you're invited to sing hymns all day. Have a barbecue chicken lunch at the Bowling Green School booth.

Take Highway 25 north from Covington to Franklinton and step back in time. It's probably the best (and one of the few) alcohol-free festivals in the state as well.

The property is open daily from 9:00 A.M. to 5:00 P.M., with tours given from 10:00 A.M. to 4:00 P.M. Tours take forty-five minutes to an hour and start on the hour. Admission.

Rosedown is a port of call for selected voyages offered by the Delta Queen Steamboat Company. Passengers can board a vessel in New Orleans and spend an afternoon exploring the mansion and grounds at Rosedown as part of their excursion.

To learn about artist John James Audubon, visit *Oakley House* (225–635–3739 or 888–677–2838), the focal point of the *Audubon State Historic Site* located at 11788 Louisiana Highway 965. West Feliciana's location on the Mississippi Valley flyway lures migrating birds, and Audubon created many of his bird studies while working here as a tutor. Numerous first-edition Audubon prints line the walls at Oakley, restored as a museum with surrounding formal gardens, nature trails, and wildlife sanctuary. Each year during the third weekend in March, St. Francisville hosts an *Audubon Pilgrimage* featuring tours of area plantation homes and gardens. Modest admission. Except for Thanksgiving, Christmas, and New Year's days, hours run from 9:00 A.M. to 5:00 P.M. daily.

Afterward, follow Route 965 to *The Bluffs Country Club and Resort* (225–634–5222 or 888–634–3410) with suites within walking distance of golf, tennis, pool, and restaurant. Rates are moderate. Travelers can enjoy steaks, seafood, and more at Cocodrie's Restaurant on the premises.

Designed by Arnold Palmer, the championship golf course continues to collect accolades. Hundreds of azaleas and native dogwoods supplement the sylvan setting and enhance sweeping swaths of greenery punctuated by high bluffs. Advance tee times are required. Check out www.thebluffs.com.

From the Bluffs, follow State Route 10 east to Jackson, which offers a host of historical attractions and a winery. In a colonnaded Spanish mission-style structure at 1848 Charter Street (also State Route 10), travelers can stop by the *Feliciana Cellars Winery* (225–634–7982) for free tours and tastings. Under the direction of Devin Barringer, the winery currently makes several muscadine vintages plus a sparkling wine and a dry white wine, Blanc du Bois.

In the gift shop, decorated with big, bright banners, you'll also find muscadine grape jellies, jams, and bar supplies. Except for major holidays, the facility opens daily, closing at 5:00 P.M. From Monday through Saturday, hours start at 10:00 A.M.. and on Sunday at 1:00 P.M. See www.felicianacellars.com.

Nearby at 1740 Charter Street, the *Old Centenary Inn* (225–634–5050) offers rooms furnished with antiques and equipped with whirlpool baths. Owner Leroy Harvey imported the life-size statue of a Scottish Highlander from the British Isles to symbolize the parish's Anglo-Saxon heritage. The handsome mahogany bar embellished with stained glass and brass once served an English pub, and the grilled lift that takes you to the upstairs guest rooms also came from England. The inn offers eight lovely antique-filled rooms and an inviting courtyard plus a full Southern breakfast. Rates are moderate. Check out the property at www.oldcentenaryinn.com.

Don't miss the *Republic of West Florida Museum* (225–634–7444 or 225–634–7379) in Old Hickory Village at 3406 College Street, Jackson. Exhibits include vintage cars, horse-drawn carriages, a restored cotton gin from the 1880s, and a working theater pipe organ from the 1920s. Hours are 10:00 A.M. to 5:00 P.M. Thursday through Saturday and 1:00 to 5:00 P.M. on Sunday. Admission is modest. From mid-March to mid-November, the Old Hickory Railroad offers rides every Saturday and Sunday (weather permitting) at 3:00 P.M. The narrow-gauge train transports visitors from the museum to various local sites. Click on www.louisianasteamtrain.com for more details. Further information is also available from the Feliciana Chamber of Commerce at (225) 634–7155.

Continue to *Centenary State Historic Site* (225–634–7925 or 888–677–2364) at the corner of College and Pine Streets for a tour of the restored 1800s home of a former professor with exhibits on pre–Civil War education in Louisiana. Guides interpret early college life and conduct walks across campus.

A "Berry" Good Louisiana Breakfast

While in Jackson, don't miss **Milbank Historic House** (225–634–5901), a ca. 1836 classic Greek Revival town home that housed the town's first bank. Located at 3045 Bank Street, the home boasts museum-quality antiques. Guests sleep in Mallard beds and sit down to a full breakfast at a table graced with a candelabra commissioned by Napoleon III.

In the far-reaching aftermath of Hurricane Katrina on August 29, 2005, Milbank House offered shelter to many people escaping the storm, said manager Marjorie Collamer, including historian Julie Martin. She "found her way to us after losing her home, The Old Spanish Customs House, ca. 1787, the oldest building in Bay St. Louis, Mississippi," Collamer said. "She was very grateful to have found us, and we are left humbled by this experience."

Hours for Milbank House tours and the Old Post Office Gift Shop run Monday through Saturday from 10:00 A.M. to 5:00 P.M., and on Sunday from 1:00 to 4:00 P.M. Visit www.milbankbandb.com or e-mail milbankinn01@bellsouth.net.

Milbank offers bed-and-breakfast accommodations, and rates are moderate. The home is also open for historic tours. Overnight guests can enjoy delicious homemade breakfast bread, featuring local seasonal blueberries, strawberries, or ripened persimmons. But, in case you can't wait, here's the recipe:

Leila's Strawberry Bread

3 cups all-purpose flour
1½ teaspoons baking soda
1 pinch salt
1 tablespoon cinnamon
1½ cups sugar
3 eggs

1¼ cups vegetable oil
3 cups fresh Louisiana strawberries, sliced
1 cup Louisiana pecans, chopped
1 teaspoon vanilla

In a mixing bowl, combine dry ingredients. Add eggs, oil, strawberries, and pecans. Stir until all ingredients are moist. Place in well-greased loaf pans and bake at 350 degrees for 1 hour or until done. Check with toothpick. Enjoy!

On the way to West Wing Dormitory (complete with historical graffiti), you'll see the remains of the East Wing. Except for major holidays, the site is open daily from 9:00 A.M. to 5:00 P.M., and admission is modest.

In Clinton, which became the parish seat in 1824, you'll see the **East Feliciana Parish Courthouse.** This stately Greek Revival structure, with twenty-eight columns and a domed, octagonal cupola atop a hipped roof, serves as the town's centerpiece. Be sure to walk around to the back of the

naturewalk

St. Tammany Parish has the **Northlake Nature Center,** with a pleasant marked nature trail through varying terrain, on Highway 190 near the entrance to Fontainebleau State Park.

courthouse, where you'll see a row of Greek Revival buildings that date from 1840 to 1860. These cottages, collectively known as Lawyers' Row, have also been designated a National Historic Landmark. Nearby, you can take in the Community Street Market held year-round on the first Saturday of each month from 8:00 A.M. to 1:00 P.M.

From Clinton take Route 10 east until you intersect Interstate 55. Travel south toward Hammond and then take the Springfield exit.

Turf and Swamp

Near Hammond you can visit ***Kliebert's Alligator & Turtle Farm*** (985–345–3617), an interesting stop (unless you're traveling during winter when alligators hibernate). Located at 41067 West Yellow Water Road, this unique facility is the world's largest working alligator farm. Harvey Kliebert and his son-in-law, Bruce Mitchell, operate the reptile farm.

The family has been raising alligators for a long time. You'll probably see Big Fred, now 16 feet long, who was hatched here almost half a century ago. The farm's alligators surpass wild alligators in size because they're well fed. Feeding more than 5,000 alligators, a number of which measure from 9 to 17 feet long, requires plenty of food. The alligators eat chicken, nutria, fish, and everything Harvey, who traps in winter, brings home.

During June and July, if you're lucky, you may observe a procedure called "taking the eggs," whereby two staff members, using long sticks, retrieve the alligators' eggs. Because these reptiles do not relish relinquishing their eggs, the collection process can prove quite challenging. The eggs are then placed in incubators and hatched to restock the farm.

In addition to alligators, you'll see thousands of turtles as well as a snake pit and a bird rookery. During spring, flocks of egrets and herons nest at the farm. In the gift shop, you can buy alligator meat, sausage, and reptile novelties.

A guided walking tour of the farm takes about forty-five minutes. Except for the period from November 1 through March 1, the farm is open daily. Tours are offered starting at noon and ending around dark. Admission. Visit www.klieberttours.com and see more.

After visiting the alligators head southeast to nearby ***Ponchatoula***—population 5,475. Already recognized as "Strawberry Capital of the World," the town flaunts a new title, "America's Antique City." Located at the junction of U.S. Highway 51 and Route 22, Ponchatoula takes its name from Choctaw Indian words for "hanging hair" (a reference to the ubiquitous Spanish moss dangling from area trees).

Ponchatoula's rebirth as an antiques mecca happened in less than three years. "We went from twenty-four vacant downtown buildings to total occupancy," says local Realtor and Main Street Program manager Charlene Daniels, one of the driving forces in the town's restoration.

Well over 200 dealers offer their wares for shoppers who love poking among yesterday's treasures, antiques, crafts, bric-a-brac, and collectibles. Strolling along the sidewalk, you see changing still-life compositions—a barber pole balanced against an antique pie safe, a rocking chair draped with a crazy quilt, or a hobbyhorse, doll, and vintage buggy.

Stop by the ***Ponchatoula Country Market*** (985–386–9580) in the heart of town. Housed in an 1854 historic depot, this bazaar offers booths of handcrafted items, antiques, collectibles, homemade jellies, and pastries. Hours are 10:00 A.M. to 5:00 P.M. Monday through Saturday and noon to 5:00 P.M. on Sunday. Beside the railroad station, you can visit the Mail Car Art Gallery, a restored baggage-mail car featuring the work of local artists. You may want to say hello to the town's mascot, "Old Hardhide." Not your average alligator, this one boasts his own bank account and local newspaper column (in which he espouses opinions that others dare not). He lives in a large wire cage in front of the railroad station.

Across the street, you'll find the ***Collinswood School Museum.*** This old-fashioned schoolhouse, which dates from around 1876, contains artifacts and memorabilia pertaining to the area's history. At 180 East Pine Street, browse through ***Ponchatoula Feed and Seed*** (985–386–3506), an old-fashioned store that carries pet, farm, and garden supplies, baby chicks, hardware, wind chimes, gifts, and bedding plants.

mardigras, countrystyle

Mardi Gras, the Tuesday before Ash Wednesday, six weeks before Easter, is celebrated in Covington, Slidell, Mandeville, and Bogalusa. Even Bush has a truck parade the prior Saturday. Parade schedules will be in the *Times-Picayune* and in local papers. Bogalusa's parade is the Saturday before Mardi Gras and draws a huge crowd. If you have kids and want to catch lots of throws, consider going to Bogalusa.

While continuing your exploration in downtown Ponchatoula, stop for lunch or dinner at ***O'Donnell's Restaurant*** (985–386–4077) at 131 Southwest Railroad Avenue. Try the jumbo lump crab cake salad. Prices are moderate.

TOP ANNUAL EVENTS IN TURF AND SWAMP

Amite Oyster Festival
Amite, late March to early April
(985) 748–5161

Ponchatoula Strawberry Festival
Ponchatoula, early April
(985) 386–6677 or (800) 542–7520

The Great Louisiana Bird Fest
Covington, mid-April
(800) 634–9443.

Independence Italian Festival
Highway 40 East at Pine Street
Independence, third weekend in April
(800) 542–7520

Bayou Lacombe Pirogue Races
Slidell, first Saturday in June
(800) 634–9443

Wooden Boat Festival
Madisonville, mid-October
(800) 634–9443

Tangipahoa Parish Fair
Amite, first weekend in October
(800) 542–7520 or (985) 748–8632
www.tangifair.org

Washington Parish Free Fair
Franklinton, third week in October
(985) 839–5228

Fanfare
Southeastern Louisiana University
Hammond, October
(985) 543–4366

Three Rivers Art Festival
Covington, second weekend in
November
(800) 634–9443

Store hours in town generally run from 10:00 A.M. to 5:00 P.M. Wednesday through Sunday. (About half the shops close on Monday and Tuesday.) Visit www.ponchatoulachamber.com for upcoming events.

On your way out, stop by *Taste of Bavaria,* a bakery and restaurant on the town's western outskirts. You can pick up some great German breads and pastries to go or enjoy a meal on the premises.

From Ponchatoula, take Route 22 east to St. Tammany Parish and the New Orleans Northshore. Here, you'll find charming towns, recreation options galore, enchanting bed-and-breakfasts, dining gems, and more. Stop first in Madisonville, a lovely waterside town on the northern shore of Lake Pontchartrain with several fine restaurants, shops, and an interesting maritime museum with artifacts from the town's boat-building era, all within a stroll of the riverfront.

Enjoy a casual family lunch or dinner at *Morton's Seafood Restaurant* (985–845–4970) at 702 Water Street. A red and white sign alerts diners to HOT BOILED SEAFOOD WHEN ARROW IS FLASHING.

Don't miss *Friends Coastal Restaurant* (985–845–7303), located at 407 St. Tammany Street. The seafood is scrumptious, and you can look out over the Tchefuncta River as you dine.

The restaurant opens at 11:00 A.M. Tuesday through Sunday. It closes at 9:00 P.M. on weeknights and Sunday, and at 10:00 P.M. on Friday and Saturday. Prices are moderate, and reservations are recommended.

Save time for touring *Lake Pontchartrain Basin Maritime Museum* (985–845–9200), which also serves as a research center. Located at 133 Mabel Drive, the facility takes you back to days when the town served as a center for shipbuilding and riverboat traffic between New Orleans and the Northshore. You'll see a full-sized replica of the first Civil War submarine, the *Pioneer,* predecessor of the famed CSS *Hunley.* The restoration enthusiast will enjoy the collection of vintage and fully operational 1940s–era outboard motors—Johnson Sea Horses, Evinrudes, and Mercurys.

Hours are Tuesday through Saturday from 10:00 A.M. to 4:00 P.M., and on Sunday from noon to 4:00 P.M. Modest admission. For more information on exhibits and activities, click on www.lpbmaritimemuseum.org.

Two miles east of Madisonville on Route 22, you'll find *Fairview-Riverside State Park* (985–845–3318 or 888–677–3247), which offers great fishing, camping, and picnicking, as well as an old summer home available for touring. Continue on to Mandeville, almost within shouting range.

A short distance southeast of Mandeville at 62883 Highway 1089, you'll discover *Fontainebleau State Park* (985–624–4443 or 888–677–3668), which covers 2,700 acres on the shores of Lake Pontchartrain. The park features the brick ruins of an old sugar mill, and the *Tammany Trace* runs through this property. Hours are 7:00 A.M. to 9:00 P.M. year-round. To better accommodate campers, closing time is 10:00 P.M. on Friday and Saturday.

Because Hurricane Katrina badly damaged the property, the park is not fully functional at this time. Currently, the facility offers limited camping, but no pool or beach use. Plans are in the works to rebuild picnic pavilions and offer future amenities. Call before visiting to learn how repairs are progressing.

You'll want to explore the Tammany Trace, the state's first rails-to-trails project, which stretches almost 31 miles and connects Covington, Abita Springs, Mandeville (crossing through Fontainebleau State Park), Lacombe, and Slidell. A good place to start is the *Mandeville Trailhead* (985–624–3147) at 675 Lafitte Street with parking, restroom facilities, and information. Learn more at www.mandevilletrailhead.com. By the way, if you visit this site on Saturday morning between 9:00 A.M. and 1:00 P.M., you'll find a community market with home-baked goods and fresh produce from local vendors.

Head to the *Kickstand Coffee House Café* (985–626–9300) at 690 Lafitte Street to rent a bike for the Trace, as locals call it, or to ride along the nearby lakefront—now a site of ongoing construction as homeowners repair hurricane damage.

At the Kickstand, you can savor an ice-cream cone or go upstairs to enjoy an espresso or specialty coffee while checking e-mail on your laptop or admiring the artwork. The eatery, which also delivers, offers sandwiches and wraps, soups, salads, and freshly baked desserts. Check out www.kickstand.bz.

For a brunch you won't forget, call ***Benedict's Plantation*** (985–626–4557) and make reservations. You'll find the restaurant at 1144 North Causeway Boulevard just behind the Channel 4 news office near the traffic light on Brookside (actually on Mandeville's Lovers' Lane, but apparently lovers find the sign irresistible because it keeps disappearing).

The late chef Benny (Benedict) Deluzain and his wife, Shirley purchased this home, once the focal point of a plantation, and started their business here in 1989. Their son Nicholas, who trained under his father, now serves as chef. He prefers the classic dishes, and so does the crowd, because the restaurant stays booked. "No nouveau for me," he says.

The Sunday champagne brunch starts with flaky homemade biscuits and chicken-vegetable or other soup du jour, followed by a house salad. Then comes your choice of several entrees including the signature pecan-smoked prime rib. Or you might prefer eggs Nicole (named for the chef's twin sister), which consists of poached eggs on a Louisiana blue-crab cake drizzled with traditional hollandaise sauce and served with cheese grits. The menu also features such items as corn-crusted trout, grits and grillades, and crawfish omelette. Coffee, homestyle bread pudding, and live music complete the experience.

You'll have to go on Sunday because the restaurant caters for private parties other days. Benedict's offers a lovely banquet facility behind the main house. After Hurricane Katrina worked her chaos throughout the area, Shirley responded to the governor's request and provided breakfast, lunch, and dinner for rescue and cleanup crews as long as her services were needed—even though the restaurant was without power for a while.

Louisiana inventor and artist, John Preble puts his own zany spin on recycling at the state's most eccentric museum. You'll find the ***UCM Museum*** (985–892–2624 or 888–211–5731), pronounced *"you-see-em-mu-se-um,"* at 22275 Highway 36 in Abita Springs just 1 block east of the town's only traffic light.

A family visit to Albuquerque's Tinkertown inspired this Southern version, says John, who certainly proves that art can be fun. Visitors enter an old service station and browse through a series of buildings, including a Louisiana Creole cottage that dates back almost a century, an exhibition hall, and a kaleidoscopic house of shards made from thousands of pottery and china fragments.

"It's a kick," said a local, describing this place that takes roadside attractions to a new level. On the grounds, you'll see handmade folk art featuring animated Louisiana scenes such as a Mardi Gras parade, New Orleans jazz funeral, rhythm and blues dance hall, haunted Southern plantation, and more—all made with found and recycled objects. John suggests bringing a sense of humor and an open mind. E-mail John at ucm@ucmmuseum.com. Except for major holidays, the museum opens daily from 10:00 A.M. until 5:00 P.M. Modest admission "if you are over three years old."

While here, pop into *Abita Brew Pub* (985–892–5837) for a burger and Turbodog (a national magazine ranked it America's #1 beer) or a more serious lunch or dinner. Notice the large colorful mural, which depicts real people doing real things here—like biking the Trace. Hours run 11:00 A.M. to 9:00 P.M. Tuesday through Thursday with closing time at 10:00 P.M. on the weekends. The brew pub closes on Monday.

Abita Brewing Company (800–737–2311 or 985–893–3143) started on the premises here but outgrew the building and relocated farther up the road to 21084 Highway 36. Brewery tours are offered on the weekend. Check out www.abita.com for more about brews.

Before leaving Abita Springs, you'll want to enjoy a spectacular meal at *The Longbranch* (985–871–8171), located in a parklike setting of moss-trimmed trees at 21516 Highway 36. Owners Allison Vines-Rushing and Slade Rushing left stellar culinary careers in the Big Apple to return to their southern roots and start their own restaurant here.

With Slade as co-chef, Allison won the James Beard Foundation's Rising Star Chef of the Year award in 2004. You may have read about the couple in *Bon Appetit, Food & Wine, Good Housekeeping,* and other publications.

After the purchasing the property in Abita Springs, the young chefs (who met while working in the kitchen of a New Orleans restaurant) set about sprucing up the two-story nineteenth-century building and landscaping the spacious grounds. Then they browsed through nearby antiques shops for unusual pieces and tableware for The Longbranch.

Oyster lovers will enjoy one of the signature menu items, oysters Rockefeller deconstructed, a lighter version of this traditional dish. As for dessert, try the banana pudding brûlée, another popular choice here.

Dinner hours run 5:30 to 10:00 P.M. Wednesday through Saturday, and a Sunday brunch is served from 11:00 A.M. to 2:00 P.M. The lunch schedule is now being finalized. Call for reservations soon. Expensive. Visit www.thelong branchrestaurant.com.

For a glorious getaway and a grand base from which to explore the Northshore, make reservations at *Maison Reve Farm* (985–769–8103), a tucked-away treasure at 76251 Highway 1077. At this bed-and-breakfast in the Folsom/Covington area, JoAnn and Dan Gray offer southern hospitality at its finest, and—not to spoil any surprises, you'll leave with a bit of lagniappe.

Guests at Maison Reve (which translates to dream house) can be grateful the owners visited Ireland, but especially a certain bed-and-breakfast in Kilkenny. It was over breakfast there that JoAnn looked into the eyes of her husband and told him she wanted a bed-and-breakfast in her future. Now, lucky guests can enjoy hospitality in a French-inspired villa, which the Grays designed and built themselves. So enticing is this setting that some visitors, who arrive with the idea of making forays into nearby New Orleans, change their itinerary to savor the solitude. They bribe the Grays' pet rabbit, Trick Bunny, with carrots to see his backward hops, watch deer emerge from the nearby woodland, and feed the ducks. Birders especially enjoy the property, which spreads over thirty acres.

From master storyteller to master craftsman, Dan amazes guests with his repertoire; ask him about his grilling techniques. JoAnn teaches gourmet cooking classes in her spacious kitchen—and there's a waiting list. Maison Reve is only forty-five minutes from New Orleans and less than an hour's drive to JoAnn's "favorite restaurant in the whole world, Commanders Palace." You can pay a little visit to www.maisonrevefarm.com, but you won't smell the cookies baking. Moderate to deluxe rates.

While tooling around the Northshore, save plenty of time for Covington, a town that oozes with artsy charm and lures travelers with its great restaurants and shops, inviting bed-and-breakfasts, and a unique microbrewery.

In the town's historic district, you may want to stop by some of the *Lee Lane Shops.* These Creole cottages, dating from the nineteenth century, have been converted to specialty shops, which carry antiques, art, gifts, clothing, and other items.

At 221 Lee Lane, Carolyn Gray and Kathy Ferguson offer yesteryear's treasures at *Walker House, Ltd.* (985–893–4235). Furniture, china, crystal, and home accessories fill room after room. Step out back and wander about the patio area brimming with plants, topiaries, statuary, and accent pieces for the garden enthusiast. Hours are 10:00 A.M. to 5:00 P.M. Monday through Saturday and Sunday by chance.

Don't miss *H. J. Smith's Son General Store* (985–892–0460), located at 308 North Columbia Street in downtown Covington. This old-time country store, which also features a museum, sells everything from ox yokes and cast-iron stoves to plantation bells. On the front porch you'll see a buckboard and an inviting swing. Other merchandise consists of cypress swings, oak rockers, wood-burning stoves, and various hardware and farm supplies. Inside the store a corncrib more than 150 years old serves as a display area for kerosene lamps, crockery, and cast-iron cookware.

"There are not a lot of stores like ours left," says Jack Smith, who remembers the "old guys sitting in rocking chairs on the front porch and spinning yarns." Jack, his brothers, and their father carry on a family business that started in 1876.

The museum contains hundreds of items from yesteryear, such as an old metal icebox, a century-old cypress dugout boat, and a cast-iron casket. A hand-operated wooden washing machine, old cotton scales, and various vintage tools are also on display.

Also in Covington, you'll find *Etoile Restaurant* (985) 892–4578 at 407 North Columbia Street, which offers great food as well as a feast for the eyes. While dining on rosemary chicken salad or rare ahi tuna, you can admire the fascinating art of James Michalopoulos. Noted for his distinctive architectural renderings and vibrant dancing colors, his work finds its way into discriminating collections across the country. Restaurant hours run 11:00 A.M. to 3:00 P.M. Monday, 11:00 A.M. to 9:00 P.M. Tuesday through Thursday, and 11:00 A.M. to 10:30 P.M. Friday and Saturday.

Nearby, *Heiner Brau Microbrewery* (985–893–2884 or 888–910–2997), a walk-in brewery and museum in a century-old building at 226 Lockwood Street, makes an interesting stop. Owner and brewmaster Henryk Orlik, who started his brewing career at age sixteen in Germany, practices the art of European brewing here.

Orlik, who launched his operation the week before Katrina hit, waited out the storm on the premises. "Next time a hurricane comes," he says, "I'm out of here!" A mesmerizing storyteller and one of only a few select German brewmasters in the country, Orlik will keep you enthralled with his anecdotes and observations. For a list of his premium beers, like Kolsch and Kellerbier, offered year-round, see www.heinerbrau.com. In a joint venture, Orlik and the monks at St. Joseph Abbey in Benedict are reviving the ancient art of monastery brewing. Brew buffs will want to look for St. Joseph's Kloster Festbier in grocery stores, pubs, and restaurants.

Drive along Rutland Street in the downtown historic district, and you'll see some of Covington's charming homes like *Camellia House Bed & Breakfast* (985–893–2442 or 985–264–4973). Innkeepers Linda and Don Chambless welcome guests to their raised Louisiana-style cottage at 426 East Rutland Street, a great place to swing on the porch or float in the pool. See more at www.camellia house.net. Linda may share some bone-chilling hurricane stories with you.

Nearby, at 505 East Rutland Street, you'll see *Blue Willow Bed & Breakfast* (985–892–0011), fronted by a white picket fence and an inviting front

Alligators—Up Close and Personal

Picture yourself holding an alligator, or feeding one, or even watching one hatch from an egg. These adventures and more await at *Insta-Gator Ranch & Hatchery* (985–892–3669 or 888–448–1560), where "you can get up close and personal with alligators," promises owner John Price. Located at 23440 Lowe Davis Road in Covington, the facility features some 2,000 alligators swimming in crystal-clear water.

Both entertaining and educational, the tour starts with an interesting overview of the life of the alligator—all the way back to dinosaur days. Afterward, when the tour guide hops into the pen and brings out an alligator (and yes, he tapes the mouth shut), you can get your picture taken holding it.

John and his staff work closely with Louisiana Wildlife and Fisheries in this program, developed to conserve the American Alligator species and save the state's wetlands. Louisiana leads the world in alligator production—and preservation. "It's a win-win situation," says John, describing an alligator ranching program that results in a population twice as large as would otherwise occur. Visitors get a first-person report of the alligator industry and see action film footage made in the wild, which shows the egg harvesting. In only one year, hatchlings grow from less than 1 foot to alligators more than 4 feet long. John harvested his first stock of alligator eggs in 1989—and still has all ten fingers.

Reservations are recommended. Tours take place at 11:00 A.M. and 2:00 P.M. Tuesday through Saturday, but more may be added soon; call ahead for tour times. Admission. Click on www.insta-gatorranch.com for more information on this exciting program and to view a virtual tour movie.

porch. Hosts Maureen and Tom Chambless invite you to slow down the pace here, sip coffee in a private plant-filled courtyard, and enjoy a Continental-plus breakfast at your leisure. (Maybe they'll give you a ginger plant to take home for your garden.) Visit the property at www.bluewillowbandb.com.

Before leaving Covington, enjoy some fine dining and French cuisine at *Annadele's Plantation Restaurant* (985–809–7669) at 71495 Chestnut Street. Beef lovers will want to order the special-cut filet that arrives on a sizzling platter. Try the blue-cheese mashed potatoes, a popular side item here. For a look at the tantalizing menu, check out www.annadeles.com. Moderate to expensive. This former plantation home on the Bogue Falaya River also offers bed-and-breakfast accommodations with four spacious suites upstairs. Deluxe rates.

St. Tammany Parish boasts a wonderfully remote and mysterious spot for getting off the beaten path—*Honey Island Swamp* on the eastern edge of the parish between Louisiana and Mississippi.

To reach Honey Island Swamp, head toward Slidell in the state's southeastern corner. A good way to explore this pristine wilderness is to take one of

Dr. Wagner's Honey Island Swamp Tours (985–641–1769 or 504–242–5877). Tours depart from Crawford Landing, about 5 miles east of Slidell on the West Pearl River. Dr. Paul Wagner is a wetlands ecologist who started the business, retired, and entrusted the tour company to longtime staff members who will introduce you to this wild 250-square-mile region.

Because it attracted large swarms of honeybees, early settlers called the place Honey Island. One of America's least explored swamps, this area is home to a large variety of plants and wildlife—and maybe even the mysterious swamp monster, Wookie. Some hunters and anglers swear that they've seen the creature, which they consistently describe as about 7 feet tall and covered with short hair, longer at the scalp. Wookie supposedly walks upright and leaves four-toed tracks. So far nobody on the tours has spotted said creature, but if it exists, then this wild and dense area seems an appropriate environment.

Although you may miss Wookie, you'll see some of the swamp's resident and migratory birds: herons, ibis, egrets, bald eagles, owls, and wild turkeys. Crawfish, turtles, alligators, wild boar, deer, and otter also live here.

Biologist Paul Trahan and a staff of naturalist native guides serve as stewards of the Louisiana Nature Conservancy's White Kitchen Preserve, and the tour includes a visit to this beautiful area, teeming with wildlife. This area contains a rookery, a wood-duck roost, and an active bald eagle nest where generations of eagles have come for some fifty years.

A number of visitors return to see the swamp's seasonal changes. In spring and summer, the place becomes lush like a rain forest, but cool-weather months offer improved visibility. Regular tours are offered morning and afternoon, by reservation. Additional tours, also requiring reservations, are available. A typical tour takes about two hours. The staff offers a hotel pickup service from New Orleans—complete with narration to and from the swamp. Credit cards are not accepted. Call for tour rates and reservations.

Only five minutes from Honey Island, travelers will find sanctuary and a warm welcome at ***Woodridge Bed & Breakfast*** (985–863–9981 or 877–643–7109). Set against a backdrop of century-old live oak trees, this former academy at 40149 Crowe's Landing in Pearl River offers five spacious suites. Debbi and Tim Fotsch rescued the private school, which closed in the early 1990s, and transformed it into an inviting bed-and-breakfast.

You'll be welcomed by friendly felines, Garfield and Dammit (well, if you *must* know, a guest returning from a late night in New Orleans called him that, and the name stuck). Be sure to notice the intricate Mardi Gras gowns and trains (one with a Greek theme) handstitched by Debbi, a doll collection, and other interesting exhibits. A balcony, where early birds can enjoy coffee and pastries, affords access to the suites, each with a motif of its own. Later, a

OTHER ATTRACTIONS WORTH SEEING IN TURF AND SWAMP

Global Wildlife Center
26389 Highway 40
Folsom
(985) 796–3585
Guided covered-wagon tours over 900 acres and a variety of species to see. Kids will enjoy the visit.

Greensburg
Take Highway 16 off I–55 west to Greensburg (stop off at the Bear Creek Steakhouse in Montpelier for music and a meal if you like). At Greensburg you can see an old jail and the original Florida Parishes land office, where claims were settled after the area joined the state of Louisiana.

Highway 51
Tangipahoa Parish was only formed in 1867, carved out from adjoining parishes to form a corridor along the Illinois Central Railroad. Towns are dotted at 10-mile intervals along Highway 51, which follows the train route. Ponchatoula has antiques stores; Hammond has the campus of Southeastern Louisiana University; Independence has a rich Italian heritage;

Amite has a pleasant residential section and a bed-and-breakfast mansion, Blythewood (985–748–5886). Near Tangipahoa is Camp Moore, a Civil War military camp with museum exhibits.

Military Road, Highway 21
This highway north of Covington going toward Bogalusa is lovely in spring. Azaleas bloom along the fences and wisteria and Cherokee roses climb along the pine trees for what seems like miles.

The Tammany Trace
This biking and hiking path on an old railroad right-of-way is a good venue for getting out in the country for a stroll. Start in Abita Springs (and have a sip of the famous spring water before you begin).

Zemurray Gardens
23115 Zemurray Garden Drive
Loranger
(985) 878–2284
Azalea garden is glorious in spring. Wander among the trees and shrubbery on the trail around the lake.

gourmet breakfast is served family style. Moderate rates. View the property at www.woodridgebb.com.

Continue to nearby Slidell. Since Hurricane Katrina's visitation, you can expect heavier traffic than usual throughout this area, especially with many former New Orleanians now commuting from nearby towns. You'll see plenty of post-hurricane rebuilding in and around Slidell, the hardest hit town on the Northshore.

In Slidell's *Olde Town,* look for the ***Passionate Platter Cooking School*** (985–781–HERB or 985–781–4372), a business that rebounded in record time. Located in an eggplant-colored house at 2104 First Street, the facility offers hands-on cooking classes for kids and adults, lunch and garden tours, private gourmet meals, aromatherapy, garden and planting supplies, and more. Owner and chef Linda Franzo, who provides recipes with all classes, also posts some of her favorites at www.passionateplatter.com, and you'll find a schedule of activities here as well. Class prices vary depending on the size.

Leaving Slidell puts you on the doorstep of New Orleans, a city anticipating your visit more than ever. So take nearby I–10 and cross the twin-span bridge over the end of Lake Pontchartrain into America's Paris.

Crescent City Realm

New Orleans, famous for its food, music, festivals, architecture, and history, is a city like no other. New Orleans has been described as magical, rambunctious, debonair, flamboyant, seductive, and, yes, decadent—but most of all, it's fascinating.

Spring is an ideal time to visit New Orleans—it's no secret that summer days can fall in the sweaty and sweltering category.

Before beginning your exploration of the Crescent City, throw away your compass. New Orleans's confusing geography takes a while to master. Natives refer to upriver as uptown and downriver as downtown; the two other major directions are lakeside (toward Lake Pontchartrain) and riverside. You can get a good view of the crescent from *Moonwalk,* a promenade that fronts the French Quarter and overlooks the Mississippi River.

New Orleans Wants *You!*

The best way to hug New Orleans now is by visiting—the first chance you get. Wherever you go in the city, people say, "Spread the word. We want our visitors."

Most of the things (95 percent) for which you come to this city are just waiting for you. You can still enjoy fine dining at most of the city's stellar restaurants, start your day with cafe au lait and beignets at Cafe du Monde, and dig into red beans and rice at Tujaque's on Monday. You'll still find magic and great music here–and all this without fighting the crowds you last encountered.

Therein lies the problem. New Orleans relies on tourism, which accounts for 40 percent of its annual tax revenues. Also, tourism employed 85,000 people before Katrina, making it the city's top industry.

"You walk around downtown," said a local, "and you don't even know there was a hurricane. The city is just as viable as ever. People need to realize you can come down here and still have a good time, but a lot of people are afraid. They think we are living in devastation."

So, the best way to show your support for this unique city is by coming on down and having fun. Savor the celebrated cuisine. Dance to the music. Now how hard is that?

A word of caution: As you explore New Orleans, it's best to stick to the beaten path, avoiding any questionable areas. New Orleans can appear deceptively safe, so don't forget to exercise the same caution that you would in any major city.

If New Orleans is your exclusive destination, consider coming by plane or train. An Amtrak excursion with sleeping car, which includes meals and other amenities, will allow you to arrive rested and ready to tackle the Big Easy. For reservations and information call (800) 872–7245 or click on www.amtrak.com. In this city of precious parking (not to mention the French Quarter's narrow streets), a car has definite drawbacks. United Cabs offer reliable and courteous service; call (504) 522–9771. Also, the St. Charles Streetcar, listed on the National Register of Historic Places, affords an entertaining and inexpensive way to get about. You may want to purchase a pass for a day of unlimited rides.

For comfort and convenience with some marbled opulence thrown in for good measure, plan to stay at *Le Pavillon Hotel* (800–535–9095 or 504–581–3111). Fronted by large columns and ornamented with sculptures and cast terra-cotta garlands, Le Pavillon stands at 833 Poydras Street on the corner intersecting Baronne. A member of Historic Hotels of America, this 1907 architectural classic offers spacious rooms and suites along with friendly service. The lobby's crystal chandeliers came from Czechoslovakia and its marble railings from the Grand Hotel in Paris. Each of the hotel's seven deluxe suites features a different decor. From antique to Art Deco, all furnishings, paintings, and accents carry out the room's theme.

Guests can take a dip in the rooftop pool and relax on the patio with its sweeping view of the Mississippi River. After a night on the town, stop by the lobby for a complimentary late-night snack of peanut butter and jelly sandwiches with a glass of milk or hot chocolate. You can compensate for the fat grams with free sessions in the fitness center. Rates are moderate to deluxe.

After settling in, start your sight-seeing session in the nearby French Quarter with beignets and cafe au lait at *Cafe du Monde* (504–587–0840). Located in the French Market at 800 Decatur Street, the eatery is open twenty-four hours daily (except Christmas Day). Afterward, stroll through the Vieux Carré (*view-ka-ray*), as the old French Quarter also is known. Save some time to watch the street performers in Jackson Square with its famous artists' fence. Clopping through the quarter, straw-hatted mules pull surreys and carriages—a relaxing way to see the stately tri-towered *St. Louis Cathedral,* outdoor cafes, and "frozen lace" galleries.

While in the French Quarter with its many enticements, consider touring the *Beauregard-Keyes House* (504–523–7257) at 1113 Chartres Street just across from the Old Ursuline Convent. Frances Parkinson Keyes (*kize*), author of fifty-one books, lived here while writing *Dinner at Antoine's, Blue Camel-*

Hurricane Katrina Tour

A disaster tour sounds pretty gruesome, right? Gray Line offers one here and gets plenty of takers. Many people admit to mixed feelings about this. Some find it offensive and see no point in gawking at the ruins. Others say you cannot comprehend the level of destruction unless you see it with your own eyes. Participants hear how oil and gas pipelines, manmade levee protection, and America's disappearing coastline combined to create this catastrophe.

"We want people to see this, so they won't forget. We want every member of Congress to come here. It's unbelievable. Even if you stayed glued to the TV during Katrina's landfall and aftermath with the levees breaking, and you saw all the news reports over and over, you don't realize the magnitude of it all," said a tour guide. "The destruction extends from here to the Mississippi Gulf Coast.

"The storm cut across all lines; it did not discriminate between rich and poor, black and white," she continued. "The media tried to portray this as a black and white issue. It is not. The real issue boiled down to one of owners and renters. Owners want to save their investments; renters have nothing to save."

The Gray Line New Orleans Hurricane Katrina Tour takes people through many of the devastated low-lying neighborhoods in Lakeview, Gentilly, and near the Ninth Ward; a city ordinance prohibits tour vehicles from entering the Ninth Ward.

Roofs wear blue tarps and wait for insurance adjusters. Giant oak trees rest on houses, and broken windows gape back at you. An ominous X painted high on the front of each house indicates a completed inspection by rescue teams. (Teams did their initial inspections by boat, thus the high placement of the X.) The standardized format provides quick information: the inspection unit, date checked, and number of missing persons. You see the ubiquitous water line and messages about the fate of pets.

The tour takes you past street after street, neighborhood after neighborhood— reduced to rubble. Cleanup crews clear away debris. An occasional person, wearing a mask, pulls out possessions from a ravaged home. Pyramids of household furnishings wait for curbside pickup–refrigerators, sofas, beds, and clothing. For the most part, the scene resembles a war-torn country with devastation in every direction.

Every person here has a story to tell. One woman uprighted a china cabinet, which had toppled face down, to discover the entire set of Limoges china from her grandmother still intact; everything else was destroyed.

"Nobody's the same now," noted a New Orleans restaurant owner. "The storm affected everyone in some way. Even those who escaped property damage know many people who did not."

Katrina tours last three hours and take place daily at 9:00 A.M. and 1:00 P.M. The cost is $35.00 per adult with $3.00 of the fee earmarked for one of four nonprofit organizations (which participants can choose) directly affected by the hurricane. Call Gray Line at (800) 535–7786 or (504) 569–1401 for reservations. You can also take a look at www.graylineneworleans.com.

America's Most Haunted City

New Orleans offers many ghostly sites, tours of its historic cemeteries called "cities of the dead," and a variety of Halloween activities. On your next trip to "America's Most Haunted City," check into **Hotel Monteleone** (504–523–3341 or 800–535–9595), 214 Rue Royale, a legendary French Quarter hotel. Long known as a literary landmark, the hotel staff has welcomed such guests as William Faulkner, Tennessee Williams, Truman Capote, Ernest Hemingway, and others. For more background see www.hotelmonteleone.com.

At a past news conference the hotel released findings on its ghosts and hauntings, said a staffer. A parapsychologist and his team spent several days investigating Hotel Monteleone and reported contacts with more than a dozen earthbound entities. They also checked other upscale properties including neighboring French Quarter restaurants, Brennan's and the Court of Two Sisters. For information on what may be going on during your visit, go to www.neworleansonline.com.

Speaking of the supernatural, many crew members and Delta Queen passengers report close encounters with a benevolent presence presumed to be Mary Becker Greene. One of the country's earliest women riverboat pilots, the petite lady and her husband, Captain Gordon Greene, founded what became the Delta Queen Steamboat Company. "Ma" Greene spent fifty-nine years on steamboats, charming guests with her stories. At age eighty, she danced the Virginia Reel with passengers only two days before her death, which occurred in her cabin on the Delta Queen. So it comes as no surprise when she gets credit for unusual happenings aboard her riverboat home. One case in point: When the boat's first saloon was installed after Captain Mary's death (she was a devout temperance backer), a barge rammed the Delta Queen, shattering the bar, but damaging nothing else. Crew members gasped when they saw the barge's name: CAPTAIN MARY B—named for the celebrated lady pilot.

Sign up for a voyage and admire the rich woodwork, stained glass transoms, glittering crystal chandeliers, and antique furnishings. And, as you stroll about, don't be startled if you meet a woman in a long green robe and she vanishes before your eyes. Just enjoy your holiday aboard a legendary vessel watched over, many claim, by Captain Mary. For the latest steamboatin' information, see www.deltaqueen.com.

lia, and other novels. Docents, dressed in period costume, give guided tours Monday through Saturday, from 10:00 A.M. to 3:00 P.M. on the hour. The gift shop offers a wide selection of the author's books. Admission is modest.

Afterward, take a break at nearby **Napoleon House** (504–524–9752). This interesting old building at 500 Chartres Street houses a bar and cafe. You can study the menu, printed on fans with faces of Napoleon and Josephine, while listening to classical music in the background. Try the house specialty, an Italian muffuletta—a great sandwich with meats, cheeses, and olive salad. Call ahead for hours.

For a great way to get acquainted with this fascinating section, sign up for a walking tour by a ranger from the French Quarter Visitor Center–Jean Lafitte National Historical Park and Preserve. Tours last about ninety minutes, so wear your walking shoes. Except for Christmas Day and Mardi Gras, the tours take place daily and are free. Hours run from 9:00 A.M. to 5:00 P.M., and "it's first come, first served" for the first twenty-five persons to show up, said a ranger. Call (504) 589–2636.

Bienville House Hotel (504–529–2345 or 800–535–7836) makes a convenient and cozy base for exploring the French Quarter. You'll find it at 320 Decatur Street, only a short stroll or cab ride away from antiques shops, jazz showcases, blues clubs, and great restaurants, including the hotel's own *Louisiana Heritage Cafe and School of Cooking* (where you can pick up some culinary tips to impress your family and friends).

Created from two eighteenth-century warehouses, this intimate inn, elegantly appointed with hand-painted murals, exudes an old-world ambience. Check out

The Silver Badge of Courage

Attention jewelry lovers (and spouses or significant others who might need a bit of help in the gift idea department): Look for the gallery and flagship store of **Mignon Faget** *(fah-ZHAY)* at 3801 Magazine Street. It's virtually impossible to visit New Orleans without spotting a woman wearing Faget's distinctive designs in earrings, bracelets, brooches, pendants, and more. (I own a few treasured pieces myself.)

The *fleur de lis,* a motif Faget started using during the 1970s, shines with new significance in the aftermath of Katrina. "People want to wear it as a badge of courage," the jewelry designer says. "It has never been more meaningful to us." She describes this, her most popular design, as "the symbol of New Orleans, signifying light and life."

The company sold more than 20,000 *fleur de lis* pieces in 2005, five times the previous year's number sold in her shops and on the Web site. Faget donated 10 percent of all *fleur de lis* product sales through the end of 2005 to the city's reconstruction effort.

Faget's roots go deep here, in the city she loves. Her maternal ancestors escaped to New Orleans during the French Revolution, and her paternal French ancestors were plantation owners from the West Indies.

For her designs, Faget finds inspiration in the natural and architectural forms of her native environment. Every piece reflects the beauty and culture of her city, state, and the Gulf Coast beyond. Handcrafted in her New Orleans studio, each jewelry design bears her unmistakable signature, and many items are available in both gold and sterling silver. Call the gallery at (504) 891–2005 or visit www.mignonfaget.com. Shop hours run 10:00 A.M. to 6:00 P.M. Monday through Saturday.

Arnaud's for Fine Cuisine, Jazz, and Mardi Gras

Founded by Count Arnaud Cazenave, this legendary restaurant dates to 1918 and serves a sampler of history along with superb Creole cuisine. *Arnaud's* (504–523–5433) at 813 Bienville Street draws discerning diners, who face the perennial problem of what to order—it's all so delectable. (Either before or after your jazz-enhanced dining experience, take a tour of the premises to see exhibits of Germaine's gorgeous Carnival court gowns, made in France, and other Mardi Gras memorabilia.)

Favorites here include succulent oysters Bienville, Shrimp Arnaud—chilled boiled shrimp marinated in the restaurant's famous remoulade sauce—Arnaud's air-puffed Pommes Souflee with a tarragon-infused béarnaise dipping sauce, and trout meunière. Arnaud's shared its recipe for delectable oyster soup, which you can try for yourself. (Though the count's Remoulade recipe remains a closely guarded secret, you can buy a bottle to take home—and if you become addicted, then visit www.arnauds.com to order more.)

Arnaud's Oyster Soup

2 dozen freshly shucked oysters, drained
1 tablespoon plus ¼ cup (2 ounces, ½ stick) unsalted butter
2 ribs celery, finely chopped
6 green onions, white and light green parts only, finely chopped
½ small onion, finely chopped
1 small clove garlic, very finely chopped

¼ teaspoon fresh thyme leaves, or ⅛ teaspoon dried thyme
⅛ teaspoon cayenne
1 bay leaf
¾ cup heavy whipping cream
2 cups whole milk
½ cup all-purpose flour
1 teaspoon Kosher or sea salt
¼ teaspoon ground white pepper

In a medium saucepan, bring 3½ cups of water to a boil, then reduce the heat so the water is just simmering. Add the oysters and cook for 3 minutes. Immediately remove the oysters with a slotted spoon; reserve the oysters and the poaching water separately.

Place a large heavy pot such as a Dutch oven over medium heat, and add 1 tablespoon of the butter. When it foams, add the celery, green onions, and onion. Cook, stirring frequently, for about 3 minutes, until tender but not browned. Add 2½ cups of the reserved oyster-poaching liquid, the garlic, thyme, cayenne, and bay leaf. Bring to a boil, then stir in the cream. Lower the heat and simmer for 5 minutes. Stir in the milk and return to a slow simmer.

Meanwhile, melt the remaining ¼ cup of butter in a small saucepan over low heat. Thoroughly stir in the flour, and continue stirring for about 3 minutes, but do not let the mixture brown (lower the heat even further, if necessary). The mixture will be thick.

Stir about ¼ cup of the milk mixture into this blond roux (the butter-flour paste), then return the entire mixture to the larger saucepan of soup. Use a balloon whisk briefly, if necessary, to be sure there are no lumps. Simmer for 5 minutes, then, if the soup is too thick for your liking, add a little more of the reserved oyster-poaching liquid to thin. Add the oysters, salt, and white pepper, and simmer for about 2 minutes to heat the oysters through. Discard the bay leaf and ladle into soup cups or bowls, distributing the oysters evenly. Serves 4 to 6.

upcoming events and make bookings via www.bienvillehouse.com/reservations. Moderate to deluxe.

After browsing through the French Quarter's antiques shops, art galleries, and boutiques, consider taking a stroll along Riverwalk and visiting *Aquarium of the Americas* (504–565–3033), where you can get nose to nose with a shark, see white alligators, and hold a parrot in the Amazon rain forest. Except for Monday when the aquarium closes, hours are 10:00 A.M. to 5:00 P.M. daily. Admission.

Afterward, head for Canal Street, a few blocks away. This wide avenue divides the French Quarter from "American territory" in uptown New Orleans. On Canal, hopefully you can catch the St. Charles Streetcar for a ride through the *Garden District.* Bumping along you'll see handsome nineteenth-century villas, Greek Revival mansions, and raised cottages surrounded by magnolias and ancient live oaks. This lovely area, with its lush landscaping and extravagant gardens dotted with statuary and fountains, makes a fine place to stroll. By walking you can better admire the ornamental iron fences with their geometric and plant motifs.

fishing

Everyone who fishes in Louisiana and is between the ages of sixteen and sixty is required to have a fishing license. You can purchase one at most sporting goods stores and bait shops; a one-day license is available for about $5.00 (add $15.00 for salt water) for out-of-state visitors.

Or, you can take a short stroll to *Commander's Palace* (504–899–8221), one of the city's renowned restaurants. Housed in a Victorian mansion at 1403 Washington Avenue, the famous eatery is closed for repairs and remodeling after Hurricane Katrina. Chances are, by the time of your next visit, you can again enjoy the spectacular Creole cuisine and superb seafood Commander's Palace built its reputation on.

For another delightful place to hang your hat in this area, head to the *Josephine* (504–524–6361 or 800–779–6361), located just at the edge of the

Outdoor Living in the City

One of Louisiana's most popular state parks is *Bayou Segnette* (suh-NET), 7777 Westbank Expressway in Westwego (888–677–2296 or 504–736–7140). The park took a triple hit with hurricanes Cindy, Katrina, and Rita, so most of it remains in a state of rebuilding. At press time, the wave pool is open (from Memorial Day though Labor Day), but no picnic facilities, cabins, or campsites are available. For updated information on the park, about thirty minutes from downtown New Orleans, call (877) 226-7652.

Garden District. Owned by Mary Ann Weilbaecher and husband, Dan Fuselier, this guest house stands at 1450 Josephine Street at the corner of Prytania. The Italianate-style home dates from 1870 and houses such striking antiques as "the jewel of the Josephine," an ornate ebony bed with inlaid ivory designs of danc-

Tujague's Tantalizing Tastes

Something about New Orleans spells food, and while you're exploring the French Quarter, stop by 823 Decatur Street. The city's second oldest restaurant, *Tujague's* (504–525–8676) opened its doors in 1856 and soon became a favorite spot for workers from the nearby French Market. Be sure to step into the antique bar to see the massive ornate mirror, shipped from Paris in 1856.

Presidents Roosevelt, Truman, and Eisenhower, and French president de Gaulle have enjoyed Tujague's, and so can you. From appetizer through dessert, today's owners carry on the Tujague family's tradition of serving fine fare in the Creole manner. The restaurant's seven-course meals evolve from such staples as shrimp remoulade and a superb brisket of beef presented with a red horseradish sauce.

Straight from this classic New Orleans neighborhood restaurant to you, here's Tujague's signature dish:

Tujague's Boiled Brisket of Beef

6–7 pounds choice brisket of beef	1 tablespoon salt
2 onions, quartered	15 black peppercorns
1½ ribs celery, quartered	2 green onions, quartered
1 head garlic, peeled	1 carrot, quartered
1 bay leaf	1 bell pepper, quartered

NOTE: Here are the two most important steps to produce a tender, juicy, tasty brisket:

(1) Buy a quality, well-trimmed brisket, never frozen.

(2) Simmer the meat (not a hard boil).

Place the brisket in a large soup pot, cover with cold water, add the remaining ingredients, and simmer for 3–4 hours until beef is tender. Remove beef and slice. Serve with a sauce made by combining 1 cup ketchup, ½ cup prepared horseradish, and ¼ cup Creole mustard.

For vegetable soup, skim and strain the beef stock. Add 3 tablespoons tomato paste, 2 sliced tomatoes, and your favorite vegetables. Cook until tender and serve. We have found a little okra adds a distinctive taste to the soup. Cut and cook okra first in the oven or a saucepan to remove slime.

Any stock left after soup is made can be frozen and stored for future soups and sauces. Makes approximately 1 gallon soup.

ing nymphs. The bed, which Dan calls "a bit on the risqué side," has been featured in a bridal magazine.

Mary Ann, who studied cookery in Paris, makes fresh breads, which she serves with juice and cafe au lait on Wedgwood china and presents on a silver tray. The couple offers recommendations and makes reservations for guests. "We like to help dock our guests," says Dan. Rates are moderate to deluxe.

On St. Charles Avenue you may want to visit **Audubon Park** in a pretty setting with ancient live oaks, flower-filled gardens, and wandering lagoons. The 400-acre urban park also offers a golf course, tennis courts, and picnic facilities as well as walking and jogging paths. At Cascade Stables in the park, you can rent a horse and go galloping off along a tree-shaded trail that offers glimpses of St. Charles Avenue.

Don't miss nearby **Audubon Zoo** (504–861–2537). Noted for its simulated barrier-free natural habitats, the zoo also makes a delightful outing, complete with peanuts, popcorn, and more than 1,800 animals. Zoo hours are 10:00 A.M. to 4:00 P.M. Tuesday through Friday and 10:00 A.M. to 5:00 P.M. Saturday and Sunday. Visit www.auduboninstitute.org for details.

Magazine Street, which runs parallel to the Mississippi River, offers some of the country's most unique shopping opportunities. You can stroll along 6 miles of intriguing antiques shops, art galleries, boutiques, clothing stores, home decor shops, and more. Fortunately, Magazine Street survived Katrina without flooding.

Located at 2109 Magazine Street, **Bush Antiques** (504–891–2005) features an interesting and extensive inventory, which includes antique beds and religious artifacts. You can check it out at www.bushantiques.com. At 3033 Magazine Street, **As You Like It Silver Shop** (504–897–6915) offers strictly estate silver and specializes in matching flatware patterns for both discontinued and active patterns. You'll also find sterling silver tea services, tureens, goblets, bowls, and other hollowware items. Hours are 10:00 A.M. to 5:00 P.M. Monday through Saturday. At 5415 Magazine Street you can browse through **British Antiques** (504–895–3716). Hours are 10:00 A.M. to 4:30 P.M. Monday through Friday, and until 5:00 P.M. on Saturday.

You'll come across some excellent buys in both English and French antiques, furniture, paintings, china, crystal, silver, collectibles, and souvenirs. You'll also pass brass dealers, bookstores, restaurants, and specialty shops. Even though most of the stores don't have fancy facades (some even resemble junk shops), you can find some quality merchandise at bargain prices.

At some point during your visit, schedule a boat ride to experience the mighty Mississippi's romance and majesty. Describing the Mississippi, Mark

Making Groceries

New Orleans is a city that, like Napoleon's army, moves on its stomach. To get in the spirit of things, learn to "make groceries"—a local expression that's a rough translation of the French *faire le marche*.

There is a farmers' market every Saturday from 8:00 A.M. to noon on the corner of Girod and Magazine Streets featuring fresh produce, a local chef using market goods to prepare dishes for tasting, lots of baked goods, jellies, and more. There's also coffee so you can make this a breakfast. There is an uptown farmers' market Tuesday from 10:00 A.M. to 1:00 P.M. at Broadway and Leake Avenue and a mid-city version on Thursday evening from 4:00 to 6:00 P.M. at Orleans Avenue by Bayou St. John.

Langenstein's (504–899–9283), uptown on the corner of Pitt and Arabella Streets off St. Charles Avenue, is the uptown grocery of choice. It has good meats, seafoods, and produce and a deli department that prepares lots of local specialties: boiled seafood, gumbo, red beans and rice, oyster dressing for your turkey, and pies. They will ship for you.

Most eccentric supermarket? **Dorignac's** (504–837–4650), 710 Veterans Boulevard, Metairie. Although the late "Mr. Joe" Dorignac no longer sits in the coffee shop consulting the *Racing Form* (at one point he owned a good string of runners), his all-inclusive inventory still holds. The aisles are jam-packed, and you can find one of every local product here first. There's an incredible array of vegetables, including things like those hard-to-find artichoke stalks that make a special dish around St. Joseph's Day. Good butchers, too.

For health food try the **Whole Foods Market** (504–899–9119) at 5600 Magazine Street. It is a full-size grocery with organic vegetables and meat and a deli with fresh-made New Orleans specialties, albeit in healthful form. For wines consult **Martin's Wine Cellar** (504–899–7411) for a huge selection and a regular schedule of tastings each Saturday. Three locations: 3500 Magazine Street, 714 Elmeer at Veteran's Boulevard in Metairie, and 2895 Highway 190 in Mandeville.

Twain called it "not a commonplace river, but in all ways remarkable." For a taste of Mr. Twain's river, you can choose a short ferry trip or a longer excursion on the *Creole Queen,* the *Natchez,* or another of the local riverboats. Some cruises combine sight-seeing with jazz, dinner, or Sunday brunch.

For a real taste of the river, grab your bag and head for the **Delta Queen Steamboat Company** (800–543–1949), located on the river behind the Convention Center. Here you can set off on a fun-filled cruise from New Orleans aboard the *Delta Queen,* the *Mississippi Queen,* or the *American Queen,* the biggest steamboat ever built.

For a unique vacation, you can choose a cruise out of New Orleans in the spring and winter on one of the company's legendary boats. Spend a holiday

Mardi Gras

The Carnival season runs from January 6 (Feast of the Epiphany, Three Kings Day) to Mardi Gras. There are lots of street parades throughout the area. Endymion on Saturday night, Baccchus on Sunday, and Orpheus on Monday are big, glitzy parades with giant floats and Hollywood kings. For a glimpse of the old-fashioned, small-float type of parade, catch Thoth on Sunday afternoon, uptown on Henry Clay Avenue or Magazine Street. This is what New Orleans Mardi Gras used to look like: very human-sized and still fun.

Saints' Days

St. Patrick's Day, March 17, is celebrated with parades and green beer. St. Joseph, patron saint of Italians, is celebrated on his feast day, March 19, with parades and with altars piled high with special foods and displayed to the public. There will be one at St. Alphonsus Church on Constance Street. (Writer Anne Rice is very active at St. Alphonsus, and you may see her there.) African-Americans who costume as Mardi Gras Indians also parade on St. Joseph's Day. All Saints Day, November 1, is the day for cleaning and decorating graves, so New Orleans cemeteries will be filled with families bearing chrysanthemums. All cemeteries have guards then, so it's a good day to visit.

Tennessee Williams Festival

225 Baronne Street, mid- to late March. Literary happenings— panel discussions, walking tours, performances—all concerning writing and writers with an emphasis on Williams. Don't miss the Stanley-Stella yelling contest in Jackson Square. (504) 581–1144 www.tennesseewilliams.net

French Quarter Festival

400 North Peters Street, mid-April. Food and music all over the French Quarter. (504) 522–5730.

Jazzfest

New Orleans Jazz and Heritage Festival, last weekend of April, first weekend of May. If you can only get to one New Orleans event in a lifetime, make it Jazzfest. The weekend music and crafts festival at New Orleans Fair Grounds racetrack has lots of stages, booths, big-name musicians, all sorts of bands, and lots of food. A crowd of 90,000 is not unusual, yet it is a safe and remarkably mellow occasion. Anyone of any age will find something to enjoy. Plus, there are concerts in the evenings, and all the musicians will be sitting in at clubs around town. (504) 522–4786 www.nojazzfest.com

New Orleans Film and Video Festival

225 Baronne Street, second week of October. Showcases new and experimental films and videos. (504) 523–3818 www.neworleansfilmfest.com

Christmas in New Orleans

December. Besides holiday events, this includes special room rates at many hotels. Ask for the "Papa Noel" rate. Also, many restaurants serve a prix-fixe Reveillon Dinner, which can be a good value. Be sure to ask.

OTHER ATTRACTIONS WORTH SEEING IN CRESCENT CITY REALM

ART

The New Orleans Museum of Art in City Park at the end of Esplanade Avenue (504–488–2631) has interesting holdings, especially in decorative arts, with a good selection of European as well as South American and African work to complement its American collections.

While you're there, be sure to check out NOMA's handsome new *Sydney and Walda Bestoff Sculpture Garden,* which is free to the public and open Wednesday through Sunday, 10:00 A.M. to 4:30 P.M. The seven-acre setting showcases a world-class collection of modern and contemporary sculpture set among City Park's moss-festooned oaks.

You'll find *Contemporary Arts Center* at 900 Camp Street (504–523–1216), in what is fast becoming New Orleans's art district, just a few blocks above the French Quarter. The C.A.C. hosts theater as well as art exhibits. Be sure to stroll the galleries of Julia Street—New Orleans has a vibrant and active art community.

Art lovers can explore a neighborhood of museums, galleries, and more in the Warehouse Arts District, sometimes called "the Soho of the South." Prominent in the area's arts explosion is the new *Ogden Museum of Southern Art* featuring five floors of the world's most comprehensive collection of Southern art. (Tip: Start on the top floor and work your way down.)

Louisiana ArtWorks on Howard Avenue and Carondelet Street, is where, under one roof, you can visit fifty artists' studios.

The big art event, *Art of Art's Sake,* takes place the first Saturday in October at all galleries.

Consider headquartering at the *Renaissance Arts Hotel,* (504) 613–2330 at 700 Tchoupitoulas Street. A virtual art gallery in itself, the hotel features rotating exhibits and original art in each room. Three Dale Chihuly chandeliers hang in its handsome lobby, and the Arthur Roger Gallery is located on the first floor.

in the Old South with stops at history-filled Natchez (especially delightful during Spring Pilgrimage) and Vicksburg, Mississippi, as well as other towns along the river. Or explore Baton Rouge's impressive sites and tour Louisiana plantations like Laura and Oak Alley.

Along with stellar dining and accommodations, you'll see stage production shows with a four-member musical theater ensemble—*Showboatin' Jubilee* fea-

BATTLE OF NEW ORLEANS SITE

The *Chalmette Battlefield* is now part of the many-sited Jean Lafitte National Park. Military history buffs will enjoy this one: Here's where the Duke of Wellington's brother-in-law, General Pakenham, came to his end during the British defeat. This is what started Andrew Jackson on the road to the White House.

From the French Quarter go east on Rampart Street, then on St. Claude Avenue, which actually becomes St. Bernard Highway and leads you right to the park. A few miles farther is the *Isleños Center,* also in Jean Lafitte National Park. Here you can learn the history of the Canary Islanders who settled the area. Sometimes the local docent demonstrates how to skin a nutria or coypu, a local wild rodent. Warning: It's not for the squeamish.

THE NATIONAL WORLD WAR II MUSEUM

Located at 945 Magazine Street, interactive exhibits and galleries take visitors through the period leading up to World War II's D-Day and honor the men and women who fought for American freedom.

HOUSE MUSEUMS

New Orleans has such a rich stock of nineteenth-century housing, it can offer the very best in accurately furnished period homes. Try *Gallier House,* 1133 Royal Street, home of architect James Gallier, or the *Hermann-Grima House*, 820 St. Louis Street (both at 504–525–5661).

There is also one in-town plantation, the *Pitot House* on Bayou St. John, 1440 Moss Street (504–482–0312).

MUSIC

Traditional jazz can be heard nightly at *Preservation Hall* at 726 St. Peter Street (504–522–2841) where fans sit on benches and pay a modest fee for pure music. Visit the *Louisiana State Museum*'s Jazz and Mardi Gras displays in the Old Mint Building on Esplanade Avenue at the Mississippi River to ground yourself in history. (Louis Armstrong's first horn is there.)

If you decide to hit the clubs, expect to be out late—New Orleans music hits its stride after midnight. There is sometimes a van service that operates between clubs; ask at a club to see if it is still rolling.

turing nineteenth-century costuming and riverboat-related music from Stephen Foster through Jerome Kern; *Memories* with popular music of the twentieth century; *It's My Party,* focusing on rock and pop favorites of the '50s, '60s, and '70s; and *Last of the Red Hot Mamas,* with music from the era of Sophie Tucker and Bessie Smith—a cabaret show, and theme-related entertainment, such as a Mark Twain impersonator or a classic country artist.

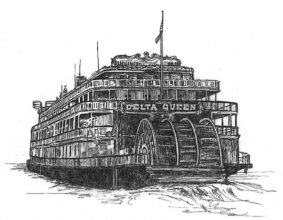

The *Delta Queen*

Connect with www.deltaqueen.com today and start planning your riverboat getaway. Excursions range from three to eleven nights. Call for seasonal rates and special packages. Prices include all onboard meals and entertainment plus port, ground handling, and fees, including taxes. Rates are deluxe.

Rare Treasures on Royal Street

The Travel Channel named Royal Street America's top antiques shopping destination in 2004. Here, in the French Quarter, you'll find six blocks of the country's finest antiques shops, unparalleled art galleries, superb restaurants, and more. Royal Street Guild merchants offer a unique experience when it comes to antiquing.

Serious collectors should not miss *M. S. Rau Antiques* (504–523–5660 or 800–544–9440) at 630 Royal Street. With an inventory that equals or surpasses many museums, M. S. Rau ranks as one of the world's premier dealers in antiques. The huge showrooms carry everything from silver pieces by Tiffany & Co., original Renoir and Monet paintings, and exquisite estate jewelry to mirrors, Venetian glass chandeliers, and stunning historic pieces like the rare Henry Clay Rosedown Plantation armoire, originally created for the White House. Pull up www.rau antiques.com and browse through recent acquisitions.

Bays and Bayous

You can take the Jackson Avenue ferry (when available; call 504–376–8100 or 504–376–8180 to check schedule) from the edge of New Orleans' Garden District over the river to *Gretna,* once a small community of railroad workers and German immigrants. Near the river is the City of Gretna Visitor Center in the old depot area (504–363–1580 or 888–4–GRETNA). There is a railroad exhibit there and nearby is the Gretna Historical Society Museum, 209 Lafayette Street, which encompasses three nineteenth-century cottages, properly furnished, and the David Crockett Fire House, built in 1859. The pumper wagon still shines, and even if the Dalmatian on board is ceramic, the costumed volunteer firemen are real—most are current or former volunteer firemen. Nearby, you'll find a blacksmith shop and the *German American Cultural Center* (504–363–4202). The Gretna Heritage Festival takes place here the first full weekend in October.

"It's an exciting time in Gretna," said Virgie Ott, tourism coordinator. "We have a lot of people moving here from the Ninth Ward and St. Bernard Parish—people who lost their homes because of Katrina. They're enjoying our weekly farmers' market and other activities." The Gretna Farmers' Market, located on Huey P. Long Avenue at Fourth Street, takes place every Saturday from 8:30 A.M. to 12:30 P.M. with a monthly Art Walk scheduled the second Saturday of each month from September through May. Visit www.gretnala.com for more information.

When it's time for a break from boisterous New Orleans, head for the banks of Bayou Barataria, about 30 miles south. The little fishing village of *Jean Lafitte* "where there be dragons" (just like the kind bordering the unknown on ancient maps), makes an excellent escape. The local dragons must be the gentle sort, because people in Lafitte don't feel the need to lock doors and often leave keys in their cars. The year's big crime might involve a shady aluminum-siding deal.

For your own dragon-embellished map with directions on how to find Lafitte, call Dale or Roy Ross at *Victoria Inn* (504–689–4757 or 800–689–4797) on Highway 45. Dale welcomes guests to her West Indies–style cottage at 4707 Jean Lafitte Boulevard with refreshments on arrival. Roy, a former construction company owner, built the lovely guest houses as well as the couple's nearby home.

Early risers will find coffee in the kitchen from 5:00 A.M. on. Breakfast specialties range from a wonderful interpretation of eggs Benedict called eggs Victoria, made with local hand-picked lump crab, to pecan waffles, crabmeat omelette, and "mosquito toast" (inspired by cuisine in Roy's native Belize) accompanied by bacon and a fruit compote. Rates are moderate.

TOP ANNUAL EVENTS IN BAYS AND BAYOUS

Louisiana Iris Festival
Jean Lafitte Park and Lafitte
mid-March
(800) 689–4797

Blessing of the Shrimp Fleet
Lafitte, last Sunday in April
(504) 689–4101

The Restaurant at Victoria Inn offers specialties by chef Matt Regan. Hours run Wednesday through Sunday from 6:00 to 9:30 P.M.

Both Gulf and inland fishing charters are available locally, and the inn's staff can help with sea-plane and fishing packages.

Only ten minutes away you'll find the ***Jean Lafitte National Park Barataria Unit,*** 6588 Barataria Boulevard, Marrero (504–589–2330). You'll see an interpretive center with a good video on early area inhabitants and extensive displays on the local environment and the cypress timber industry (which decimated the indigenous trees in the area). Other enticements include several hiking trails, all of them enjoyable. As for recent hurricane damage, Katrina knocked down some of the park's smaller trees, and Rita produced a salt water surge. There is also a canoe trail, and close by are canoes for rent. Rangers guide regular free tours.

The most popular trail is the Bayou Coquille–Marsh Overlook, especially spectacular when ringed with iris in spring (unless salt water intrusion prevents it, as proves to be the case following active hurricane seasons). It ends on high ground with an aerial view of the marsh and the skyscrapers of New Orleans in the background—and perhaps an alligator nearby. Those little black "pickles" you see are nutria droppings. Watch for the rooting armadillos with their little piggy ears. If you have one afternoon to go to the country, go here.

Hungry? On the West Bank of the Mississippi and downriver from New Orleans, look for boiled seafood such as shrimp, crabs, and crawfish. You may have to be shown how to pick a boiled crab, but it's worth it. Add some crackers and cold beer and you have an instant picnic.

Stop at small bakeries for fresh French bread. Look for homemade hogshead cheese (Creole Country is a good New Orleans brand). Be on the lookout for roadside stands that sell "Creole" (home-grown) tomatoes or strawberries in season.

A po'boy sandwich on French bread can be ordered dressed (with lettuce and tomato) and with gravy (for roast beef). Po'boy Nirvana? Softshell crab.

At ***Voleo's Seafood Restaurant*** (504–689–2482) 5134 Nunez Street, about 1 mile past Goose Bayou Bridge, you can sample either German or Cajun cuisine. Consider ordering the stuffed eggplant with fish, shrimp, oysters, and jambalaya. The restaurant opens at 11:00 A.M. and closes at 9:00 P.M. every day except Sunday and Tuesday. Prices are moderate.

Other local eateries include ***Boutte's Bayou Restaurant*** (504–689–3889) overlooking Bayou Barataria and ***Restaurant des Familles*** (504–689–7834), which specializes in authentic Cajun cuisine and serves local seafood.

Places to Stay in Southeast Louisiana

SWAMPLAND

Cajun Holiday Motel
1737 Highway 1
Grand Isle
(985) 787–2002

Coco Marina
106 Pier 56 Court
Cocodrie
(985) 594–6626 or
(800) 648–2626

Fairfield Inn by Marriott
1530 Martin Luther King
Boulevard
Houma
(985) 580–1050

Grand Bayou Noir
1143 Bayou Black Drive
Houma
(985) 868–0956

Hampton Inn
1728 Martin Luther King
Boulevard
Houma
(985) 873–3140

Holiday Inn–Holidome
210 South Hollywood Road
Houma
(800) HOLIDAY

Howard Johnson Motel
201 North Canal Boulevard
Thibodaux
(985) 447–9071 or
(800) 952–2968

PLANTATION COUNTRY

Holiday Inn LaPlace
3900 Main Street
LaPlace
(985) 652–5544

Madewood
4250 Highway 308
Napoleonville
(985) 369–7151 or
(800) 375–7151

Nottoway
30970 Highway 405
White Castle
(225) 545–2730

"RED STICK"

Baton Rouge Marriott
5500 Hilton Avenue
Baton Rouge
(225) 924–5000 or
(800) 842–2961

**The Cook Hotel &
Conference Center**
LSU Campus
3848 West Lakeshore Drive
Baton Rouge
(225) 383–2665 or
(866) 610–COOK
www.thecookhotel.com

Hampton Inn
4646 Constitution Avenue
Baton Rouge
(800) HAMPTON

**The Stockade Bed &
Breakfast**
8860 Highland Road
Baton Rouge
(225) 769–7358 or
(888) 900–5430
www.thestockade.com

FRENCH CREOLE COUNTRY

Holiday Inn Express
131 Lobdell Highway
I–10 and Highway 415
Port Allen
(225) 343–4821 or
(800) HOLIDAY

Jubilee!
11704 Pointe Coupee Road
New Roads
(225) 638–8333

THE FELICIANAS

Asphodel
4626 Highway 68
Jackson
(225) 658–8808

**Best Western St. Francis
Hotel on the Lake**
Highway 61
St. Francisville
(225) 635–3821 or
(800) 826–9931

Butler Greenwood
8345 Highway 61
St. Francisville
(225) 635–6312

FOR MORE INFORMATION

SWAMPLAND

Grand Isle Tourist Commission
2757 Highway 1
Grand Isle 70358
(985) 787–2997
www.grand-isle.com

Houma Area Convention and Visitors Bureau
114 Tourist Drive
Gray 70359
(800) 688–2732
info@houmatourism.com
www.houmatravel.com

Lafourche Parish Tourist Commission
P.O. Box 340
Raceland 70394
(985) 537–5800 or (877) 537–5800

Local newspapers: *Houma Daily Courier* (owned by the New York Times Corporation) and the *Thibodaux Daily Comet*. Check both for events.

PLANTATION COUNTRY

Ascension Parish Tourist Commission
6967 Highway 22
Sorrento 70778
(225) 675–6550 or (888) 775–7990

Gonzales Welcome Center
2410 Tanger Boulevard
Gonzales 70737
(225) 621–9659

St. Charles Parish Economic Development Department
P.O. Box 302
Hahnville 70057
(985) 783–5140

St. James Tourist Center
P.O. Box 629
Gramercy 70052
(800) 367–7852

St. John Parish President's Office
1801 West Airline Highway
LaPlace 70068
(985) 652–9569

"RED STICK"

Baton Rouge Area Convention and Visitors Commission
730 North Boulevard
Baton Rouge 70802
(800) LA–ROUGE
www.visitbatonrougetour.com

Newspapers: *Baton Rouge Advocate*. Check the Friday "Fun" section for events, restaurant reviews, etc. Also, check the LSU student paper, the *Daily Reveille*.

FRENCH CREOLE COUNTRY

Pointe Coupee Office of Tourism
500 East Main Street
New Roads 70760
(225) 638–3998 or (800) 259–2468

West Baton Rouge Tourist Commission
2750 North Westport Drive
Port Allen 70767
(225) 344–2920 or (800) 654–9701

Newspapers: The *Pointe Coupee Banner* of New Roads, the *West Side Journal* of Port Allen. Check the Friday "Fun" section of the *Baton Rouge Advocate* for events.

THE FELICIANAS

East Feliciana Chamber of Commerce
P.O. Box 667
Jackson 70748
(225) 634–7155

West Feliciana Parish Tourist Commission
P.O. Box 1548
St. Francisville 70775
(225) 635–6769

Newspapers: *St. Francisville Democrat, Zachary Plainsman–News,* the *Watchman* in Clinton. The *Baton Rouge Advocate* Friday "Fun" section will cover events.

TURF AND SWAMP

Bogalusa Chamber of Commerce
608 Willis Avenue
Bogalusa 70427
(985) 735–5731

St. Tammany Tourist & Convention Commission
68099 Highway 59
Mandeville 70471
(800) 634–9443
www.neworleansnorthshore.com

Tangipahoa Parish Tourist Commission
42271 South Morrison Boulevard
Hammond 70403
(985) 542–7520 or (800) 542–7520

Newspapers: *Bogalusa Daily News, Franklinton Era Leader, Amite Tangi–Digest, Hammond Daily Star, St. Tammany Farmer, St. Tammany News* in Covington, *Covington News–Banner, Kentwood News–Ledger, St. Helena Echo* in Greensburg, and the *Ponchatoula Times.* The *Times–Picayune* puts out a Northlake edition with local events. The Friday "Lagniappe" (*lanyap*—a little something extra) section also covers this area.

CRESCENT CITY REALM

New Orleans Convention and Visitors Bureau
2020 St. Charles Avenue
New Orleans 70130
(800) 672–6124 or (800) 748–8695
www.neworleansinfo.com

New Orleans Tourism Marketing Corporation
365 Canal Street
Suite 1120
New Orleans 70130
(504) 210–1218
www.neworleansonline.com

Newspapers: The *Times–Picayune* has a daily calendar of events and on Friday has a "Lagniappe" section with lots of news on entertainment and music. The *Gambit Weekly* has another event calendar. *Off–Beat* newspaper has music listings. WWOZ community radio (FM 90.7) sponsors a phone line for recorded information on performances: (504) 840–4040.

BAYS AND BAYOUS

Jean Lafitte National Park
Barataria Unit
6588 Barataria Boulevard
Marrero 70072
(504) 589–2330

Jefferson Convention and Visitors Bureau
6640 Riverside Drive, Suite 160
Metairie 70003
(504) 731–7089 or (877) J–PARISH
www.jptourism.com

Newspapers: The *Times–Picayune* covers this area. Check Friday's "Lagniappe" section for events.

Cottage Plantation
10528 Cottage Lane
St. Francisville
(225) 635–3674

Greenwood Plantation
6838 Highland Road
St. Francisville
(225) 655–3850

Milbank Historic House
3045 Bank Street
Jackson
(225) 634–5901

Myrtles
7747 Highway 61
St. Francisville
(225) 635–6277

Old Centenary Inn
1740 Charter Street
Jackson
(225) 634–5050

Shadetree Inn
Ferdinand and Royal Streets
St. Francisville
(225) 635–6116

St. Gemme de Beauvais
4302 Quiet Lane
Ethel
(225) 634–3245 or
(225) 721–1514
www.stgemmedebeauvais
.com

**TURF AND SWAMP
NEW ORLEANS
NORTHSHORE**

**Annadele's Plantation Bed
& Breakfast**
71495 Chestnut Street
Covington
(985) 809–7669
www.annadeles.com

Baymont Inn
794 East I–10 Service Road
Slidell
(985) 643–9770 or
(800) 531–5900

**Best Western
Northpark Inn**
625 North Highway 190
Covington
(985) 892–2681 or
(877) 766–6700

**Blue Willow
Bed & Breakfast**
505 East Rutland Street
Covington
(985) 892–0011
www.bluewillowbandb.com

**Camellia House
Bed & Breakfast**
426 East Rutland Street
Covington
(985) 893–2442
www.camelliahouse.net

Holiday Inn
2000 South Morrison
Boulevard
Hammond
(985) 345–0556 or
(800) HOLIDAY

**Land–O–Pines Family
Campground**
17145 Million Dollar Road
Covington
(800) 443–3697

Maison Reve Farm
76251 Highway 1077
Folsom
(985) 769–8103
www.maisonrevefarm.com

**Woodridge Bed &
Breakfast**
40149 Crowe's Landing
Pearl River (near Slidell)
(985) 863–9981 or (877)
643–7109
www.woodridgebb.com

CRESCENT CITY REALM

Bienville House Hotel
320 Decatur Street
New Orleans
(504) 529–2345 or
(800) 535–7836

Grand Victorian
2727 St. Charles Avenue
New Orleans
(504) 895–1104

Hampton Inn
3626 St. Charles Avenue
New Orleans
(800) 426–7866

InterContinental Hotel
444 St. Charles Avenue
New Orleans
(504) 525–5566

Josephine
1450 Josephine Street
New Orleans
(504) 524–6361 or
(800) 779–6361
www.josephine.us

Le Pavillon Hotel
833 Poydras Street
New Orleans
(504) 581–3111 or
(800) 535–9095

The Monteleone
214 Royal Street
New Orleans
(800) 535–9595

Renaissance Arts Hotel
700 Tchoupitoulas Street
New Orleans
(504) 613–2330

St. Charles Guest House
1748 Prytania Street
New Orleans
(504) 523–6556

Sully Mansion
2631 Prytania Street
New Orleans
(504) 891–0457

BAYS AND BAYOUS

Best Western Westbank
1700 Lapalco Boulevard
Harvey
(504) 366–5369 or
(800) 528–1234

Travelodge Hotel Westbank
2200 Westbank Expressway
Harvey
(504) 366–5311 or
(800) 578–7878

Victoria Inn
4707 Jean LaFitte Boulevard
Lafitte
(504) 689–4757

Places to Eat in Southeast Louisiana

SWAMPLAND

Bayou Delight
4038 Bayou Black Drive
Houma
(985) 876–4879

Christiano Ristorante
724 High Street
Houma
(985) 223–1130 or
(985) 223–1103

The Jolly Inn
1507 Barrow Street
Houma
(985) 872–6114

Lighthouse Restaurant
Coco Marina
106 Pier 56 Court Chauvin
Cocodrie
(985) 594–6626 or
(800) 648–2626

1921 Seafood Restaurant
1522 Barrow Street
Houma
(985) 868–7098

Politz's Restaurant
535 St. Mary Street
Thibodaux
(985) 448–0944

PLANTATION COUNTRY

The Cabin Restaurant
Corner of Highways 44
and 22
Burnside
(225) 473–3007

Latil's Landing Restaurant
at Houma House Plantation
40136 Highway 942 (River Road)
Darrow
(225) 473–7841

Madewood
4250 Highway 308
Napoleonville
(985) 369–7151 or
(800) 375–7151

Nottoway
30970 Highway 405
White Castle
(225) 545–2730

Oak Alley Plantation Restaurant and Inn
3645 Highway 18
Vacherie
(225) 265–2151 or
(800) 44–ALLEY

"RED STICK"

Capital City Grill
3535 South Sherwood
Forest Boulevard
Baton Rouge
(225) 291–2233

100 Lafayette Street
The Shaw Center
Baton Rouge
(225) 381–8140

Drusilla's
3482 Drusilla Lane
Baton Rouge
(225) 923–0896

LSU Faculty Club
Highland Road
Baton Rouge
(225) 578–2356

Mike Anderson's
1031 West Lee Drive
Baton Rouge
(225) 766–7823

Tsunami
The Shaw Center
100 Lafayette Street
6th Floor
Baton Rouge
225–346–5100

FRENCH CREOLE COUNTRY

Joe's "Dreyfus Store" Restaurant
2741 Maringouin Road West
Livonia
(225) 637–2625

Morel's
210 Morrison Parkway
New Roads
(225) 638–4057

My Mama's Kitchen
124 West Main Street
New Roads
(225) 618–2424

THE FELICIANAS

The Bluffs Country Club and Resort
Route 965
St. Francisville
(225) 634–3410 or
(888) 634–3410

Magnolia Cafe
5687 Commerce Street
St. Francisville
(225) 635–6528

Oxbow Restaurant
7193 US 61
St. Francisville
(225) 635–6276

St. Francisville Inn
5720 North Commerce Street
St. Francisville
(225) 635–6502

The Surrey Restaurant at Bear Corners
1674 Charter Street
Jackson
(225) 634–7655

Varnadoe's Carriage House Restaurant
at the Myrtles Plantation
7747 US 61 North
St. Francisville
(225) 635–2635

TURF AND SWAMP NEW ORLEANS NORTHSHORE

Abita Brew Pub
72011 Holly Street
Abita Springs
(800) 737–2311

Acme Oyster House
519 East Boston Street
Covington
(985) 898–0667

Annadele's Plantation Restaurant
71495 Chestnut Street
Covington
(985) 809–7669
www.annadeles.com

Benedict's Plantation
1144 N. Causeway Boulevard
Mandeville
(985) 626–4557

Coffee Rani
234–A Lee Lane
Covington
(985) 893–6158

Dakota Restaurant
629 Highway 190
Covington
(985) 892–3712

Etoile Restaurant
407 North Columbia Street
Covington
(985) 892–4578

Friends Coastal Restaurant
407 St. Tammany Street
Madisonville
(985) 845–7303

The House of Seafood Buffet
Highway 21
Bush
(985) 886–2231

Judice's
421 East Gibson Street
Covington
(985) 892–0708

Juniper
301 Lafitte Street
Mandeville
(985) 624–5330 or
(985) 624–3422

Kickstand Coffee House Cafe
690 Lafitte Street
Mandeville
(985) 626–9300

The Longbranch
21516 Highway 36
Abita Springs
(985) 871–8171

Middendorf's
30160 Highway 51
Manchac (Akers)
(985) 386–6666

O'Donnell's Restaurant
131 Southwest
Railroad Avenue
Ponchatoula
(985) 386–4077

Ristorante Del Porto
205 North New Hampshire
Street
Covington
(985) 875–1006

CRESCENT CITY REALM

Arnaud's
813 Bienville Street
New Orleans
(504) 523–5433

The Besh Steak House at Harrah's
Canal at the River
New Orleans
(504) 533–6111

Brennan's
417 Royal Street
New Orleans
(504) 525–9713

Café Adelaide & the Swizzle Stick Bar
Loews New Orleans Hotel
300 Poydras Street
New Orleans
(504) 595–3305
www.cafeadelaide.com

Cafe du Monde
800 Decatur Street
New Orleans
(504) 587–0840

Commander's Palace
1403 Washington Avenue
New Orleans
(504) 899–8221

Emeril's Restaurant
800 Tchoupitoulas Street
New Orleans
(504) 528–9393

Galatoire's
209 Bourbon Street
New Orleans
(504) 525–2021

K–Paul's Louisiana Kitchen
416 Chartres Street
New Orleans
(504) 596–2530

Mother's
401 Poydras Street
New Orleans
(504) 523–9656

Napoleon House
500 Chartres Street
New Orleans
(504) 524–9752

Rio Mar
800 South Peters Street
New Orleans
(504) 525–FISH
www.riomarseafood.com

Tujague's
823 Decatur Street
New Orleans
(504) 525–8676

Upperline Restaurant
1413 Upperline Street
New Orleans
(504) 891–9822

BAYS AND BAYOUS

Boutte's Bayou Restaurant
Lafitte
(504) 689–3889

Copeland's Restaurant
1700 Lapalco Boulevard
Harvey
(504) 364–1575

Restaurant des Familles
7163 Barataria Boulevard
Crown Point
(504) 689–7834

Voleo's Seafood Restaurant
5134 Nunez Street
Lafitte
(504) 689–2482

Indexes

Entries for Bed-and-Breakfasts, Plantation Homes, Restaurants, and Recipes appear in special indexes on pages 186–88.

Swamp Gardens, 105
Sydney and Walda Bestoff Sculpture
Garden, 168

Tallulah, 36
Tammany Trace, 149, 156
Teche Drugs & Gifts, 88
Telephone Pioneer Museum
of Louisiana, 77
Tensas River National Wildlife
Refuge, 34–36
Thibodaux, 120
Three States Marker, 3
Toledo Bend Lake, 44
Touchstone Wildlife and
Art Museum, 14
Town, A. Hays, 97
Transylvania General Store, 36–37
Trinity Parish Church, 47
Tunica Hills, 135

UCM Museum, 150
University of Louisiana at Monroe,
The, 34
U.S.S. *Kidd*, 128

Vermilionville, 85, 87
Vieux Carré. *See* French Quarter.
Voice of the Wetlands, 114

W. H. Tupper General Merchandise
Museum, 77
Walker House, Ltd., 152
Walter B. Jacobs Memorial
Nature Park, 4–5
Washington, 81–82
Washington Parish Free Fair, 143
Watermark Saloon, 31
Webb and Webb Commissary, 12
West Baton Rouge Museum, 136
West Baton Rouge Parish Tourist
Commission Office, 136
West Feliciana Historical Society
Museum, 138
West Monroe, 25
Wetlands Acadian Cultural
Center, 120
White Castle, 124
White Castle of Louisiana,
The, 125
Whole Food Market, 166
Wildlife Gardens, 113
Winter Quarters State
Historic Site, 38–39

Ya-Yas, 58

Zemurray Gardens, 156
Zigler Art Museum, 75–76
Zwolle Tamale Festival, 44
Zydeco Festival, 83

BED-AND-BREAKFASTS

Annadele's Plantation Bed &
Breakfast, 154
Aunt Ruby's Bed & Breakfast, 72
Bittersweet Plantation, 124
Blue Willow Bed & Breakfast, 153–54
Butler Greenwood, 139
C. A.'s House Bed and Breakfast, 72
Camelia Hosue Bed & Breakfast, 153
Captain's Quarters, The, 31
Chrétien Point Plantation, 83–84
Cottage Plantation, 141

Eddy House Bed and Breakfast, 72
Estorge-Norton House, 102
Fairfield Place, 6–7
Grand Bayou Noir, 115
Greenwood Plantation, 141
Josephine, 163–65
Jubilee!, 135–36
leRosier Country Inn, 101
Madewood, 120
Maison Reve Farm, 151–52
Milbank Historic House, 145

PLANTATION HOMES

RESTAURANTS

RECIPES

About the Author

Gay N. Martin, who has lived in several southeastern states, now makes her home in Alabama. She has published hundreds of articles in national newspapers and magazines and especially enjoys writing about food and travel in the Southeast.

Before she made a New Year's resolution to turn her writing hobby into a career, Martin taught high school for eleven years, served as resource coordinator of her school's gifted program, and sponsored the school newspaper. Her work has appeared in *Modern Bride, Boston Herald, Kiwanis,* the *Writer, Seventeen, Atlanta Journal-Constitution,* the *Times-Picayune, Far East Traveler,* the *London Free Press, St. Petersburg Times,* and other publications. She is the author of Globe Pequot's *Alabama Off the Beaten Path* and *Alabama's Historic Restaurants and Their Recipes,* published by John F. Blair.

Martin belongs to the Society of American Travel Writers and the International Food, Wine, and Travel Writers Association. Visit her Web site at www.gnmartintravels.com.

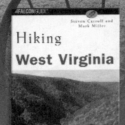
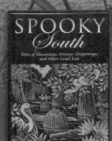

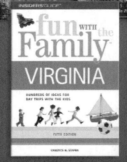
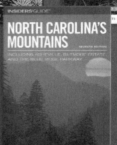